LIFE IN THE WORLD UNSEEN

ANTHONY BORGIA

FOREWORD

by Mike Rigby

Dear Reader:

As the Publisher of this work. I feel it necessary to explain that we have tried to put this book out without changing much of the original text. We have made every effort to reproduce it, as we found it.

You may find that the author's language feels a bit flowery at times. But this is due to his English background and the fact that he wrote extensively. It should be remembered that the author's profession was that of a priest and that his earthly enlightenment was limited. His knowledge, which has grown enormously, is still restricted in some areas because of his lack of spiritual progression, which he rapidly admits.

It will become apparent to the reader that much of the writing is what the author calls fact, based on what he sees, touches, tastes and hears. He then draws some conclusions from these facts that are based on his judgment with respect to the knowledge, and spirituality that he feels he now possesses.

It will be up to you the reader to determine the amount of truth which can be gleaned from this work. We hope that you find it refreshing and reassuring in its positive approach to life after death.

PREFACE

KNOWLEDGE is the best antidote for fear, especially if that fear should be of the possible or probable state of existence after we have made the change from this life to the next.

To discover what kind of place is the next world, we must inquire of someone who lives there, and record what is said. That is what has been done in the present volume.

The communicator, whom I first came to know in 1909—five years before his passing into the spirit world—was known on earth as Monsignor Robert Hugh Benson, a son of Edward White Benson, former Archbishop of Canterbury.

Until the present scripts were written he had never communicated with me directly, but I was once told (by another spirit friend) that there were certain matters he wished to set right. The difficulties of communication were explained to him by spirit friends and advisers, but he held to his purpose. And so when a suitable time was reached, he was told that he could communicate through a friend of his earthly days, and it has been my privilege to act as his recorder.

The first script was composed under the title of Beyond This Life; the second under that of The World Unseen.

In the former, the communicator gives, in a general survey, an account of his passing and his subsequent travels through various parts of spirit lands. In the latter script he deals at much greater length with a number of important and interesting facts and facets of spirit life, upon which previously he had touched only lightly or in passing.

For example: in Beyond This Life he mentions the highest realms and the lowest. In The World Unseen he actually visits them and describes what he saw and what took place in both regions. Although each of the two scripts is complete in itself, the second greatly extends and amplifies the first, and together they form a composite whole.

We are old friends, and his passing hence has not severed an early friendship; on the contrary, it has increased it, and provided many more opportunities of meeting than would have been possible had he remained on earth. He constantly expresses his delight upon his ability to return to earth in a natural, normal, healthy, and pleasant manner, and to give some account of his adventures and experiences in the spirit world, as one who 'being dead (as many would regard him), yet speaketh'. A.B.

CONTENTS

PART I Beyond This Life

PART II The World Unseen

Beyond This Life!

I. MY EARTH LIFE

WHO I am really matters not. Who I was matters still less. We do not carry our earthly positions with us into the spirit world. My earthly importance I left behind me. My spiritual worth is what counts now, and that, my good friend, is far below what it should be and what it can be. Thus much as to who I am. As to who I was, I should like to give some details concerning my mental attitude prior to my passing here into the world of spirit.

My earth life was not a hard one in the sense that I never underwent physical privations, but it was certainly a life of hard mental work. In my early years I was drawn towards the Church because the mysticism of the Church attracted my own mystical sense. The mysteries of religion, through their outward expression of lights and vestments and ceremonies, seemed to satisfy my spiritual appetite in a way that nothing else could. There was much, of course, that I did not understand, and since coming into spirit I have found that those things do not matter. They were religious problems raised by the minds of men, and they have no significance whatever in the great scheme of life. But at the time, like so many others, I believed in a wholesale fashion, without a glimmering of understanding, or very little. I taught and preached according to the orthodox text-books, and so I established a reputation for myself. When I contemplated a future state of existence I thought—and that vaguely—of what the Church had taught me on the subject, which was infinitesimally small and most incorrect. I did not realize the closeness of the two worlds—ours and yours—although I had ample demonstration of it. What occult experiences I had were brought about, so I thought, by some extension of natural laws, and they were rather to be considered as incidental than of regular occurrence, given to the few rather than to the many.

The fact that I was a priest did not preclude me from visitations of what the Church preferred to look upon as devils, although I never once, I must confess, saw anything remotely resembling what I could consider as such. I did not grasp the fact that I was what is called, on the earth-plane, a sensitive, a

7

psychic—one gifted with the power of 'seeing', though in a limited degree.

This incursion of a psychic faculty into my priestly life I found to be considerably disturbing since it conflicted with my orthodoxy. I sought advice in the matter from my colleagues, but they knew less than I knew, and they could only think of praying for me that these 'devils' might be removed from me. Their prayers availed me nothing—that was to be expected as I now see. Had my experiences been upon a high spiritual plane there is the chance that I should have been regarded in the light of a very holy man. But they were not so; they were just such experiences as occur to the ordinary earthly sensitive. As happening to a priest of the Holy Church they were looked upon as temptations of 'the devil'. As happenings to one of the laity they would have been regarded as dealings with 'the devil', or as some form of mental aberration. What my colleagues did not understand was that this power was a gift—a precious gift, as I understand now—and that it was personal to myself, as it is to all those who possess it, and to pray to have it removed is as senseless as to pray that one's ability to play the piano or paint a picture might be removed. It was not only senseless, it was unquestionably wrong, since such a gift of being able to see beyond the veil was given to be exercised for the good of mankind. I can at least rejoice that I never prayed for release from these powers. Pray I did, but for more light on the matter.

The great barrier to any further investigation of these faculties was the Church's attitude towards them, which was—and is—unrelenting, unequivocal, narrow, and ignorant. However long were any investigations or in whatever direction, the Church's final judgment was always the same, and its pronouncements unvarying—'such things have their origin in the devil'. And I was bound by the laws of that Church, administering its sacraments and delivering its teachings, while the spirit world was knocking upon the door of my very existence, and trying to show me, for myself to see, what I had so often contemplated—our future life.

Many of my experiences of psychic happenings I incorporated into my books, giving the narratives such a twist as would impart to them an orthodox religious flavor. The truth was there, but the meaning and purpose were distorted. In a larger work I felt that I had to uphold the Church against the assaults of those who believed in the spiritual survival of bodily death, and that it was possible for the spirit world to communicate with the earth world. And in that larger work I ascribed to 'the devil'—against my better judgment—what I really knew to be nothing other than the working of natural laws, beyond and entirely independent of any orthodox religion, and certainly of no evil origin.

To have followed my own inclinations would have entailed a complete upheaval in my life, a renunciation of orthodoxy, and most probably a great material sacrifice, since I had established a second reputation as a writer. What I had already written would then have become worthless in the eyes of my readers, and I should have been regarded as a heretic or a madman. The greatest opportunity of my earthly life I thus let pass. How great was that opportunity, and how great were my loss and regret, I knew when I had passed into this world whose inhabitants I had already seen so many times and on so many different occasions. The truth was within my grasp, and I let it fall. I adhered to the Church. Its teachings had obtained too great a hold upon me. I saw thousands believing as I did, and I took courage from that, as I could not think that they could all be wrong. I tried to separate my religious life from my psychic experiences, and to treat them as having no connection with one another. It was difficult, but I managed to steer a course that gave me the least mental disturbance, and so I continued to the end, when at last I stood upon the threshold of that world of which I had already had a glimpse. Of what befell me when I ceased to be an inhabitant of the earth and passed into the great spirit world, I hope now to give you some details.

II. PASSING TO SPIRIT LIFE

THE actual process of dissolution is not necessarily a painful one. I had during my earth life witnessed many souls passing over the border into spirit. I had had the chance of observing with the physical eyes the struggles that take place as the spirit seeks to free itself forever from the flesh. With my psychic vision I had also seen the spirit leave, but nowhere was I able to find out—that is, from orthodox sources—what exactly takes place at the moment of separation, nor was I able to gather any information upon the sensations experienced by the passing soul. The writers of religious text-books tell us nothing of such things for one very simple reason—they do not know.

The physical body many times appeared to be suffering acutely, either from actual pain or through labored or restricted breathing. To this extent such passings had all the appearance of being extremely painful. Was this really so?—was a question I had often asked myself. Whatever was the true answer I could never really believe that the actual physical process of 'dying' was a painful one, notwithstanding that it appeared so. The answer to my question I know I would have one day, and I always hoped that at least my passing would not be violent, whatever else it might be. My hopes were fulfilled. My end was not violent, but it was labored, as were so many that I had witnessed.

I had a presentiment that my days on earth were drawing to a close only a short while before my passing. There was a heaviness of the mind, something akin to drowsiness, as I lay in my bed. Many times I had a feeling of floating away and of gently returning. Doubtless during such periods those who were concerned with my physical welfare were under the impression that, if I had not actually passed, I was sinking rapidly. During such lucid intervals that I had I endured no feelings of physical discomfort. I could see and hear what was going on around me, and I could 'sense' the mental distress that my condition was occasioning. And yet I had the sensation of the most extraordinary exhilaration of the mind. I knew for certain that my time had come to pass on, and I was full of eagerness to be gone. I had no fear, no misgivings, no doubts, no regrets—so far—at thus leaving the earth world. (My regrets were to come later, but of these I shall speak in due course.) All that I wanted was to be away.

I suddenly felt a great urge to rise up. I had no physical feeling whatever, very much in the same way that physical feeling is absent during a dream, but I was mentally alert, however much my body seemed to contradict such a condition. Immediately I had this distinct prompting to rise, I found that I was actually doing so. I then discovered that those around my bed did not seem to perceive what I was doing, since they made no effort to come to my assistance, nor did they try in any way to hinder me. Turning, I then beheld what had taken place. I saw my physical body lying lifeless upon its bed, but here was I, the real I, alive and well. For a minute or two I remained gazing, and the thought of what to do next entered my head, but help was close at hand. I could still see the room quite clearly around me, but there was a certain mistiness about it as though it were filled with smoke very evenly distributed. I looked down at myself wondering what I was wearing in the way of clothes, for I had obviously risen from a bed of sickness and was therefore in no condition to move very far from my surroundings. I was extremely surprised to find that I had on my usual attire, such as I wore when moving freely and in good health about my own house. My surprise was only momentary since, I thought to myself, what other clothes should I expect to be wearing? Surely not some sort of diaphanous robe. Such costume is usually associated with the conventional idea of an angel, and I had no need to assure myself that I was not that!

Such knowledge of the spirit world as I had been able to glean from my own experiences instantly came to my aid. I knew at once of the alteration that had taken place in my condition; I knew, in other words, that I had 'died'. I knew, too, that I was alive, that I had shaken off my last illness sufficiently to be able to stand upright and look about me. At no time was I in any mental distress, but I was full of wonder at what was to happen next, for here I was, in full possession of all my faculties, and, indeed, feeling 'physically' as I had never felt before.

Although this has taken some time in the telling, in order that I might give you as much detail as possible, the whole process must have taken but a few minutes of earth time.

As soon as I had had this brief space in which to look about me and to appreciate my new estate, I found myself joined by a former colleague—a priest—who had passed to this life some years before. We greeted each other warmly, and I noticed that he was attired like myself. Again this in no way seemed strange to me, because had he been dressed in any other way I should have felt that something was wrong somewhere, as I had only known him in clerical attire. He expressed his great pleasure at seeing me again, and for my part I foresaw the gathering up of the many threads that had been broken by his 'death'.

For the first moment or so I allowed him to do all the talking; I had yet to accustom myself to the newness of things. For you must remember that I had just relinquished a bed of final sickness, and that in casting off the physical body I had also cast off the sickness with it, and the new sensation of comfort and freedom from bodily ills was one so glorious that the realization of it took a little while to comprehend fully. My old

11

friend seemed to know at once the extent of my knowledge, that I was aware that I had passed on, and that all was well.

And here let me say that all idea of a 'judgment seat' or a 'day of judgment' was entirely swept from my mind in the actual procedure of transition. It was all too normal and natural to suggest the frightful ordeal that we must go through after 'death'. The very conception of 'judgment' and 'hell' and 'heaven' seemed utterly impossible. Indeed, they were wholly fantastic, now that I found myself alive and well, 'clothed in my right mind', and, in fact, clothed in my own familiar habiliments, and standing in the presence of an old friend, who was shaking me cordially by the hand, and giving me greeting and good wishes, and showing all the outward—and in this case—genuine manifestations of being pleased to see me, as I was pleased to see him. He, himself, was in the best of spirits as he stood there giving me such a welcome as, upon the earth-plane, two old friends accord each other after long separation. That, in itself, was sufficient to show that all thoughts of being marched off to my judgment were entirely preposterous. We both were too jolly, too happy, too carefree, and too natural, and I, myself, was waiting with excitement for all manner of pleasant revelations of this new world, and I knew that there could be none better than my old friend to give them to me. He told me to prepare myself for an immeasurable number of the pleasantest of surprises, and that he had been sent to meet me on my arrival. As he already knew the limits of my knowledge, so his task was that much the easier.

As soon as I managed to find my tongue, after our first breaking the silence, I noticed that we spoke just as we had always done upon the earth, that is, we simply used our vocal cords and spoke, quite as a matter of course. It required no thinking about, and indeed I did not think about it. I merely noted that it was so. My friend then proposed that as we had no further need or call to stay in the surroundings of my passing, we might move away, and that he would take me to a very nice 'place' that had been made ready for me. He made this reference to a 'place', but he hastened to explain that in reality I was going to my own house, where I should find myself immediately 'at home'. Not knowing, as yet, how one proceeded, or, in other words, how I was to get there, I placed myself entirely in his hands, and that, he told me, was precisely what he was there for!

I could not resist the impulse to turn and take a last look at the room of my transition. It still presented its misty appearance. Those who were formerly standing round the bed had now withdrawn, and I was able to approach the bed and gaze at 'myself'. I was not the least impressed by what I saw, but the last remnant of my physical self seemed to be placid enough. My friend then suggested that we should now go, and we accordingly moved away.

As we departed, the room gradually became more misty until it faded farther from my vision; and finally disappeared. So far, I had had the use, as usual, of my legs as in ordinary walking, but in view of my last illness and the fact that, consequent, upon it, I should need some period of rest before I exerted myself too much, my friend said that it would be better if we did not use the customary means of locomotion—our legs. He then told me to take hold of his arm firmly, and to have no fear, whatever. I could, if I wished, close my eyes. It would, he said, perhaps be better if I did so. I took his arm, and left the rest to him as he told me to do. I at once experienced a sensation of floating such as one has in physical dreams, though this was very real and quite unattended by any doubts of personal security. The motion seemed to become more rapid as time went on, and I still kept my eyes firmly closed. It is strange with what determination one can do such things here. On the earth-plane, if similar circumstances were possible, how many of us would have closed our eyes in complete confidence? Here there was no shadow of doubt that all was well, that there was nothing to fear, that nothing untoward could possibly take place, and that, moreover, my friend had complete control of the situation.

After a short while our progress seemed to slacken somewhat, and I could feel that there was something very solid under my feet. I was told to open my eyes. I did so. What I saw was my old home that I had lived in on the earth-plane; my old home—but with a difference. It was improved in a way that I had not been able to do to its earthly counterpart. The house itself was rejuvenated, as it seemed to me from a first glance, rather than restored, but it was the gardens round it that attracted my attention more fully.

They appeared to be quite extensive, and they were in a state of the most perfect order and arrangement. By this I do not mean the regular orderliness that one is accustomed to see in public gardens on the earth-plane, but that they were beautifully kept and tended. There were no wild growths or masses of tangled foliage and weeds, but the most glorious profusion of beautiful flowers so arranged as to show themselves to absolute perfection. Of the flowers themselves, when I was able to examine them more closely, I must say that I never saw either their like or their counterpart, upon the earth, of many that were there in full bloom. Numbers were to be found, of course, of the old familiar blossoms, but by far the greater number seemed to be something entirely new to my rather small knowledge of flowers. It was not merely the flowers themselves and their unbelievable range of superb colorings that caught my attention, but the vital atmosphere of eternal life that they threw out, as it were, in every direction. And as one approached any particular group of flowers, or even a single bloom, there seemed to pour out great streams of energizing power which uplifted the soul spiritually and gave it strength, while the heavenly perfumes they exhaled were such as no soul clothed in its mantle of flesh has ever experienced. All these flowers were living and breathing, and they were, so my friend informed me, incorruptible.

There was another astonishing feature I noticed when I drew near to them, and that was the sound of music that enveloped them, making such soft harmonies as corresponded exactly and perfectly with the gorgeous colors of the flowers themselves. I am not, I am afraid, sufficiently learned, musically, to be able to give you a sound technical explanation of this beautiful phenomenon, but I shall hope to bring to you one with knowledge of the subject, who will be able to go into this more fully. Suffice it for the moment, then, to say that these musical sounds were in precise consonance with all that I had so far seen—which was very little—and that everywhere there was perfect harmony.

Already I was conscious of the revitalizing effect of this heavenly garden to such an extent that I was anxious to see more of it. And so, in company with my old friend, upon whom I was here relying for information and guidance, I walked the garden paths, trod upon the exquisite grass, whose resilience and softness were almost comparable to 'walking on air'; and tried to make myself realize that all this superlative beauty was part of my own home.

There were many splendid trees to be seen, none of which was malformed, such as one is accustomed to see on earth, yet there was no suggestion of strict uniformity of pattern. It was simply that each tree was growing under perfect conditions, free from the storms of wind that bend and twist the young branches, and free from the inroads of insect life and many other causes of the misshapenness of earthly trees. As with the flowers, so with the trees. They live forever incorruptible, clothed always in their full array of leaves of every shade of green, and forever pouring out life to all those who approach near them.

I had observed that there did not appear to be what we should commonly call shade beneath the trees, and yet there did not appear to be any glaring sun. It seemed to be that there was a radiance of light that penetrated into every corner, and yet there was no hint of flatness. My friend told me that all light proceeded directly from the Giver of all light, and that this light was Divine life itself, and that it bathed and illumined the whole of the spirit world where lived those who had eyes spiritually to see.

I noticed, too, that a comfortable warmth pervaded every inch of space, a warmth perfectly even and as perfectly sustained. The air had a stillness, yet there were gentle perfume-laden breezes—the truest zephyrs—that in no way altered the delightful balminess of the temperature.

And here let me say to those who do not care much for 'perfumes' of any sort: Do not be disappointed when you read these words, and feel that it could never be heaven to you if there were something there you do not like. Wait, I say, until you witness these things, and I know that then you will feel very differently about them.

I have gone into all these things in a rather detailed fashion because I am sure there are so many people who have wondered about them.

I was struck by the fact that there were no signs of walls or hedges or fences; indeed, nothing, so far as I could see, to mark off where my garden began or ended. I was told that such things as boundaries were not needed, because each person knew instinctively, but beyond doubt, just where his own garden ended. There was therefore no encroaching upon another's grounds, although all were open to any who wished to traverse them or linger within them. I was wholeheartedly welcome to go wherever I wished without fear of intruding upon another's privacy. I was told I should find that that was the rule here, and that I would have no different feelings with respect to others walking in my own garden. I exactly described my sentiments at that moment, for I wished, then and there, that all who cared would come into the garden and enjoy its beauties. I had no notions whatever of ownership personally, although I knew that it was my own 'to have and to hold'. And that is precisely the attitude of all here—ownership and partnership at one and the same time.

Seeing the beautiful state of preservation and care in which all the garden was kept, I inquired of my friend as to the genius who looked after it so assiduously and with such splendid results. Before answering my question he suggested that as I had but so very recently arrived in the spirit land, he considered it advisable that I should rest, or that at least I should not overdo my sightseeing. He proposed, therefore, that we should find a pleasant spot—he used the words in a comparative sense, because all was more than pleasant everywhere—that we should seat ourselves, and then he would expound one or two of the many problems that had presented themselves to me in the brief time since I had passed to spirit.

Accordingly, we walked along until we found such a 'pleasant' place beneath the branches of a magnificent tree, whence we overlooked a great tract of the countryside, whose rich verdure undulated before us and stretched far away into the distance. The whole prospect was bathed in glorious celestial sunshine, and I could perceive many houses of varying descriptions picturesquely situated, like my own, among trees and gardens. We threw ourselves down upon the soft turf, and I stretched myself out luxuriously feeling as though I were lying upon a bed of the finest down. My friend asked me if I was tired. I had no ordinary sensation of earthly fatigue, but yet I felt somewhat the necessity for a bodily relaxation. He told me that my last illness was the cause of such a desire, and that if I wished I could pass into a state of complete sleep. At the moment, however, I did not feel the absolute need for that, and I told him that for the present I would much prefer to hear him talk. And so he began.

"'Whatsoever a man soweth,'" he said, "'that shall he reap.'" Those few words describe exactly the great eternal process by which all that you see, actually here before you, is brought about. All the trees, the flowers, the woods, the houses that are also the happy homes of happy people—everything is the visible result of "whatsoever a man soweth." This land, wherein you and I are now living, is the land of the great harvest, the seeds of which were planted upon the earth-plane. All who live here have won for themselves the precise abode they have passed to by their deeds upon the earth.'

I was already beginning to perceive many things, the principal one of which, and that which touched me most closely, being the totally wrong attitude adopted by religion in relation to the world of spirit. The very fact that I was lying there where I was, constituted a complete refutation of so much that I taught and upheld during my priestly life upon earth. I could see volumes of orthodox teachings, creeds, and doctrines melting away because they are of no account, because they are not true, and because they have no application whatever to the eternal world of spirit and to the great Creator and Upholder of it. I could see clearly now what I had seen but hazily before, that orthodoxy is manmade, but that the universe is God-given.

My friend went on to tell me that I should find living within the homes, that we could see from where we were lying, all sorts and conditions of people; people whose religious views when they were on the earth were equally varied. But one of the great facts of spirit life is that souls are exactly the same the instant after passing into spirit life as they were the instant before. Death-bed repentances are of no avail, since the majority of them are but cowardice born of fear of what is about to happen—a fear of the theologically-built eternal hell that is such a useful weapon in the ecclesiastical armory, and one that perhaps has caused more suffering in its time than many other erroneous doctrines. Creeds, therefore, do not form any part of the world of spirit, but because people take with them all their characteristics into the spirit world, the fervid adherents to any particular religious body will continue to practice their religion in the spirit world until such time as their minds become spiritually enlightened. We have here, so my friend informed me—I have since seen them for myself—whole communities still exercising their old earthly religion. The bigotry and prejudices are all there, religiously speaking. They do no harm, except to themselves, since such matters are confined to themselves. There is no such thing as making converts here!

Such being the case, then, I supposed that our own religion was fully represented here. Indeed, it was! The same ceremonies, the same ritual, the same old beliefs, all are being carried on with the same misplaced zeal—in churches erected for the purpose. The members of these communities know that they have passed on, and they think that part of their heavenly reward is to continue with their man-made forms of worship. So they will continue until such time as a spiritual awakening takes place. Pressure is never brought to bear upon these souls; their mental resurrection must come from within themselves. When it does come they will taste for the first time the real meaning of freedom.

My friend promised that if I wished we could visit some of these religious bodies later, but, he suggested, that as there was plenty of time it would be better if first of all I became quite accustomed to the new life. He had, so far, left unanswered my question as to who was the kindly soul who tended my garden so well, but he read my unspoken thought, and reverted to the matter himself.

Both the house and the garden, he told me, were the harvest I had reaped for myself during my earth life. Having earned the right to possess them, I had built them with the aid of generous souls who spend their life in the spirit world performing such deeds of kindness and service to others. Not only was it their work, but it was their pleasure at the same time. Frequently this work is undertaken and carried out by those who, on earth, were expert in such things, and who also had a love for it. Here they can continue with their occupation under conditions that only the world of spirit can supply. Such tasks bring their own spiritual rewards, although the thought of reward is never in the minds of those who perform them. The desire of being of service to others is always uppermost.

The man who had helped to bring this beautiful garden into being was a lover of gardens upon the earth-plane, and, as I could see for myself, he was also an expert. But once the garden was created there was not the incessant toil that is necessary for upkeep, as with large gardens upon the earth. It is the constant decay, the stresses of storm and wind, and the several other causes that demand the labor on earth. Here there is no decay, and all that grows does so under the same conditions as we exist. I was told that the garden would need practically no attention, as we usually understand the term, and that our friend the gardener would still keep it under his care if I so wished it. Far from merely wishing I expressed the hope that he certainly would do so. I voiced my deep gratitude for his wonderful work, and I hoped that I might be able to meet him and convey to him my sincere appreciation and thanks. My friend explained that that was quite a simple matter, and that the reason why I had not already met him was the fact of my very recent arrival, and that he would not intrude until I had made myself quite at home.

My mind again turned to my occupation while on earth, the conducting of daily service and all the other duties of a minister of the Church. Since such an occupation, as far as I was concerned, was now needless, I was puzzled to know what the immediate future had in store for me. I was again reminded that there was plenty of time in which to ponder the subject, and my friend suggested that I should rest myself and then accompany him upon some tours of inspection—there was so much to see and so much that I should find more than astonishing. There were also numbers of friends who were waiting to meet me again after our long separation. He curbed my eagerness to begin by saying that I must rest first, and for which purpose, what better place than my own home?

I followed his advice, therefore, and we made our way towards the house.

III. FIRST EXPERIENCES

I HAVE already mentioned that when I was first introduced to my spirit home I observed that it was the same as my earth home, but with a difference. As I entered the doorway I saw at once the several changes that had been brought about. These changes were mostly of a structural nature and were exactly of the description of those that I had always wished I could have carried out to my earthly house, but which for architectural and other reasons I had never been able to have done. Here, earthly needs had no place, so that I found my spirit home, in general disposition, exactly as I had ever wished it to be. The essential requisites indispensably associated with an earthly homestead were, of course, completely superfluous here, for example, the severely mundane matter of providing the body with food. That is one instance of the difference. And so with others it is easy enough to call to mind.

As we traversed the various rooms together, I could see many instances of the thoughtfulness and kindness of those who had labored so energetically to help me reconstruct my old home in its new surroundings. While standing within its walls I was fully aware of its permanence as compared with what I had left behind me. But it was a permanence that I knew I could end; permanent only so long as I wished it to be so. It was more than a mere house; it was a spiritual haven, an abode of peace, where the usual domestic cares and responsibilities were wholly absent.

The furniture that it contained consisted largely of that which I had provided for its earthly original, not because it was particularly beautiful, but because I had found it useful and comfortable, and adequately suited my few requirements. Most of the small articles of adornment were to be seen displayed in their customary places, and altogether the whole house presented the unmistakable appearance of occupancy. I had truly 'come home'.

In the room that had formerly been my study I noticed some well-filled bookshelves. At first I was rather surprised to see such things, but upon further thought I could see no reason, if such as this house could exist at all with all its various adjuncts, why books should not also have their place within the scheme. I was interested to learn what was the nature of the books, and so I made a closer examination. I found that conspicuous among them were my own works. As I stood in front of them I had a clear perception of the reason, the real reason, for their being there. Many of these books contained those narratives that I spoke of earlier, in which I had told of my own psychic experiences after giving them the necessary religious turn. One book in particular seemed to stand out in my mind more than the others, and I came to the full realization that I now wished that I had never written it. It was a distorted narrative, where the facts, as I had really known them, were given unfair treatment, and where the truth was suppressed. I felt very remorseful, and for the first time since coming into this land I had regret. Not regret that I had, at last, arrived in the spirit world, but sorrow that, with the truth before me, I had deliberately cast it aside to place in its stead falsehood and misrepresentation. For I knew that so long as my name lived, that is, so long as it had any commercial value, that book would continue to be reproduced and circulated and read—and regarded as the absolute truth. I had the unpleasant knowledge that I could never destroy what I had thus done.

There was, at no time, any sense of condemnation over this.

On the contrary, I could feel a distinct atmosphere of intense sympathy. Whence it came, I knew not, but it was real and concrete nevertheless. I turned to my friend, who, during my inspection and discovery, had been standing discreetly and understandingly at a little distance apart, and I asked for his help. It was instantly forthcoming. He then explained to me that he knew exactly what had lain before me concerning this book, but that he was debarred from making any reference to it before I made the discovery for myself. Upon my doing so, and upon my subsequent appeal for his help, he was at once enabled to come to my aid.

My first question was to ask him how I could put this matter right. He told me that there were several ways in which I could do so, some more difficult—but more efficacious—than others. I suggested that perhaps I could go back to the earth-plane and tell others of this new life and the truth of communication between the two worlds. Many, many people, he said, had tried, and were still trying, to do so, and how many were believed? Did I think that I should have any better fortune? Certainly none of those who read my books would ever come within miles of receiving or crediting any communication from me. And did I realize, also, that if I were to present myself to such people they would at once call me a 'devil', if not the very Prince of Darkness himself!

'Let me,' he continued, 'place a few considerations before you concerning this subject of communication with the earth world. You know full well that such is possible, but have you any conception of the difficulties surrounding it?

'Let us assume that you have found the means to communicate. The first thing you will be called upon to do will be to furnish clear and definite identification of yourself. Quite probably, upon your first declaring who you are, there will be some hesitation at accepting your name simply because it carried weight when you were incarnate. However important or famous we happen to be when upon the earth-plane, as soon as we are gone to the spirit-plane, we are referred to in the past tense! Whatever works of a literary nature we may leave behind us are then of far greater importance than their authors, since to the earth world we are "dead". To the earth, the living voice is gone. And although we are still very much alive—to ourselves as well as to others here—to the earth people we have become memories, sometimes permanent, more often than not

21

memories that rapidly fade, leaving mere names behind them. We know, moreover, that we are very much more alive than we have ever been before; the majority of earth people will consider that we could never be more "dead"!

'You will be commanded, then, to provide a great deal of identification. That is quite proper in such circumstances, provided it is not carried to extremes as so often it is. After fulfilling this condition what next? You will wish to intimate that you are alive and well. If the people with whom you are communicating are no mere dabblers, no doubt will be placed upon your statement. But if you wish to send such news to the world in general through the customary channels, those who believe it is really you who have spoken will be those who already know of, and practice communication with, the spirit world. For the rest, who will believe it is you? None—certainly none of your former readers. They will say that it cannot be you, but that it is a "devil" impersonating you. Others will quite probably take no notice whatever. There would, of course, be a number who would imagine that, because you have passed into the world of spirit, then you will at once have become endowed with the profoundest wisdom, and that all you say will be infallible utterances. You can see some of the difficulties that will confront you in this simple matter of telling the truth to those who still sit in the darkness of the earth world.'

My friend's forecast grieved me considerably, but I appreciated the extreme difficulties, and I was persuaded to leave the project for the time being. We would consult others wiser than ourselves, and perhaps some course would be outlined whereby I could achieve my desires. I might find that with the passage of time—speaking in a mundane sense—my wishes might change. There was no need to distress myself. There was much that I could see and do, and much experience to be gained that would be invaluable to me if, in the end, I resolved to try and carry out my intentions. His best advice was that I should have a thorough rest, during which time he would leave me. If, when I was quite refreshed, I would send out my thought to him, he would receive it and return to me at once. So, making myself 'comfortable' upon a couch, I sank into a delightful state of semi-sleep, in which I was fully conscious of my surroundings, yet at the same time I could feel a downpouring of new energy, which coursed through my whole being. I could feel myself becoming, as it were, lighter, with the last traces of the old earth conditions being driven away forever

How long I remained in this pleasant state, I have no knowledge, but eventually I fell into a gentle slumber from which I awoke in that state of health which in the spirit world is perfect. I at once remembered my friend's proposal, and I sent out my thoughts to him. Within the space of a few seconds of earth time he was walking in through the door. His response was so bewilderingly rapid that my surprise sent him into merry laughter. He explained that in reality it was quite simple. The spirit world is a world of thought; to think is to act, and thought is instantaneous. If we think ourselves into a certain place we shall travel with the rapidity of that thought, and that is as near instantaneous as it is possible to imagine. I should find that it was the usual mode of locomotion, and that I should soon be able to employ it.

My friend at once noticed a change in me, and he congratulated me upon my regaining my full vigor. It is impossible to convey, even in a small measure, this exquisite feeling of supreme vitality and well-being. When we are living upon the earth-plane we are constantly being reminded of our physical bodies in a variety of ways—by cold or heat, by discomfort, by fatigue, by minor illnesses, and by countless other means. Here we labor under no such disabilities. By that I do not mean that we are just unfeeling logs, insensible to all external influences, but that our perceptions are of the mind, and that the spirit body is impervious to anything that is destructive. We feel through our minds, not through any physical organs of sense, and our minds are directly responsive to thought. If we should feel coldness in some particular and definite circumstances, we undergo that sensation with our minds, and our spirit bodies in no way suffer. We are never continuously reminded of them. In the realm of which I am now speaking, all is exactly attuned to its inhabitants—its temperature, its landscape, its many dwellings, the waters of the rivers and streams, and, most important of all, the inhabitants one with another. There is therefore nothing that can possibly create any unhappiness, unpleasantness, or discomfort. We can completely forget our bodies and allow our minds to have free play, and through our minds we can enjoy the thousands of delights that the same minds have helped to build up.

At times we may feel saddened—and at times we are amused—by those who, still upon the earth, ridicule and pour scorn and contempt upon our descriptions of the spirit lands. What do these poor minds know? Nothing! And what would these same minds substitute for the realities of the spirit world? They do not know. They would take away from us our beautiful countryside, our flowers and trees, our rivers and lakes, our houses, our friends, our work, and our pleasures and recreations. For what? What conception can these dull minds have of a world of spirit? By their own stupid admissions, no conception whatever. They would turn us into wraiths, without substance, without intelligence, and merely surviving in some dim, shadowy, vaporous state, dissevered from everything that is human. In my perfect health and abounding vitality, and living among all the beauties of this world of strict reality—a mere hint of which I have only so far given you—I am forcibly impressed by the magnitude of ignorance shown by particular minds upon earth.

The time had come, I felt, when I would like to see something of this wonderful land, and so, in company with my friend, we set forth on what was, for me, a voyage of discovery. Those of you who have travelled the earth for the sake of seeing new lands will understand how I felt at the outset.

To obtain a wider view, we walked to some higher ground, whence a clear panorama unfolded before the eyes. Before us the countryside reached out in a seemingly unending prospect. In another direction I could clearly perceive what had all the appearance of a city of stately buildings, for it must be remembered that all people here do not possess a uniformity of tastes, and that even as on earth, many prefer the city to the country, and vice versa, while again some like both. I was very keenly interested to see what a spirit city could be like. It seemed easy enough to visualize the country here, but cities seemed so essentially the work of man in a material world. On the other hand, I could advance no logical reason why the spirit world should not also build cities. My companion was greatly amused by my enthusiasm, which, he declared, was equal to a schoolboy's. It was not his first acquaintance with it, however; most people when they first arrive are taken in the same way! And it affords our friends a never-ending pleasure to show us round.

I could see a church in the distance built on the usual lines externally, and it was proposed that we might go in that direction, and include other things on the way. And so we set off.

We followed a path that led for part of the way beside a brook, whose clear water sparkled in the light of the heavenly sun. As the water pursued its course it gave forth many musical notes that constantly changed and weaved themselves into a medley of the most dulcet sounds. We drew to the edge that I might look at it closer. It seemed to be almost like liquid crystal, and as the light caught it, it scintillated with all the colors of the rainbow. I let some of the water run over my hand, expecting it, by its very look, to be icy cold. What was my astonishment to find that it was delightfully warm. But still more it had an electrifying effect which extended from my hand right up the arm. It was a most exhilarating sensation, and I wondered what would it be like to bathe fully within it. My friend said that I should feel myself being charged with energy, but there was not a sufficient depth of water to immerse myself in it properly. I should have the opportunity, as soon as we came to a larger body of water, to indulge in a bathe. When I withdrew my hand from the brook, I found that the water flowed off in flashing drops, leaving it quite dry!

We resumed our walk, and my friend said he would like to take me to visit a man who lived in a house which we were now approaching. We walked through some artistically laid out gardens, crossed a well-turfed lawn, and came upon a man seated at the outskirts of a large orchard. As we drew near he rose to meet us. My friend and he greeted one another in the most cordial fashion, and I was introduced as a new arrival. It was explained to me that this gentleman prided himself upon the fruit in his orchard, and I was invited to sample some of it. The owner of this pleasant retreat seemed to be a man of middle years, as far as I could judge, though he could have been much older than he appeared to be at first sight. I have since learned that to try to guess the ages of people here is a difficult and almost dangerous task! For you must know—to digress a little— that it is the law that, as we progress spiritually, so do we shake off the semblance of age as it is known on earth. We lose the wrinkles that age and worldly cares have marked upon our countenances, together with other indications of the passage of years, and we become younger in appearance, while we grow older in knowledge and wisdom and spirituality. I am not suggesting that we assume an exterior of extreme juvenility, nor do we lose those external indications of personality. To do that would make us all of a deadly uniformity, but we do, in truth, return—or advance, according to our age when we pass into spirit—towards what we have always known as 'the prime of life'.

To resume. Our host led us into the orchard where I beheld many trees in a high state of cultivation, and in full fruit. He looked at me for a moment, and then he took us to a splendid tree that looked strongly like a plum tree. The fruit was perfect in shape, with a deep rich coloring, and it hung in great clusters. Our host picked some of it, and handed it to us, telling us that it would do us both good. The fruit was quite cool to the touch, and it was remarkably heavy for its size. Its taste was exquisite, the flesh was soft without being difficult or unpleasant to handle, and a quantity of nectar-like juice poured out. My two friends watched me closely as I ate the plums, each bearing upon his face an expression of mirthful anticipation. As the juice of the fruit streamed out, I fully expected to spill an abundance of it upon my clothes. To my amazement, although the juice descended upon me I could find, upon examination, no traces of it. My friends laughed uproariously at my astonishment, and I thoroughly enjoyed the joke, but I was much mystified. They hastened to explain to me that as I am now in an incorruptible world anything that is 'unwanted' immediately returns to its own element. The fruit juice that I thought I had spilled upon myself had returned to the tree from which the fruit was plucked.

Our host informed me that the particular type of plum which I had just eaten was one that he always recommends to people who have but newly arrived in spirit. It helps to restore the spirit, especially if the passing has been caused by illness. He observed, however, that I did not present the appearance of having had a long illness, and he gathered that my passing had been fairly sudden—which was quite true. I had had only a very short illness. The various fruits that were growing were not only for those who needed some form of treatment after their physical death, but all enjoyed eating thereof for its stimulating effect. He hoped that, if I had no fruit trees of my own—or even if I had !—I should come as often as I liked and help myself. 'The fruit is always in season,' he added, in great amusement, 'and you will never find any of the trees without plenty of fruit upon them.' In response to my question as to how they grow, he replied that like so many other questions in this land, the answer was only possible from those of the higher realms, and even if we were told that answer, there is more than a strong probability that we should not understand until such time as we, ourselves, went to dwell in those realms. We are quite content, he said in effect, to take so many things just as they are, without inquiring into how they come about, and we know that those things provide a never-failing supply because they come from a never-failing Source. There is no real need to delve into such matters, and most of us are quite content to enjoy them with heartfelt thanks. As to the actual supply of fruit, our host said that all he knew was that as he picked his fruit other fruit came and took its place. It never over-ripened because it was perfect fruit, and, like ourselves, imperishable. He invited us to walk through the orchard where I saw every kind of fruit-known to man, and many that were known only in spirit. I sampled some of the latter, but it is impossible to give any indication of the delicious flavor of them because there is no earthly fruit that I know of with which comparison can be made. We can only, at any time, give such an indication to the senses by comparison with that which we have already experienced. If we have not had that experience then we are at a complete and absolute loss to convey any new sensation, and nowhere is this more appreciable than in the sense of taste.

My friend explained to our genial host that he was escorting me round to show me the land of my new life, and the latter gave us many good wishes to speed us upon our way. He repeated his invitation to visit him whenever I wished, and even if he were not about at the time of any call I might make, I was to help myself to the fruit to my heart's content. He said I should find that the fruit trees would perform the duties of a host as well as—even better than—he could! And so with further expressions of thanks and goodwill, we again set forth.

We returned to our former path beside the brook, and continued our walk in the direction of the church. After we had proceeded for a little way, I noticed that the brook began to broaden out until it expanded into the dimensions of a fair-sized lake. We could see many groups of happy people gathered at the side of the water, some of whom were bathing. The lake was bounded by an encirclement of trees, and there were flowers in abundance arranged in such a way that although a certain orderliness was observable, yet there was no hint of distinct ownership. They belonged to all in equal right, and I observed most particularly that no attempt was made by anyone to pick, or root up, or otherwise disturb them. One or two people were to be seen with both their hands placed round some of the blooms in almost a caressing manner, an action which seemed to me so unusual that I asked my friend for enlightenment on the matter. He replied by taking me over to a young girl who was thus curiously occupied. I was rather diffident of so intruding, but I was told to 'wait and see.' My friend bent down beside her, and she turned her head and gave him a friendly word and smile of welcome. I concluded that they were old friends, but such was not the case. In fact, he told me afterwards that he had never seen her before, and he explained that here in spirit we need no formal introductions; we constitute one large united gathering in the matter of ordinary 'social intercourse. After we have been here a little while, and become accustomed to our new environment and mode of living, we find that we never intrude since we can read at once the mind of a person who wishes for a period of seclusion. And when we see people out in the open—in garden or countryside—we are always welcome to approach and hold friendly converse with them.

This young lady was, like myself, a new-comer, and she told us how some friends had shown her the method of gathering from the flowers all that the flowers had so lavishly to give. I bent down beside her, and she gave me a practical demonstration of what to do. By placing the hands, she said, round the flower so as to hold it in a sort of cup, I should feel the magnetism running up my arms. As I moved my hands towards a beautiful bloom, I found that the flower upon its stem moved towards me! I did as I was instructed, and I instantly felt a stream of life rushing up my arms, the while a most delicate aroma was exhaled by the flower. She told me not to pick the flowers because they were for ever growing; they were part of this life, even as we are ourselves. I was very grateful for her timely admonition, since it was the most natural thing in the world to pick flowers that were already in such profusion. It was not quite the same in the case of the fruit, I learned, because the fruit was meant to be consumed. But the flowers were themselves decorative and to cut down the flower by picking it was equivalent to cutting down the fruit trees. There were flowers, however, that were growing expressly for the purpose of being picked, but these under immediate consideration had as their principal function that of health-giving. I inquired of our young friend if she had tried some of the good fruit we had just sampled, and she replied that she had.

My friend suggested that I might like to go closer to the water's edge, and that if the young lady were alone, perhaps she would care to join us in our excursions. She responded that nothing would give her greater pleasure, and so we all three moved towards the lake. I explained to her that my friend was a seasoned inhabitant of these lands, and that he was acting as my guide and adviser. She seemed to be glad of our company, not that she was lonely, for such a thing does not exist in this realm, but she had had few friends while on earth and had always lived something of a solitary life, although she had never, on that account, been indifferent to, or unmindful of, the cares and sorrows of others. Since coming into spirit she had found so many kindly souls of a similar disposition to herself, and she supposed that perhaps we had been in like case. I told her briefly a few things about myself, and as I was still wearing my earthly attire—that is to say, its counterpart!—she knew me, more or less, for what I had been professionally. My friend being similarly clothed, she laughingly said that she felt she was in safe hands!

It was recalled to my mind what had been said about bathing, but I was rather at a loss how to broach the matter of the necessary equipment for the purpose. However, my friend saved the situation by referring to it himself.

All we needed for the purpose of enjoying a bathe was the necessary water in which to bathe! Nothing could be simpler. We were just to go into the water precisely as we were. Whether we could swim or not, was of no consequence. And I must say I was astonished at this strange departure from the usual procedure, and I naturally hesitated a little. However, my friend quite calmly walked into the lake until he was thoroughly immersed, and the two of us followed his example.

What I was expecting to result from this I cannot say. At least I anticipated the customary effect of water upon one in similar circumstances on earth. Great, then, was my surprise—and my relief—when I discovered that the water felt more like a warm cloak thrown round me than the penetration of liquid. The magnetic effect of the water was of like nature to the brook into which I had thrust my hand, but here the revivifying force enveloped the whole body, pouring new life into it. It was delightfully warm and completely buoyant. It was possible to stand upright in it, to float upon it, and of course, to sink completely beneath the surface of it without the least discomfort or danger. Had I paused to think I might have known that the latter was inevitably bound to be the case. The spirit is indestructible. But beyond this magnetic influence there was an added assurance that came from the water, and that was its essential friendliness, if I may so call it. It is not easy to convey any idea of this fundamentally spiritual experience. That the water was living one could have no doubt. It breathed its very goodness by its contact, and extended its heavenly influence individually to all who came within it. For myself, I experienced a spiritual exaltation, as well as a vital regeneration, to such an extent that I quite forgot my initial hesitancy and the fact that I was fully clothed. The latter now presented a perfectly natural situation, and this was further enhanced by my observing my two companions. My old friend, of course, was perfectly used to the water, and our new friend seemed to have accommodated herself rapidly to new usages.

My mind was saved further perturbation when I recalled that as I withdrew my hand from the brook the water ran off it, leaving it quite dry. I was already prepared, then, for what ensued as we came out of the lake. As I emerged the water merely ran away, leaving my clothes just as they were before. It had penetrated the material just as air or atmosphere on earth will do, but it had left no visible or palpable effect whatever. We and our clothes were perfectly dry!

And now another word about the water. It was as clear as crystal, and the light was reflected back in every ripple and tiny wave in almost dazzlingly bright colors. It was unbelievably soft to the touch, and its buoyancy was of the same nature as the atmosphere, that is to say, it supported whatever was on it, or in it. As it is impossible to fall here by accident, as one does on earth, so it is impossible to sink in the water. All our movements are in direct response to our minds, and we cannot come to harm or suffer accident. It is, I am afraid rather difficult to give a description of some of these things without going beyond the range of earthly minds and experience. So much has to be witnessed at first hand to gain any adequate idea of the wonders of these lands.

A short walk brought us to the church that I had seen in the distance, and which I had expressed a keenness to visit.

It was a medium-sized building in the Gothic style, and it resembled the 'parish church' familiar on earth. It was situated in pleasant surroundings, which seemed the more spacious by the absence of any railings or walls to define its ecclesiastical limits. The surface of the stone of which it was constructed had the newness and freshness of recent building, but in point of fact, it had been in existence many years of earth time. Its exterior cleanliness was merely consonant with all things here—there is no decay. Nor is there any smoky atmosphere to cause blackening and discoloration! There was, of course, no churchyard attached. Even though some people cling so tenaciously to their old earthly religious predilections and practices here, it is hardly to be supposed that in erecting a church in which to carry them on, they would also include an entirely useless burial-ground!

Close beside the main door there was the customary notice board, but this gave only the nature of the services, which were those of the Established Church. No mention was made at all of the times of the services, and I wondered how any congregation of this kind could possibly assemble where time, as it is known on earth has no existence. For here there is no night and day by the alternation of which time can be measured. It is perpetual day. The great celestial sun for ever shines, as I have already told you. Neither do we have the many other indications of time that force themselves upon the earthly consciousness—such, for example, as hunger and fatigue. Nor in the more lengthy passage of time such as the ageing of the physical body and the dulling of the mental faculties. Here we have no recurrent seasons of spring, autumn. and winter. Instead we enjoy the glory of perpetual summer—and we never tire of it!

As usual, I turned to my friend for information on this point of congregational assemblage. To gather the people to the church was perfectly simple, he said. Whoever is in charge has only to send out his thoughts to his congregation, and those that wish to come forth will assemble! There was no need for bell-ringing. The emission of thought is far more thorough and exact! That is simple so far as the congregation is concerned. They have merely to wait until the thought reaches them, either in a direct call to attend, or by the urge to attend. But where does the ministering clergyman obtain his indication of the approach of service-time? That question, I was told, raised a much greater problem.

With the absence of earth-time in the spirit world, our lives are ordered by events; events, that is, that are part of our life. I

31

do not refer now to incidental occurrences, but to what, on earth, would be regarded as recurrent happenings. We have many such events here, as I hope to show you as we proceed, and in doing so you will see how we know that the performance of certain acts, individually or collectively, are clearly brought to our minds. The establishment of this church we were now inspecting saw also the gradual building up of a regular order of services, such as those who belong to its particular denomination on earth are familiar with. The clergyman who is acting as pastor to this strange flock would feel, by his duties on earth, the approach of the usual 'day' and 'time' when the services were held. It would be, in this respect, instinctive. It would, moreover, grow stronger with practice, until this mental perception would assume absolute regularity, as it is considered on the earth-plane. With this firmly established, the congregation have but to await the call from their minister.

The notice-board gave a list of the usual services commonly seen outside an earthly church of the same denomination. One or two items were noticeably absent, however; such as the provision for marriages and baptisms. The former omission I could understand; the latter could only imply that baptism was unnecessary, since only the baptized would be in 'heaven'— where presumably they deemed this church to be situated!

We went within, and found ourselves in a very lovely building, conventional in design, and containing little that is not to be seen in any such church upon the earth-plane. There were some beautiful stained-glass windows portraying scenes in the lives of the 'saints', through which the light poured evenly from all sides of the church at the same time, producing a strange effect in the air from the colors of the window-glass. Provision for heating the building was, of course, quite superfluous. There was a fine organ at one end, and the main altar, built of stone, was richly carved. Beyond this, there was a certain plainness which in no way detracted from its general beauty as a piece of architecture. Everywhere was there evidence of a lavish care being expended upon it, which, considering where this church was existing, is not surprising, when it is remembered under what dispensation such a building can exist at all!

We sat down for a little while, finding a calm and peaceful air about the whole place, and then we decided that we had seen all there was to be seen, and we made our way out into the open.

IV. HOME OF REST

As we walked along, at least two of us pondered upon what we had seen—and its implications. Our young friend—who told us her name was Ruth—put a number of questions to us, but I withheld any attempt to answer, since I was but a new-comer myself, in favor of my friend, whose name—Edwin—I have omitted to give so far.

Ruth, it appeared, had never been an active 'churchgoer' whilst on earth, but she was a kindly soul, as it was plain to see, and it was plain to see, also, that her abstention from church-going had made no difference to her ultimate destination as viewed by the earth. Her service to others had done more for her spiritual welfare than all the outward display of congregational religion, which so often is but outward display. Like myself, she was very surprised to find, here in spirit, the complete paraphernalia of orthodox religion. Edwin told her that she had only seen one example of it so far, and there were plenty of others. Having seen this, however, one had seen them all, more or less. Each denomination, of course, holds to its own particular creed and formularies, such as it had on earth, with a few minor differences, as we had just seen.

Such spiritual somnolence is no novelty in spirit. The earth world is to blame. Religious contentions and controversies are at the bottom of all the ignorance and lack of knowledge that so many people bring with them into the spirit world, and if the minds of such people are stubborn and they are unable really to think for themselves, then do they remain shackled to their narrow religious views, thinking it to be all the truth, until a day of spiritual awakening dawns for them. Then they will see that their slavish adherence to their creeds is holding them back. It is to be so much lamented that for every one who leaves, forever, these misguided congregations, another will come to fill his place—until the time comes when the whole earth knows the truth of the world of spirit. Of course they do no harm as they are, here, beyond retarding their own spiritual progression. Once they realize what they are doing to themselves, and take the first step forward, their joy knows no bounds. They will realize the 'time' they have apparently wasted.

Now it may be asked, if, with the acquisition of knowledge

and truth, these extensions of earthly religions into the spirit world are better done away with, what will you put in their place? It sounds like a condemnation of communal worship.

By no means. We have our communal worship here, but it is purged of every trace of meaningless creeds, of doctrines and dogmas. We worship the Great and Eternal Father in truth, absolute truth. We are of one mind, and one mind only. And no one is called upon to believe blindly—or to profess to do so—something which is utterly incomprehensible to any mind. There are many, many things here which we do not understand—and it will take eons of time before we even have a faint gleam of understanding them. But we are not asked to understand them; we are asked to take them as they are. It makes no difference whatever to our soul's progression. We shall be able to progress far—and far beyond that—before we shall ever need to think about understanding such things. And so we have one mind in our worship of the All-highest.

Such are the matters we discussed—it was Edwin who expounded—as we walked along in the beautiful air of God's heaven.

Ruth espied a rather stately building set among some well-wooded grounds, which also aroused my curiosity. On appealing to our guide, Edwin told us that it was a home of rest for those who had come into spirit after long illness, or who had had a violent passing, and who were, in consequence, suffering from shock. We wondered if it would be possible to peep inside, without appearing to be curiosity-seekers. He assured us that it would be quite in order to do so, as he had given his services there, and was therefore persona grata. Added to which was the fact that he knew we had that necessary sympathy which would banish any thought of inquisitiveness. As we drew near I could see that the building was in no sense a 'hospital' in outward semblance, whatever its functions might be. It was built in the classical style, two or three stories high, and it was entirely open upon all sides. That is to say, it contained no windows as we know them on earth. It was white in color as far as the materials of its composition were concerned, but immediately above it there was to be seen a great shaft of blue light descending upon, and enveloping, the whole building with its radiance, the effect of which was to give a striking blue tinge to the whole edifice. This great ray was the downpouring of life—a healing ray—sent to those who had already passed here, but who were not yet awake. When they were fully restored to spiritual health, there would be a splendid awakening, and they would be introduced into their new land.

I noticed that there was quite a number of people seated upon the grass in the grounds, or walking about. They were relatives and friends of those who were undergoing treatment within the hall of rest, and whose awakening was imminent. Although, doubtless, they could have been summoned upon the instant when necessary, yet, following their old earthly instinct, they preferred to wait close at hand for the happy moment. They were all supremely joyful, and very excited, as could be seen by the expressions on their faces, and many were the friendly smiles we received as we walked among them. Many of them, too, came forward to welcome us among them, thinking that we had come for the same reason as themselves. We told them of our true purpose, however, and they sped us on our way.

I observed that most of the people waiting in the gardens were not habited in their earth clothes, and I assumed that most of them had been in spirit for some considerable time. Such was not necessarily the case, Edwin told us. They had the right to wear their spirit robes by virtue of the fact that they were inhabitants of this realm we were now in. And the robes they wore were eminently suited to both the place and the situation. It is difficult to describe this costume because so much rests in being able to give some comparison with a particular earthly fabric. Here we have no such materials, and all outward appearances are produced, not by the texture of the material, but by the kind and degree of light that is the essence of a spirit robe. Those that we now saw were in 'flowing' form and of full length, and the colors—blue and pink in varying degrees of intensity—seemed to interweave themselves throughout the whole substance of the robes. They looked very comfortable to wear, and like everything here, they require no attention to keep them in a state of perfect preservation, the spirituality of the wearer alone accounting for that.

The three of us were still wearing our earthly style of raiment, and Edwin suggested that, for our present purposes, we might change to our natural element in the matter of clothes. I was quite willing, of course, to fall in with any suggestion that he might like to make, as I turned to him for everything in my lack of knowledge. Ruth also seemed very keen to try this change, but the question that puzzled us both was how it was to be accomplished.

Possibly there are people on the earth-plane who are willing to believe that such a situation as this would involve the ceremony of being formally presented with a spirit robe in the presence of a goodly gathering of celestial beings, who had come to witness the bestowing of our heavenly reward, and to be officially invited to take our 'eternal rest'.

Let me hasten to say that such was most emphatically not the case.

What did take place was very simply this: immediately I had expressed the wish to follow Edwin's suggestion of discarding my earthly style of clothes, those very clothes faded away— dissolved—and I was attired in my own particular spirit robe—of the same description as those I could see about me. Edwin's had changed likewise, and I noticed that his seemed to send out a greater strength of color than mine. Ruth's was the same as mine, and needless to say, she was full of joyful delight with this new manifestation of the spirit. My old friend had experienced the change before, so his costume was not new to him. But speaking for myself—and I am sure for Ruth—I never at any moment felt the slightest embarrassment or strangeness or self-consciousness in this revolutionary—as it might seem to be— alteration in our external appearance. On the contrary, it seemed quite natural and perfectly in order, and unquestionably it was in proper keeping with our present surroundings, the more so, as I soon discovered when we walked into the home of rest. Nothing would have been more incongruous than earthly apparel in such a building, which in its interior disposition and accommodations was totally unlike anything to be seen upon the earth-plane.

As we entered, Edwin was greeted as an old friend by one who came forward to meet us. He briefly explained his mission and our presence there, and we were made welcome to see all that we wished.

An outer vestibule led into a lofty hall of considerable dimensions. The space that would ordinarily be devoted to windows was occupied by tall pillars set some distance apart, and this arrangement was carried out through all four walls. There was very little in the way of interior decoration, but it must not be supposed from this that the apartment had a cold, barrack-like appearance. It was anything but that. The floor was carpeted with some very soft covering in a sober design, and here and there a handsomely wrought tapestry was hanging upon the walls. Occupying the whole of the floor space were extremely comfortable-looking couches, each of which bore a recumbent form, quite still, and obviously sleeping profoundly. Moving quietly about were a number of men and women intent upon watching the different couches and their burdens.

I noticed as soon as we entered this hall that we came under the influence of the blue ray, and its effect was one of pronounced energizing as well as tranquility. Another noticeable quality was the entire absence of any idea of an institution with its inevitable officialdom. There was no question of patronage, nor did I feel the least shade of being among strangers. Those in attendance upon the sleepers did so, not in the attitude of a certain task to be done willy-nilly, but as though they were performing a labor of love in the sheer joy of doing it. Such, indeed, was precisely the case. The glad awakening of these sleeping souls was an ever recurrent joy to them, no less than to the people who had come to witness it.

I learned that all the 'patients' in this particular hall had gone through lingering illnesses before passing over. Immediately after their dissolution they are sent gently into a deep sleep. In some cases the sleep follows instantly—or practically without break—upon the physical death. Long illness prior to passing into the spirit world has a debilitating effect upon the mind, which in turn has its influence upon the spirit body. The latter is not serious, but the mind requires absolute rest of varying duration. Each case is treated individually, and eventually responds perfectly to its treatment. During this sleep-state the mind is completely resting. There are no unpleasant dreams, or fevers of delirium.

While gazing upon this perfect manifestation of Divine Providence, the thought came to me of those absurd earthly notions of 'eternal rest,' 'everlasting sleep', and the many other equally foolish earthly conceptions, and I wondered if, by some chance or other, this sleep I was now beholding had been distorted by earthly minds into a state of eternal slumber, whither all souls pass at dissolution, there to await, in countless years' time, the awful 'last day'—the dread 'Day of Judgment'. Here was the visible refutation of such a senseless belief.

Neither of my two friends had awakened in this—or other— hall of rest, so they told me. Like myself, they had suffered no lengthy illness, and the end of their earth lives had come quite quickly and quite pleasantly.

The patients resting upon their couches looked very peaceful. Constant watch is kept upon them, and at the first flutterings of returning consciousness, others are summoned, and all is ready for the full awakening. Some will wake up partially, and then sink back again into slumber. Others will shake off their sleep at once, and it is then that those experienced souls in attendance will have, perhaps, their most difficult task. Until that moment, in fact, it has been mostly a matter of watching and waiting. In so many cases it has to be explained to the newly awakened soul that he has 'died' and is alive. They will remember usually their long illness, but some are quite unaware that they have passed over into spirit, and when the true state of affairs has been gently and quietly explained to them, they often have an urgent desire to go back to the earth, perhaps to those who are sorrowing, perhaps to those for whose care and welfare they were responsible. They are told that nothing can be done by their going back, and that others of experience will take care of those circumstances that are so distressing them. Such awakenings are not happy ones by comparison with those who wake up with the full realization of what has taken place. Were the earth more enlightened, this would be the more often the case, and there would be a great deal less distress to the newly awakened soul.

The earth world thinks itself very advanced, very 'civilized'. Such estimation is begotten of blind ignorance. The earth world, with all things appertaining thereto, is looked upon as of the very first importance, and the spirit world is regarded as something dim and distant. When a soul finally arrives there, it is quite time enough to begin thinking about it. Until that time comes there is no need even to bother about it. That is the attitude of mind of thousands upon thousands of incarnate souls, and here, in this hall of rest, we witnessed people awakening from their spirit sleep. We saw kind and patient spirits trying so hard to convince these same people that they had really 'died'. And this hall of rest is but one place out of many where the same service is being carried on unceasingly, and all because the earth world is so very superior in knowledge!

We were shown another large hall similarly appointed, where those whose passing had been sudden and violent were also in their temporary sleep. These cases were usually more difficult to manage than those we had just seen. The suddenness of their departure added far greater confusion to the mind. Instead of a steady transition, the spirit body had in many cases been forcibly ejected from the physical body, and precipitated into the spirit world. The passing over had been so sudden that there seemed to them to be no break in their lives. Such people are taken in hand quickly by bands of souls who devote all their time and the whole of their energies to such work. And in the hall of rest we could now see the results of their labors. Had so many of these souls had but a small knowledge of spirit matters, these awakenings would have been so much the happier.

I do assure you it is not a pleasant sight to see these gentle, patient helpers wrestling mentally—and sometimes almost physically—with people who are wholly ignorant of the fact that they are 'dead'. It is a most saddening sight, which I can vouch for from first hand evidence, for have I not seen it? And who is to blame for this state of affairs? Most of these souls blame themselves when they have been here long enough to appreciate their new condition, or alternatively, they blame the world they have but recently left for tolerating such blindness and stupidity.

Edwin hinted that perhaps we had seen all that we wished, and truth to tell, both Ruth and I were not sorry to leave. For it must be recalled that we were both comparatively new arrivals, and we had not yet sufficient experience to be able to withstand sights that were in themselves distressing. So we passed out into the open again, and we took a path that skirted a large orchard of fruit trees, similar to, though much more extensive than, that wherein I had had my first taste of celestial fruit. It was close at hand for the use of the newly awakened—and, of course, for anyone else who wished to partake of the stimulating fruit.

It occurred to me that Edwin was expending a good deal of his time upon us, perhaps at the expense of his own work. But he told us that what he was now doing, was, in many respects, his usual work—not only to help people to become accustomed to their new surroundings, but to help those who were just beginning to shake off their old religious ideas, and break away from the stifling of their minds as members of orthodox communities here. I was glad to know this, because it meant that he would continue to be our cicerone.

Now that we were again in the open, the question arose: should we continue to wear our spirit dress, or should we go back to our old attire? As far as Ruth was concerned, she would not hear of any changing back. She declared her perfect satisfaction with what she was wearing, and demanded of us to know what possible earthly costume could ever improve upon it. In the face of such a powerful argument, we were bound to submit. But what of Edwin and me? My friend had only reverted to his earthly cassock to keep me company and to help me feel at home. And so I decided that I would stay as I now was—in my spirit apparel.

As we walked along we fell to chatting about the various earthly notions touching the personal appearance of spirit people. Ruth mentioned 'wings' in connection with 'angelic beings', and we were all at once agreed that such an idea was nothing less than preposterous. Could any means of locomotion be more clumsy or ponderous, or thoroughly unpracticable? We supposed that artists of ancient days must have been largely responsible for this wide departure from actuality. One presumes they thought that some means of personal locomotion was essential for spirit people, and that the ordinary mundane method of using one's legs was far too earthly to be admitted, even as a remote possibility, into the heavenly realms. Having no knowledge whatever of the power of thought here, and its direct application in the literal movement of ourselves through these realms, they were thrown back upon the only means of movement through space known to them—the use of wings. One wonders if there are still earth people who really believe that we are only partly removed from some form of large bird! Among the thinking, modern science has managed to dispel some of the absurd conceptions so long prevalent.

We had not gone very far when Edwin bethought him that we might like to make our way to the city which we could see plainly not too far away. I say 'not too far away', but that should not be misunderstood into meaning that distance here is of any account. It certainly is not! I mean that the city lay sufficiently close for us to visit it without making any deviation from our general direction. Ruth and I agreed at once that we should like to proceed there forthwith, as a city of the spirit world must be something of a new revelation to us in itself.

Then the question came to our minds: should we walk, or should we employ a faster method? We both felt that we should like to try exactly what the power of thought can do, but as before, in other circumstances, we were both devoid of any knowledge of how to put these forces into action. Edwin told us that once we had performed this very simple process of thinking, we should have no difficulty whatever in the future. In the first place, it was necessary to have confidence, and in the second, our concentration of thought must not be a half-hearted affair. To borrow an earthly allusion, we 'wish ourselves' there, wherever it may be, and there we shall find ourselves! For the first few occasions it may be required to make something of a conscious effort; afterwards we can move ourselves whithersoever we wish—one might almost say, without thinking! To recall earthly methods, when you wish to sit down, or walk, or perform any one of the many earthly actions that are so familiar, you are not conscious of making any very definite effort of thought in order to bring about your desires. The thought very rapidly passes through your mind that you wish to sit down, and you sit down. But you have given no heed to the many muscular movements, and so on, involved in the simple action. They have become as second nature. And so it is precisely the same with us here. We just think that we wish to be in a certain place, and we are there. I must, of course, qualify that statement by saying that all places are not open to us here. There are many realms where we are not able to enter except in very special circumstances, or only if our state of progression permits. That, however, does not affect the method of locomotion here; it merely restricts us in certain well-defined directions.

Being severely practical, I mentioned to Edwin that as we wished, all three of us, to be together, then must we not all wish to be at the same place, and must we not have some very definite locality in mind upon which to fasten our thoughts? He replied that there were several factors to be borne in mind in this particular instance. One factor was that it was our initial essay in thought locomotion, and that he would, more or less, 'take charge' of us. We should automatically remain in close contact with each other, since we had voiced the wish and intention of doing so. These two facts together were sufficient to afford us a safe and sure arrival in company at our desired destination! When we became quite proficient in these methods we should have no difficulty in this connection.

It must be remembered that thought is as instantaneous as it is possible to imagine, and there is no possibility of our losing ourselves in illimitable space! I had had my first example of travelling through space in this way immediately after my passing, but then I had moved comparatively slowly with my eyes firmly closed. Edwin then suggested that it would give us some pleasant amusement if we were to try an experiment for ourselves. He assured us that we could not, in any circumstances, come to any harm whatever. He proposed that Ruth and I should project ourselves to a small clump of trees lying about a quarter of a mile away—as measured by the earth. We all three sat on the grass, and we gazed at our objective. He suggested that if we felt at all nervous that we might hold each other's hands! Ruth and I were to go alone, while he would remain on the grass. We were just to think that we wished to be beside yonder trees. We looked at one another with a great deal of merriment, both of us wondering what would happen next, and neither of us taking the initiative. We were pondering thus, when Edwin said: 'Off you go!' His remark must have supplied the requisite stimulus, for I took Ruth's hand, and the next thing we knew we found ourselves standing beneath the trees!

We looked at one another, if not in amazement, then in something that was very much like it. Casting our eyes whence we had just come, we saw Edwin waving his hand to us. Then a strange thing happened. We both beheld immediately before our faces what seemed to be a flash of light. It was not blinding, nor did it startle us in any way. It simply caught our attention just as the earthly sun would do when coming from behind a cloud. It illumined the small space before our eyes as we stood there. We remained quite still, full of expectancy for what might transpire. Then clearly, beyond any vestige of doubt, we heard—whether with the ear or with the mind, I could not then say—the voice of Edwin asking us if we had enjoyed our brief journey, and to go along back to him in exactly the same way as we had left him. We both made some remark upon what we had heard, trying to decide if it were really Edwin we had heard speaking. Scarcely had we mentioned our perplexity at this latest demonstration of the spirit, when Edwin's voice spoke again, assuring us that he had heard us as we cogitated upon the matter! So surprised and altogether delighted were we with this fresh manifestation of the power of thought, following so swiftly upon the other, that we determined to return to Edwin upon the instant, and demand a full explanation. We repeated the procedure, and there we were, once more, seated one each side of my old friend, who was laughing joyously at our wonderment.

He was prepared for the onslaught that came—for we bombarded him with questions—and he told us that he had purposely kept this surprise for us. Here, he said, was another instance of the concreteness of thought. If we can move ourselves by the power of thought, then it follows that we should also be able to send our thoughts by themselves, unhindered by all ideas of distance. When we focus our thoughts upon some person in the spirit world, whether they be in the form of a definite message, or whether they are solely of an affectionate nature, those thoughts will reach their destination without fail, and they will be taken up by the percipient. That is what happens in the spirit world. How it happens, I am not prepared to say. That is another of the many things we take as we find, and rejoice therein. We had, so far, used our 'organs of speech' in conversing with each other. It was quite natural, and we hardly gave the matter any thought. It had not occurred either to Ruth or myself that some means of communication at a distance must be available here. We were no longer limited by earthly conditions, yet so far we had not observed anything that would take the place of the usual mode of intercommunication upon the earth. This very absence should, perhaps, have told us to expect the unexpected.

Although we can thus send our thoughts, it must not be assumed that our minds are as an open book for all to read. By no means. We can, if we so will, deliberately keep our thoughts to ourselves; but if we should think idly, as it were; if we should just let our thoughts ramble along under a loose control, then they can be seen and read by others. One of the first things to be done upon arrival here is to realize that thought is concrete, that it can create and build, and then our next effort is to place our own thoughts under proper and adequate control. But like so much else in the spirit world, we can soon learn to adjust ourselves to the new conditions if we have a mind to do so, and we shall never lack the most willing helpers in any or all of our difficulties. The latter, Ruth and I had already found out with relief and gratitude. Ruth was by now very impatient to be off to visit the city, and she insisted that Edwin should take us there immediately. And so, without further delay, we rose up from the grass, and with a word from our guide, we set forth.

V. HALLS OF LEARNING

As we approached the city, it was possible for us to gather some idea of its extensive proportions. It was, I hardly need say, totally unlike anything I had yet seen. It consisted of a large number of stately buildings each of which was surrounded with magnificent gardens and trees, with here and there pools of glittering water, clear as crystal, yet reflecting every shade of color known to earth, with many other tints to be seen nowhere but in the realms of spirit.

It must not be imagined that these beautiful gardens bore the slightest resemblance to anything to be seen upon the earth-plane. Earthly gardens at their best and finest are of the very poorest by comparison with these that we now beheld, with their wealth of perfect colorings and their exhalations of heavenly perfumes. To walk upon the lawns with such a profusion of nature about us held us spellbound. I had imagined that the beauty of the countryside, wherein I had had all my experience of spirit lands so far, could hardly be excelled anywhere.

My mind had reverted to the narrow streets and crowded pavements of the earth; the buildings huddled together because space is so valuable and costly; the heavy, tainted air, made worse by streams of traffic; I had thought of hurry and turmoil, and all the restlessness of commercial life and the excitement of passing pleasure. I had no conception of a city of eternal beauty, as far removed from an earthly city as the light of day is from black night. Here were fine broad thoroughfares of emerald green lawns in perfect cultivation, radiating, like the spokes of a wheel, from a central building which, as we could see, was the hub of the whole city. There was a great shaft of pure light descending upon the dome of this building, and we felt instinctively—without Edwin having to tell us—that in this temple we could together send up our thanks to the Great Source of all, and that there we should find none other than the Glory of God in Truth.

The buildings were not of any great height as we should measure and compare with earthly structures, but they were for the most part extremely broad. It is impossible to tell of what materials they were composed because they were essentially spirit fabrics. The surface of each smooth as of marble, yet it had the delicate texture and translucence of alabaster, while each building sent forth, as it were into the adjacent air, a stream of light of the palest shade of coloring. Some of the buildings were carved with designs of foliage and flowers, and others were left almost unadorned, as far as any smaller devices were concerned, relying upon their semiclassic nature for relief. And over all was the light of heaven shining evenly and uninterruptedly, so that nowhere were there dark places.

This city was devoted to the pursuit of learning, to the study and practice of the arts, and to the pleasures of all in this realm. It was exclusive to none, but free for all to enjoy with equal right. Here it was possible to carry on so many of those pleasant and fruitful occupations that had been commenced on the earth-plane. Here, too, many souls could indulge in some agreeable diversion which had been denied them, for a variety of reasons, whilst they were incarnate.

The first hall that Edwin took us into was concerned with the art of painting. This hall was of very great size and contained a long gallery, on the walls of which were hanging every great masterpiece known to man. They were arranged in such a way that every step of earthly progress could be followed in proper order, beginning with the earliest times and so continuing down to the present day. Every style of painting was represented, gathered from all points of the earth. It must not be thought that such a collection, as we were now viewing, is only of interest and service to people who have a full appreciation and understanding of the painter's art. Such could not be farther from the case.

There was a goodly number of people in the gallery when we entered, some of whom were moving about wherever their fancy took them. But there were many groups listening to the words of able teachers, who were demonstrating the various phases in the history of art as exemplified upon the walls, and they were, at the same time giving such a clear and interesting position that none could fail to understand.

A number of these pictures I recognized as I had seen their 'originals' in the earth's galleries. Ruth and I were astonished when Edwin told us that what we had seen in those galleries were not the originals at all. We were now seeing the originals for the first time. What we had seen was an earthly counterpart, which was perishable from the usual causes—for example, from fire or the general disintegration through the passage of time. But here we were viewing the direct results of the thoughts of the painter, created in the etheric before he actually transferred those thoughts to his earthly canvas. It could be plainly observed, in many cases, where the earthly picture fell short of that which the painter had in his mind. He had endeavored to reproduce his exact conception, but through physical limitations this exact conception had eluded him. In some instances it had been the pigments that had been at fault when, in the early times, the artist had been unable to procure or evolve the particular shade of color he wanted. But though he lacked physically, his mind had known precisely what he wished to do. He had built it up in the spirit—the results of which we were now able to see—while he had failed to do so on the material canvas.

That was one major difference that I noticed in the pictures, by comparison with what I had seen on the earth-plane. Another great point of dissimilarity—and the most important—was the fact that here all these pictures were alive. It is impossible to convey any idea of this paramount difference. These spirit pictures must be seen here to understand it. I can only just suggest an idea. These pictures, then, whether landscape or portrait, were never flat; that is, they did not seem to have been painted upon flat canvas. They possessed, on the other hand, all the completeness of relief. The subject stood forth almost as though it were a model—a model whereof one could take hold of all the elements that went to the making up of the subject of the picture. One felt that the shadows were real shadows cast by real objects. The colors glowed with life, even among the very early works before much progress had been made.

A problem came into my mind, for a solution of which I naturally turned to Edwin. It was this: as it would be undesirable, perhaps, as well as impracticable, to hang in these galleries every painting that emanated from the earth-plane, any idea of preferential treatment based upon the judgment of others did not seem quite consonant with spirit law, in so far as I was acquainted with it. What system is used for the selection of paintings to hang upon these walls? I was told that it was a question that is frequently asked by visitors to this gallery. The answer is that by the time an artist, whether he be good, bad, or just commonplace, has adjusted himself to his new life, he has no further illusions—if he ever harbored any—of his own work. Usually an extreme diffidence sets in, fostered by the immensity and the superlative beauty of this realm. So that in the end the problem becomes one of scarcity rather than superabundance!

When we gazed at the portraits of so many men and women whose names had worldwide fame, whether they lived in distant times or in the present day, it gave Ruth and me a strange feeling to think that we were now inhabitants of the same world as they, and that they, like ourselves, were very much alive, and not mere historic figures in the chronicles of the earth world.

In other parts of this same building were rooms wherein students of art could learn all that there is to be learned. The joy of these students is great in their freedom from their earthly restrictions and bodily limitations. Here instruction is easy, and the acquisition and application of knowledge equally facile to those who wish to learn. Gone are all the struggles of the student in the surmounting of earthly difficulties both of the mind and of the hands, and progress towards proficiency is consequently smooth and rapid. The happiness of all the students whom we saw, itself spread happiness to all who beheld it, for there is no limit to their endeavors when that bugbear of earthly life—fleeting time—and all the petty vexations of the mundane existence have been abandoned for ever. Is there any wonder that artists within this hall, and, indeed, in every other hall in the city, were enjoying the golden hours of their spiritual reward?

To have made a really exhaustive study of all the pictures in the gallery would have taken us too long for our present purposes, which were to acquire as comprehensive an idea of this realm as we could, so that later we could find our way about the more easily, and return to such places as had the most attraction for us. This was Edwin's idea, and Ruth and I were heartily in agreement with it. And so we tarried no longer in the hall of painting, and we passed on to another immense building.

This was the hall of literature, and it contained every work worthy of the name. Its interior was divided into smaller rooms than in the hall of painting. Edwin led us into one spacious apartment which contained the histories of all the nations upon the earth-plane. To anyone who has a knowledge of earthly history, the volumes with which the shelves of this section of the great library were filled, would prove illuminating. The reader would be able to gain, for the first time, the truth about the history of his country. Every word contained in these books was the literal truth. Concealment is impossible, because nothing but the truth can enter these realms.

I have since returned to this library and spent much profitable time among its countless books. In particular I have dipped into history, and I was amazed when I started to read. I naturally expected to find that history would be treated in the manner with which we are all familiar, but with the essential difference that now I should be presented with the truth of all historical acts and events. The latter I soon discovered to be the case, but I made another discovery that for the first moment left me astounded. I found that side by side with the statements of pure fact of every act by persons of historical note, by statesmen in whose hands was the government of their countries, by kings who were at the head of those same countries, side by side with such statements was the blunt naked truth of each and every motive governing or underlying their numerous acts—the truth beyond disputation. Many of such motives were elevated, many, many of them were utterly base; many were misconstrued, many distorted. Written indelibly upon these spirit annals were the true narratives of thousands upon thousands of human beings, who, whilst upon their earthly journey, had been active participants in the affairs of their country. Some were victims to others' treachery and baseness; some were the cause or origin of that treachery and baseness. None was spared, none omitted. It was all there for all to see—the truth, with nothing extenuated, nothing suppressed. These records had no respect for persons, whether it be king or commoner, churchman or layman. The writers had just set down the veridical story as it was. It required no adornment, no commentary. It spoke for itself. And I was profoundly thankful for one thing—that this truth had been kept from us until such time as we stood where we were now standing, when our minds would, in some measure, be prepared for revelations such as were here at hand.

So far I have mentioned only political history, but I also delved into church history, and the revelations I received in that direction were no better than those in the political sphere. They were, in fact, worse, considering in whose Name so many diabolical deeds were committed by men who, outwardly professing to serve God, were but instruments of men as base as themselves.

Edwin had forewarned me of what to expect in consulting these histories, but I had never anticipated the degree of fullness I should find in the narration of the true facts. The supposed motives given in our earthly history books were wide of the mark of the real motives on so many numberless occasions!

Although these books bore witness against the perpetrators of so many dark deeds in the earth world's history, they also bore witness to many deeds both great and noble. They were not there specifically for the purpose of providing evidence for and against, but because literature has become part of the fabric of human life. People take pleasure in reading. Is it not quite in accord with this life that there should be books for us to read? They may not be exactly the same as the earth books, but they are in precise keeping with all else here. And it is found that the pursuit of knowledge is far greater here than upon the earth-plane, since the necessity of turning our minds to the pressing needs and exigencies of incarnate life no longer exists here.

We passed through many other rooms where volumes upon every subject imaginable were at the disposal of all who wished to study them. And perhaps one of the most important subjects is that which has been called by some truly enlightened soul 'psychic science'—for science it is. I was astonished by the wealth of literature under this heading. Upon the shelves were books denying the existence of a spirit world, and denying the reality of spirit return. Many of the authors of them have since had the opportunity of looking again at their own works—but with very different feelings! They had become, in themselves, living witnesses against the contents of their own books.

We were very much struck by the beautiful bindings in which the books were encased, the material upon which they were inscribed, and the style of inscription. I turned to Edwin for information upon these points. He told me that the reproduction of books in the world of spirit was not the same process as in the case of paintings. I had seen for myself how the truth had been suppressed in the earthly volumes either through deliberate intent or through ignorance of the real facts. In the case of the paintings the artist had desired to depict in truth, so to speak, but through no real fault of his own he had been unable to do so. They had not perpetuated untruth, therefore; on the contrary, his mind had recorded what was entirely true. An author of a book would hardly write it with intentions diametrically opposed to those expressed within it. Who, then, writes the book of truth in spirit? The author of the earthly volume writes it—when he comes into the spirit world. And he is glad to do it. It becomes his work, and by such work he can gain the progress of his soul. He will have no difficulty with the facts, for they are here for him to record, and he records them—but the truth this time! There is no need to dissemble—in fact, it would be useless.

As to inscribing the books, are there not printing machines upon the earth? Of course there are! Then surely the spirit world is not to be the worse provided for in this respect? We have our methods of printing, but they are totally unlike those of the earth. We have our experts, who are also artists at their work, and it is work they love doing, or else they would not be doing it. The method of reproduction here is wholly a process of the mind, as with all else, and author and printer work together in complete harmony. The books that result from this close co-operation are works of art, they are beautiful creations which, apart altogether from their literary contents, are lovely to look upon. The binding of the book is another expert process, carried out by more artists, in wonderful materials never seen upon the earth, since they are of spirit only. But the books thus produced are not dead things that require a concentration of the whole mind upon them. They live just as much as the paintings we saw were living. To pick up a book and begin reading from it meant also to perceive with the mind, in a way not possible on earth, the whole story as it was being told, whether it be history or science, or the arts. The book, once taken in the hand by the reader, instantly responds, in very much the same way as the flowers respond when one approaches close to them. The purpose is different, of course.

All the vast numbers of books we saw were there for all to use at their leisure and to their heart's delight. There were no restrictions, no tiresome rules and regulations. Standing with all this enormous wealth of knowledge about us, I was staggered at my own ignorance, and Ruth felt the same. However, Edwin reassured me by telling us that we must not let the sight of so much knowledge frighten us, as we have the whole of eternity before us! It was a comforting reminder, and strange to say, a fact that one is inclined to overlook. It takes time to shake off finally that feeling of impermanence, of transience, that is so closely associated with the earth life. And in consequence we feel that we must see everything as quickly as we can, in spite of the fact that time, as a factor in our lives, has ceased to function.

By now Edwin thought it due to Ruth to show her something that would have a special appeal to her, and so he took us into the hall of fabrics. This was equally spacious, but the rooms were of greater dimensions than those of the two halls we had just viewed. Here were contained the scores upon scores of beautiful materials and cloths woven throughout the centuries, and of which practically nothing remains upon the earth-plane. It was possible to see here specimens of the materials that we read about in histories and chronicles in the descriptions of state ceremonies and festive occasions. And whatever may be said for the change of style and taste that has taken place throughout the ages, the earth world has lost a vast deal of its color in exchange for a dull drabness.

The colorings in many of the old materials were simply superb, while the magnificently-wrought designs revealed to us the art that has been lost to earth. Though perishable to the earth, they are imperishable to the spirit world. After making due allowance for the etherealization of these fabrics by their being in the spirit world, there remained in our minds a sufficiently vivid conception of what these rich fabrics must have looked like in their earthly element. Here again, it was possible to observe the gradual progress made in the designing and making of earthly materials, and it must be admitted, as far as I was able to judge, that progress proceeded up to a point when a retrograde movement was noticeable. I am, of course, speaking in a general sense.

A room of tapestries contained some superb examples of the artists' genius, the earthly counterparts of which have long since gone out of existence. Annexed to this apartment were smaller rooms where many happy, industrious souls were studying and practicing the art of tapestry weaving, with other equally happy souls ever at their side to help and instruct. This was not a tedious work of pupil and teacher, but the enjoyment of pure pleasure, which both could terminate for other things at any time they so wished. Ruth said that she would dearly love to join one of the groups engaged upon a large tapestry, and she was told that she could do so whenever she wished and that she would be welcomed with all the joy in the world into this community of friends. However, she would, for the present, remain with us upon our expeditions.

It may be thought that what we had seen as yet were nothing more than celestial museums, containing, it is true, magnificent specimens not to be seen upon earth, but museums, nevertheless. Now earthly museums are rather cheerless places. They have an aroma of mustiness and chemical preservatives, since their exhibits have to be protected from deterioration and decay. And they have to be protected from man, too, by uninspiring glass cases. But here there are no restrictions. All things within these halls are free and open for all to see and hold in the two hands. There is no mustiness, but the beauty of the objects themselves sends out many subtle perfumes, while the light of heaven streams in from all quarters to enhance the glories of man's handicrafts. No, these are no museums; very far from it. They are temples, rather, in which we spirit people are conscious of the eternal thanks that we owe to the Great Father for giving us such unbounded happiness in a land of which so many upon earth deny the reality. They would sweep all this away—for what? They know not. There are many, many beauties upon the earth-plane, but we in spirit must have none! Perhaps that is another reason why such deep sympathy is felt for us when we pass into spirit—because we have left behind us for ever all that is beautiful, to pass into a state of emptiness—a celestial vacuum. All that is beautiful, then, becomes exclusive to the earth world. Man's intelligence is of no further use when once he has passed to here, because here there is nothing upon which to exercise it! Just emptiness! No wonder that the realities and the immense fullness of the spirit world come as such a shock of revelation to those who were anticipating an eternity of celestial nothingness!

It is essential to understand that every occupation and every task performed by the inhabitants of this and higher realms is done willingly, for the pure wish of doing so, and never from the attitude of having to do it 'whether they like it or not'. There is no such thing as being compelled to undertake a task. Never is unwillingness felt or expressed. That is not to say that the impossible is attempted. We may be able to see the outcome of some action or another—or if we cannot, there are others of greater wisdom and knowledge who can—and we shall know whether to commence our task or withhold for the time being. We never want here for help and advice. You may recall my own suggestion earlier of trying to communicate with the earth to set right some matters in my own life, and that Edwin advised that I should seek advice later on upon the practicability of that course. So that it is the truth to say that the wish to do and to serve is the keynote here. I mention these matters so that a better understanding may be obtained of a particular hall that

Edwin took us into after we left the hall of fabrics.

This was, to all intents and purposes, a school where souls, who had had the misfortune to miss the benefits of some earthly knowledge and learning, could here equip themselves intellectually.

Knowledge and learning, education or erudition do not connote spiritual worth, and the inability to read and write do not imply the absence of it. But when a soul has passed into this life, when he sees the great, broad spiritual thoroughfare opening before him with its opportunities both manifold and multiform, he sees also that knowledge can help him on his spiritual way. He may not be able to read. Are all those splendid books to remain for ever closed to him now that he has the opportunity to read, while lacking the ability? Perhaps it will be asked: surely it is not necessary to be able to read in the spirit world? Things being what they are, there must be some form of mental perception to be gathered from books without the material aid of printed words? The same question might be asked of pictures and of all else here. Why the need for anything tangible? If we pursue this line of thought it will take us to that state of vacuity I have just mentioned.

The man who is unable to read will feel with his mind that something is contained within the book that he takes into his hands, but he will not know instinctively, or in any other way, the contents of it. But one who can read will, immediately upon his commencing to do so, find himself en rapport with the author's thoughts as set down, and the book will thus respond to him who reads.

To be able to write is not necessary, and many who have been unable to do so before passing here, have not bothered to supply the omission after their arrival.

We found in this school many souls busy with their studies, and thoroughly enjoying themselves. To acquire knowledge here is not tedious, because the memory works perfectly—that is, unfailingly—and the powers of mental perception are no longer hampered and confined by a physical brain. Our faculties for understanding are sharpened, and intellectual expansion is sure and steady. The school was the home of realized ambitions to most of the students within it. I chatted with a number of them, and each told me that what he was studying now, he had longed to study on earth, but had been denied the opportunity for reasons that are all too familiar. Some had found that commercial activities had left no time, or that the struggle for a living had absorbed all the means to do so.

The school was very comfortably arranged; there was, of course, no hint of regimentation. Each student followed his own course of study independently of anyone else. He seated himself comfortably, or he went into the lovely gardens without. He began when he wanted, and he finished when he wanted, and the more he dipped into his studies the more interested and fascinated he became. I can speak from personal experience of the latter, since there is much that I have studied in the great library since my first introduction to it.

As we left the school, Edwin suggested that we might like to sit on the grass beneath some fine trees and rest ourselves. That was simply his way—a perfectly natural one—of expressing it. We do not suffer bodily fatigue, but at the same time we do not continue endlessly at the same occupation; that would mean monotony, and there is no monotony here such as we used to endure on earth. But Edwin knew from experience the different emotions that take place in the minds of newly arrived souls into spirit lands, and so he halted for the time being our further explorations.

VI. SOME QUESTIONS ANSWERED

EDWIN told us that a very large majority of people are no sooner arrived in spirit than a burning enthusiasm overtakes them as the spirit world reveals itself to them in the new life, and they immediately want to rush back to the earth and tell the world all about it. He had already explained to me some of the difficulties in my own suggestion of returning.

Another very natural tendency was to ask numberless questions upon this life in general, and he remarked that in this both Ruth and I had exercised quite an unusual restraint! Certainly I had refrained from asking too many questions, but then, Edwin had explained as much as we should be able to understand as we proceeded. I confessed, though, now that he broached the matter, that there were many things about which I should very much like to know. Ruth said she had the same feelings, and that doubtless many of our queries coincided. The difficulty was where to begin.

We had allowed our journeyings to bring forth their own

problems for Edwin's solution, but there were other considerations of a general nature which arose from the contemplation of spirit lands as a whole. One of the first that arose to my mind as we sat on the grass, with heavenly flowers round about us, was the extent of this realm in which we were now living. It reached as far as the eye could see—and that was a great deal farther than we could ever see upon the earth-plane on the finest and clearest day in the summer. This in itself was too wonderful for words, but it also gave an indication of the immensity of this particular realm. And we had only seen the tiniest fraction of it so far! We still thought in terms of earthly distances. Was there any boundary to this realm? Did it stretch still farther beyond the range of our vision? If there were any termination, what was beyond? Could we go and see for ourselves?

Certainly there was a boundary to this realm, Edwin explained to us. And we could go and see it for ourselves whenever we wished. Beyond this were other and still more realms. Each soul as it passed into spirit passed into that realm for which it had fitted itself when upon the earth—into that realm and no other. Edwin had in the beginning described this land as the land of the great harvest—a harvest that was sown on earth. We could judge for ourselves, then, whether we considered that harvest a good one or a poor one. We should find that there were others infinitely better—and others infinitely worse. In plain words, there are other realms immeasurably more beautiful than that in which we were now happily living; realms of surpassing beauty into which we cannot penetrate until such time as we have earned the right to enter, either as visitors or as inhabitants. But though we may not pass into them, the glorious souls who dwell in them can come into realms of less celestial rarity, and can visit us here. Edwin himself had seen some of them, and we hoped to do so as well. Indeed, they constantly make visitations to consult and converse with the dwellers here, to give advice and help, to give rewards and commendations, and there was no doubt but that my own matter could be placed before one of these master souls for his guidance upon it.

At certain times, too, these transcendent beings make special visitations when the whole realm is celebrating a great occasion, such, for example, as the two major earth festivals of Christmas and Easter. Ruth and I were very astonished at the latter, because we thought them both to be so essentially of the earth. But it was the manner of celebrating them, and not the festivals themselves, which was particular to the earth. In the spirit lands both Christmas and Easter are looked upon as birthdays: the first, a birth into the earth world; the second, a birth into the spirit world. In this realm the two celebrations synchronize with those upon the earth, since there is then a greater spiritual link between the two worlds than would be the case if the festivals were held independently of season. It is not so, however, in the higher realms, where laws of a different nature are in operation.

On the earth-plane the anniversary of Christmas has remained fixed for many centuries on a certain date. The exact day of the first Christmas has been lost, and it is impossible now to ascertain with any precision, by earthly means, when it occurred. Even were it possible, it is too late to make any alteration, since the present fixed has been established by long tradition and practice. The feast of Easter is movable—a stupid custom, since oft-times the chosen date bears no relation to the first and original date. There is some hope that a change will be made, and the feast stabilized. In no sense are we subservient to the earth in these matters, but at the same time a foolish obstinacy would lead us nowhere. Therefore it is that vexations co-operate with the earth-plane in our united rejoicing.

The higher realms have their own very good reasons for what may seem to be a departure from a recognized order. Such reasons do not concern us—until we ourselves pass to those higher states.

Beyond those two great festivals we do not have much else in common with the earth world in the matter of feasts. The most of the latter are merely ecclesiastical feasts which have no spiritual significance in the broadest sense, since so many are the outcome of religious doctrines which have no application in the spirit world. The feast of Epiphany, for example, is founded upon a very colorful story, and was in ancient times celebrated by the people in a secular fashion as well as a religious. It is now solely religious, and of very little moment here. The feast of Pentecost is another instance of the Church's blindness. The Holy Spirit—to use the Church's phrase—has been, is, and always will be descending upon all those who are worthy to receive it! Not upon one specific occasion, but always.

Both Ruth and I were very interested to learn how Christmas was celebrated in these realms, since, on the earth, beyond a few church services, the feast of the Nativity has developed into a secular affair, the main feature being that of prodigious eating and drinking. Edwin told us that in spirit we can experience the same degree of happiness as is the case on earth where that happiness is the outcome or expression of kindness; where our merrymaking is blended with the knowledge or the remembrance of whose great day we are celebrating. Those of us who wish—and there are many such—can decorate our houses and dwelling-places with evergreens, as we were accustomed to do on earth. By evergreens I mean those particular trees and shrubs that are so-called on earth. Here everything is eternally 'evergreen'! We join together in merry company, and if it is felt that the time would not be right without our having something to eat, then, is there not a superabundance of that most perfect fruit, that I have told you about, to delight the hearts of the most fastidious?

But I have only told of the more personal side of this feast. It is at this time that we have visitants of the higher realms to see us, perfect beings, among whom is he whose earthly birth we are celebrating. And these beauteous souls have but to pass upon their way to fill us with such an ecstasy of spiritual exaltation as to remain with us for long after their return to their high estate

At Easter time we have similar visitations, but there is a far greater degree of rejoicing, because to us the birth into the spirit world must, by the very nature of things, be of far greater significance. Indeed, when once we have left the earth-plane we are inclined to forget our earthly birthday, since the greater contains the lesser. It is only our earthly connections, if we have any, that will serve to remind us.

I have enlarged upon this subject somewhat to try to show you that we are not living in a state of fervid religious emotion for all eternity. We are human, though so many people still on the earth-plane would have us to be otherwise! Such people will inevitably be in the same relative position as ourselves one day, and nothing is so calculated to instill humility as the realization of what one once held as firm and decided opinions.

I have digressed a little from our first topic as we threw ourselves on the grass, but in our conversation one thing led to another until we seemed to have wandered some way from our course.

Mention has only been made of the higher realms. What of

the lower spheres that Edwin spoke about when I referred to the boundaries of this particular realm? We could visit them whenever we desired. We can always proceed to a realm lower than our own, while we cannot always mount higher. But it was by no means advisable to wander into the lower spheres except under expert guidance or before proper tuition had been given. Before informing us more fully upon this subject, Edwin advised us to see more of our own pleasant land first.

And now as to what constitutes the precise boundaries of this realm. We are accustomed to a knowledge of the rotundity of the earth and to seeing with our eyes the distant horizon. In contemplating this world of spirit we must abandon in many respects that idea of distance which we measure with the eye, since distance becomes annihilated by our immensely rapid means of transit. Any suggestion of terrestrial flatness is soon dispelled by the view of hills and rolling downs.

Again, the atmosphere is crystal clear and our sight is not limited by the instrument of a physical body. We are not confined to keeping our feet on the ground. If we can move ourselves laterally over these lands by the power of our thought, we can also move ourselves vertically—Edwin told us. And I must say that this had never occurred to Ruth and me as yet. We were still in some ways limited by our earthly notions and habits of thought. If we could sink beneath the waters without harm, but rather with enjoyment, then, of course, we must be able to mount into the 'air' with the same safety and enjoyment! Ruth did not express any very keen desire to do so just yet! She preferred to wait, she said, until she had become more thoroughly acclimatized. I wholeheartedly shared her sentiments in the matter, which caused our good friend the greatest amusement.

In alluding to these few features I have done so because the earth world has always looked upon the spirit world as being relatively up or down. These are really considerations of a highly scientific nature, and I am not competent to enlarge upon them—moreover, as an inhabitant of these lands my whole outlook, both mental and spiritual, has had to undergo sweeping and fundamental changes, in spite of the fact that I had some small knowledge before I passed over. It is really of little moment to know the precise location of the spirit world with its many realms or spheres.

Where is the boundary between the earth world and the spirit world? Upon the instant of my passing, of which you will remember, I was fully conscious, when I arose from my bed in response to a very definite urge. At that moment I was in the spirit world. The two worlds, then, must interpenetrate one another. But as I moved away under the support and able guidance of Edwin, I was conscious of moving in no definite direction. I might have been travelling up, or down, or along. Movement, there certainly was. Edwin later informed me that I had passed through the lower spheres—and unpleasant ones— but that through the authority of his mission of coming to help me into my realm, we were both fully protected from any and every description of unpleasant influence. We were, in effect , completely invisible to all but those of our own realm and higher.

The transition from one realm to another is gradual as far as outward appearance is concerned, as well as in other respects, so that it would be difficult to assign to any particular locality the designation of boundary. That is exactly how the boundaries of our own realm are situated. They seem to melt almost imperceptibly into one another.

Edwin now proposed that by way of practical illustration we should go and see one of these boundaries that had perplexed us so much. We again placed ourselves under Edwin's expert guidance, and we moved off.

At once we found ourselves upon a very wide expanse of grassland, but we both noticed that the turf felt less soft beneath our feet; it was, in fact, becoming hard as we walked along. The beautiful emerald green was fast vanishing, and the grass was taking on a dull yellow appearance, very similar to earthly grass that has been scorched by the sun and has lacked water. We saw no flowers, no trees, no dwellings, and everywhere seemed bleak and barren. There was no sign of human life, and life seemed to be rapidly disappearing from beneath our feet, as by now the grass had ceased altogether, and we were upon hard ground. We noticed, too, that the temperature had fallen considerably. Gone was all that beautiful, genial warmth. There was a coldness and dampness in the air which seemed to cling to our beings, and cast a chill over our very souls. Poor Ruth clung to Edwin's arm, and I am not ashamed to say that I did the same, and was very glad to do so. Ruth then visibly shivered, and stopped abruptly, imploring us not to go any farther. Edwin threw his arms around both our shoulders, and told us that we had no need to be the least afraid, as he had the power to protect us fully. However, he could see the state of deep depression, as well as oppression, that had fallen upon us, and so he turned us gently round, placed his arms about our waists, and we once more found ourselves sitting beneath our own lovely trees, with the glorious flowers close beside us, and our own warm air once more closing upon us with its heavenly balm.

It is perhaps superfluous to add that Ruth and I were both glad to be back again in the city. We had been only on the threshold of the lower spheres, but we had gone far enough to gather more than an inkling of what lay beyond. I knew that it would be some time yet before I would penetrate there, and I could now clearly perceive the wisdom of Edwin's admonitions.

As we were on the subject of these spiritual boundaries, and in spite of the fact that we had temporarily ceased our explorations, I could not refrain from asking Edwin about the frontiers of the higher realms. I knew that there could not possibly be anything unpleasant about these, and so I hinted that, by way of contrast and to offset our recent chilling experience in the other direction, we might perhaps visit the border through which our celestial visitants pass. Edwin said that there was no objection whatever, and so once again we started off.

Again we found ourselves upon grassland, but with a striking difference. The turf upon which we were walking was infinitely softer than that of the interior of the realm. The green of the verdure was even brighter than we had thought possible. The flowers were growing in still greater profusion, and the intensity of color, of perfume, and of health-giving power transcended anything we had encountered. The very air seemed to be imbued with rainbow tints. There were few dwellings at the spot where we were immediately standing, but behind us were to be seen some of the most stately and beautiful houses I have ever seen. In these houses, so our friend told us, lived wondrous souls who, though nominally belonging to our own realm, were by virtue of their spiritual progression and particular gifts and work, in close contact with the higher realms, into which they had full authority and the requisite power to pass upon their various occasions. Edwin promised that we should return to this place after we had seen as much of the city as we wished, and there we could discuss—in one of the houses—my future work, as well as Ruth's. He had taken Ruth under his wing, and for her part she expressed her gratitude for his kindness in doing so. It had several times crossed my mind what form of spiritual work I could engage myself upon, as soon as I had become sufficiently familiar with the new life and the new land.

Just as we had been heavy with chill and oppression at the borderline of the dark spheres, so were we now warmed and filled with such an elation that we were almost silent in wonderment. As we moved along, bathed in radiance, we felt such a spiritual exhilaration that Edwin's description of the visitations of personages from the higher realms at once came to my mind, and I almost knew what to expect when I should be fortunate enough to witness such a visitation. Standing here, one had the overwhelming desire to strive for that progression that would entitle one to inhabit one of the lovely houses, and to qualify for the honor of serving one of the dwellers in this higher sphere at whose gateway we were standing.

We walked a little way forward, but we could proceed no farther. There were no visible barriers, but we felt that we could not breathe if we went onward. The whole atmosphere was becoming so much the more rarefied the farther we penetrated, that in the end we were bound to retrace our steps on to our own ground.

I could see many souls dressed in the most tenuous of garments, the soft colors of which seemed hardly to belong to them but to float about the fabric of their robes—if fabric one can call it. Those of them who came sufficiently near smiled to us with such a friendly greeting that we knew we were not in any way intruding, and some waved their hands to us. My friend told us that they were aware of our purpose there, and for that reason they would not approach us. They would allow us to enjoy our experience by ourselves, and quietly to absorb the beauties and splendors of this wonderful borderland.

And so, rather reluctantly, we turned; and we quickly found ourselves back in the city in our former spot under the trees. We both felt more buoyant than ever after this brief visit, and I am sure Edwin did too, notwithstanding his having been in spirit so much longer than we had.

We did not speak for a little while after our return, each of us engaged upon our own thoughts, and when we finally broke our silence, it was to ply our good Edwin with questions. To enumerate all these questions would be tedious. So I will give, in a consecutive form, Edwin's answers as a whole.

First, with regard to the lower spheres, whose threshold had so depressed us. I have since visited them in company with Ruth and Edwin, and I have made expeditions through them, just as we are now making through our own realm. I therefore do not want to anticipate what I wish to say later as to our experiences there. For the present, then, I will only say that when we paid our visit to the boundary, we made our way there directly and rapidly, and we had no consciousness of the intermediate states through which we passed. It was for this reason that our sudden change of environment was so noticeable. Had we made our progress slowly we should have perceived the gradual decline of all those pleasant and enjoyable features that constitute the heaven of this realm. And those who dwelt within this area of decline are in the same relative position to ourselves in respect of movement: they would be inhibited from passing higher just as we were on the borders of that higher realm.

The same conditions obtained in our journey to the borders of the higher realm. We traversed the distance so quickly that we were unable to observe the gradual alteration in our surroundings. Otherwise we should have seen the country taking on a higher degree of etherealization, a greater intensification of color and brightness, observable not only in the physical features of the realm, but also in the spirit raiment of those whose homes approximated the more closely to the border.

To visit the lower realms it is necessary to have—for one's own protection—certain powers and symbols, of which Edwin told us he was in full possession. Such places are not for curiosity seekers, and no one would be foolish enough to go there for any purpose other than a legitimate one. Those who wander in that direction alone, without authority, are soon turned back by kindly souls whose work it is to save others from the perils that lie beyond. Many souls are continuously passing backwards and forwards across that sad border in the performance of their work. It is true that we saw no signs of anyone near us when we were there, but like ourselves, when we made our journey there, they move quickly to their destination.

At the border to the higher realms there is no need for such sentinels to keep others from crossing, because the natural law prevents it. When those of a lower realm travel to a higher, it is always by authority, either vested in the traveller, or in some other person of a higher sphere, who will act as escort. In the former case, such authority takes the form of symbols or signs that are given to the holder, who will always and upon every occasion receive—even unasked—every assistance he may need. Many of these symbols have the power in themselves of preserving the traveller from the overwhelming effects of the higher spiritual atmosphere. This latter would not damage the soul, of course, but a soul thus unprepared would find itself in much the same situation as upon earth when one emerges into brilliant sunlight after a prolonged stay in complete darkness. But as in the case of the earthly sunshine one can, after a suitable lapse of time, become again perfectly at ease in the normal bright light, it is not so in the case of the higher realms. There is no such adaptability there. The 'blinding' effect will be continuous to one of a lower state. But with a perfect dispensation, means are provided so that the visiting soul shall undergo no spiritual discomfort or unhappiness. And that is just what one would expect, since such visits are made for happy reasons, and not as tests of spiritual stamina and endurance. When it is necessary to make a journey to even higher spheres, it then becomes imperative, in many cases, that an inhabitant of those realms should, as it were, throw a cloak over his charge, in just the same way as Edwin, upon a lower scale, threw his protecting arms about us when we journeyed to the lower sphere.

Such, in substance, was what Edwin told us in reply to our many queries.

We now felt that we were sufficiently 'rested', and upon Edwin proposing that we might care to resume our inspection of the city, we accordingly did so.

V I I MUSIC

Music being such a vital element in the world of spirit, it is not surprising that a grand building should be devoted to the practice, teaching, and the fostering of every description of music. The next hall that our friend took us into was entirely dedicated to this important subject.

When I was on earth I never considered myself a musician, in an active sense, but I appreciated the art without very much understanding it. I had heard some splendid vocal music during my brief sojourns at different times in one of our metropolitan cathedrals, and I had had some very scanty experience of listening to orchestral music. Most of what I saw in this hall of music was new to me, and a great deal of it very technical. I have since added appreciably to my small knowledge, because I found that the greater the knowledge of music the more it helped one to understand so many things of the life here, where music plays so important a part. I do not suggest that all spirit people should become musicians in order to comprehend their own existence! The imposing of such a condition upon us would never be consonant with the natural laws here. But most individuals have some latent, innate musical sense, and by encouraging it here, so much the greater can be their joy. The latter, in effect, is exactly what I did. Ruth already possessed some extensive musical training, and so she felt very much at home in this great college.

The hall of music followed the same broad system as the other halls of the arts. The library contained books dealing with music as well as the scores of vast quantities of music that had been written on earth by composers who had now passed into spirit, or by those who were still upon the earth. What are called upon earth 'master-works', were fully represented among the musical scores upon the shelves, and I was interested to learn that there was hardly a work that had not since been altered by the composer himself since coming into spirit. The reasons for such 'improvements' I shall make plain later on. As before, the library provided a complete history of music from the very earliest times, and those who were able to read music—not necessarily instrumentally, but with a familiarity of what the printed notes indicated—were enabled to see before them the great strides that the art had made during the ages. Progression, it seems, has been slow, as in other arts, and freakish forms of expression have obtruded themselves. Needless to say the latter are not entertained here for reasons connected with those that inspire composers to alter their works after passing here.

Also contained in the library were so many of those books and musical works that have long since disappeared from earthly sight, or else are very scarce and so beyond the reach of so many folk. The musical antiquary will find all those things that he has sighed for on earth, but which have been denied him, and here he can consult, freely, works that, because of their preciousness, would never be allowed into his hands on earth. Many apartments were set aside for students who can learn of music in every branch, from theory to practice, under teachers whose names are known the earth world over. Some there are, perhaps, who would think that such famous people would not give their time to the teaching of simple forms of music to simple lovers of music. But it must be remembered, as with the painters, composers have a different appraisement of the fruits of their brains after passing into spirit. In common with us all here, they see things exactly as they are—including their compositions. They find, too, that the music of the spirit world is very different in outward results from music performed on earth. Hence they discover that their musical knowledge must undergo sweeping changes in many cases before they can begin to express themselves musically. In music, it can be said that the spirit world starts where the earth world leaves off. There are laws of music here which have no application to the earth whatever, because the earth is neither sufficiently progressed on the one hand, and on the other because the spirit world is of spirit, while the earth world is of matter. It is doubtful if the earth-plane will ever become ethereal enough to hear many of the forms of spirit music in the higher realms. Innovations have been tried, so I have been told, on the earth-plane, but the result is not only barbaric, but childish as well. Earthly ears are not attuned to music that is essentially of the spirit realms. By some strange chance earth people have essayed to produce such music on the earth-plane. It will never do—until the ears of those still incarnate have undergone a fundamental alteration.

The many types of musical instrument so familiar on earth were to be seen in the college of music, where students could be taught to play upon them. And here again, where dexterity of the hands is so essential the task of gaining proficiency is never arduous or wearisome, and it is, moreover, so much more rapid than upon the earth. As students acquire a mastery over their instrument they can join one of the many orchestras that exist here, or they can limit their performance to their many friends. It is not by any means surprising that many prefer the former because they can help to produce, in concert with their fellow musicians, the tangible effects of music upon a larger scale when so many more can enjoy such effects. We were extremely interested in the many instruments that have no counterpart upon the earth-plane. They are, for the most part, specially adapted to the forms of music that are exclusive to the spirit world, and they are for that reason very much more elaborate. Such instruments are only played with others of their kind for their distinctive music. For that which is common to the earth, the customary instrument is sufficient.

It is natural that this building should be possessed of a concert hall. This was a very large hall capable of seating comfortably many thousands. It was circular in shape, with seats rising in an unbroken tier from the floor. There is, of course, no real necessity for such a hall to be under cover, but the practice merely follows others in this realm—our own dwelling-houses, for example. We do not really need those, but we like them, we have grown used to them while upon earth, they are perfectly natural to life, and so we have them.

We had observed that the hall of music stood in grounds far more extensive than those we had already seen, and the reason was soon made clear to us. At the rear of the hall was the great center of concert performances. It consisted of a vast amphitheater like a great bowl sunk beneath the level of the ground, but it was so large that its real depth was not readily apparent. The seats that were farthest away from the performers were exactly upon ground level. Immediately surrounding these seats were masses of the most beautiful flowers of every possible hue, with a grassy space beyond, while the whole area of this outdoor temple of music was encompassed by a magnificent plantation of tall and graceful trees. Although the seating arrangements were upon such an expansive scale, much more so than would be at all practicable upon earth, yet there was no sense of being too far from the performers, even in the farthest seats. It will be recalled that our vision is not so restricted in spirit as upon earth.

Edwin suggested to us that we might like to hear a concert of the spirit world, and then he made a strange proposal. It was that we should not take our places in the seats of the theater, but that we should take up a position at some distance. The reason, he said, would be manifest as soon as the music began. As a concert was due to start very shortly, we followed his mysterious suggestion, and seated ourselves on the grass at some considerable distance from the actual amphitheater. I wondered whether we should be able to hear very much so far away, but our friend assured us that we should. And, indeed, we were joined by numbers of other people, at that very moment, who, doubtless, had come for the same purpose as ourselves. The whole place, which was empty when Edwin had first brought us in, now contained many people, some strolling about, and others, like us, seated contentedly on the grass. We were in a delightful spot, with the trees and flowers and pleasant people all about us, and never have I experienced such a feeling of real, genuine enjoyment as came upon me at this moment. I was in perfect health and perfect happiness, seated with two of the most delightful companions, Edwin and Ruth; unrestricted by time or weather, or even the bare thought of them; unhampered by every limitation that is common to our old incarnate life.

Edwin told us to walk over to the theater and look down over the seats once again. We did so, and to our astonishment we found that the whole vast hall was packed with people, where there was not a soul to be seen but a short time before. The musicians were in their places awaiting the entrance of their conductor, and this great audience had arrived as if by magic—or so it seemed. As it was apparent that the concert was about to begin, we returned to Edwin at once. In answer to our question as to how the audience had arrived so suddenly and unperceived, he reminded me of the method of bringing together the congregation of the church that we had visited in the first days of our travels. In the case of this concert, the organizers had merely to send out their thoughts to people at large who were particularly interested in such performances, and they forthwith assembled. As soon as Ruth and I had shown our interest and desires in these concerts, we should establish a link, and we should find these thoughts reaching us whenever they were emitted.

We could, of course, see nothing of the performers from where we were situated, and so when a hush came upon all around us, we were thus sufficiently informed that the concert was to begin. The orchestra was composed of some two hundred musicians, who were playing upon instruments that are well-known to earth, so that I was able to appreciate what I heard. As soon as the music began I could hear a remarkable difference from what I had been accustomed to hear on the earth-plane. The actual sounds made by the various instruments were easily recognizable as of old, but the quality of tone was immeasurably purer, and the balance and blend were perfect. The work to be played was of some length, I was informed, and would be continued without any break.

The opening movement was of a subdued nature as regards its volume of sound, and we noticed that the instant the music commenced a bright light seemed to rise up from the direction of the orchestra until it floated, in a flat surface, level with the topmost seats, where it remained as an iridescent cover to the whole amphitheater. As the music proceeded this broad sheet of light grew in strength and density, forming, as it were, a firm foundation for what was to follow. So intent was I upon watching this extraordinary formation that I could scarcely tell what the music was about. I was conscious of its sound, but that was really all. Presently, at equal spaces round the circumference of the theater, four towers of light shot up into the sky in long tapering pinnacles of luminosity. They remained poised for a moment, and then slowly descended, becoming broader in girth as they did so, until they assumed the outward appearance of four circular towers, each surmounted with a dome, perfectly proportioned. In the meanwhile, the central area of light had thickened still more, and was beginning to rise slowly in the shape of an immense dome covering the whole theater. This continued to ascend steadily until it seemed to reach a very much greater height than the four towers while the most delicate colors were diffused throughout the whole of the etheric structure. I could understand now why Edwin had suggested that we should sit outside the theater proper, and I could follow, also, why composers should feel impelled to alter their earthly works after they have arrived in spirit. The musical sounds sent up by the orchestra were creating, up above their heads, this immense musical thought-form, and the shape and perfection of this form rested entirely upon the purity of the musical sounds, the purity of the harmonies, and a freedom from any pronounced dissonance. The form of the music must be pure to produce a pure form.

It must not be assumed that every description of discord was absent. To lack discord would be to produce monotony, but the discords were legitimately used and properly resolved.

By now the great musical thought-form had assumed what appeared to be its limit of height, and it remained stationary and steady. The music was still being played, and in response to it the whole coloring of the dome changed, first to one shade, then to another, and many times to a delicate blend of a number of shades according to the variation in theme or movement of the music.

It is difficult to give any adequate idea of the beauty of this wonderful musical structure. The amphitheater being built below the surface of the ground, nothing was visible of audience, of performers, or of the building itself, and the dome of light and color had all the appearance of resting on the same firm ground as were we ourselves.

This has taken but a brief while in the telling, but the musical thought-form occupied such time in formation as would be taken by a full-length concert on the earth-plane. We had, during this period, watched the gradual building of the outward and visible effect of music. Unlike the earth where music can only be heard there we had both heard and seen it. And not only were we inspired by the sounds of the orchestral playing, but the beauty of the immense form it created had its spiritual influence upon all who beheld it, or came within its sphere. We could feel this although we were seated without the theater. The audience within were basking in its splendor and enjoying still greater benefit from the effulgence of its elevating rays. On the next occasion we should take our places in the huge auditorium.

The music at last came to a grand finale, and so ended. The rainbow colors continued to interweave themselves. We wondered how long this musical structure would survive, and we were told that it would fade away in roughly the same time as would be taken by an earthly rainbow—comparatively a few minutes. We had listened to a major work, but if a series of shorter pieces were played, the effect and lasting power would be the same, but the shapes would vary in form and size. Were the form of greater duration, a new form would conflict with the last, and the result to the eye would be the same as two different and unconnected pieces of music, when played together, would be to the ear.

The expert musician can plan his compositions by his knowledge of what forms the various harmonic and melodic sounds will produce. He can, in effect, build magnificent edifices upon his manuscript of music, knowing full well exactly what the result will be when the music is played or sung. By careful adjustment of his themes and his harmonies, the length of the work, and its various marks of expression, he can build a majestic form as grand as a Gothic cathedral. This is, in itself, a delightful part of the musical art in spirit, and it is regarded as musical architecture. The student will not only study music acoustically, but he will learn to build it architecturally, and the latter is one of the most absorbing and fascinating studies.

What we had witnessed had been produced upon a scale of some magnitude, the individual instrumentalist or singer can evolve on a greatly reduced scale his own musical thought-forms. In fact, it would be impossible to emit any form of musical sound deliberately without the formation of such a form. It may not take a definite shape such as we saw; that comes from more experience, but it would induce the interplay of numerous colors and blending of colors. In the spirit world all music is color, and all color is music. The one is never existent without the other. That is why the flowers give forth such pleasant tones when they are approached, as it will be remembered of my early experience with flowers. The water that sparkles and flashes colors is also creating musical sounds of purity and beauty. But it must not be imagined that with all this galaxy of color in the spirit world there is also a pandemonium of music going on unremittingly. The eye is not wearied by the fullness of color here. Why should our ears be wearied by the sweet sound the colors send forth? The answer is that they are not, because the sounds are in perfect accord with the colors, as the colors are with the sounds. And the perfect combination of both sight and sound is perfect harmony.

Harmony is a fundamental law here. There can be no confliction. I do not suggest that we are in a state of perfection. We should be an immensely higher realm if we were, but we are in perfection in so far as this realm is concerned. If we, as individuals, become more perfect than the realm in which we live, we, ipso facto, become worthy of advancing to a higher state, and we do so. But while we are where we are, in this realm or higher, we are living in a state of perfection according to the limits of that realm.

I have dwelt rather at length upon our musical experiences because of the great position of music in our lives and in the realm in which we are living. The whole attitude to music held by so many people of the earth undergoes a great change when they eventually come to spirit. Music is looked upon by many on the earth-plane as merely a pleasant diversion, a pleasant adjunct to the earthly life, but by no means a necessity. Here it is part of our life, not because we make it so, but because it is part of natural existence, as are flowers and trees, grass and water, and hills and dales. It is an element of spiritual nature. Without it a vast deal of the joy would depart out of our lives. We do not need to become master-musicians to appreciate the wealth of music that surrounds us in color and sound, but as in so many other features of this life, we accept and enjoy to the full, and in the enjoyment of our heritage we can afford to smile at those who persist in believing that we live in a world of emptiness.

A world of emptiness! What a shock so many people have upon their coming into the spirit world, and how immensely glad and relieved they are to find that it turns out quite pleasant after all; that it is not a terrifying place; that it is not one stupendous temple of hymn-singing religion; and that they are able to feel at home in the land of their new life. When this joyful realization has come to them, some of them are reminded that they looked upon the various descriptions of this life, that have come from us from time to time, as rather material and how pleased they are to discover that it is so. What is it, if it is not material? The musicians that we heard playing were playing upon very real, solid instruments from very real music. The conductor was a very real person, conducting his orchestra with a very material baton! But the beautiful musical thought-form was not so very material as were its surroundings or the means to create it, in just the same relative way as an earthly rainbow, and the sun and moisture that cause it.

At the risk of making myself very tedious I have reverted more than once to this strange fallacy that the world I am living in, here in spirit, is vague and shadowy. It is strange that some minds strive always to banish from the world of spirit every tree and flower, and the other thousand and one delights. There is something of conceit in this—that makes such things exclusive to the earth world. At the same time, if any soul thinks that such things have no business to exist in the spirit world, he is at liberty to abstain from both the sight and enjoyment of them by betaking himself to some barren spot where his susceptibilities will not be offended by such earthly objects as trees and flowers and water (and even human beings), and there he can give himself up to the state of beatific contemplation, surrounded by the heavenly nothingness that he thinks should be heaven proper. No soul is forced into an unwilling task here, nor into surroundings that he considers uncongenial. I venture to assert that it will not be long before such a soul emerges from his retreat and joins his fellows in the enjoyment of all the delights of God's heaven. There is just one fault—among one or two others—that the earth world possesses: the overwhelming superiority, in its own mind, over every other world, but principally over the spirit world. We can afford to be amused, though our amusement turns to sadness when we see the distress of souls upon their arrival here, when they realize that they are, at last, faced with eternal truth beyond all question or doubt. It is then that humility so often sets in! But we never reproach. The reproaching comes from within each soul itself.

And what, perhaps, it will be asked, has all this to do with our musical experiences? Just this: that after every new experience I have thought the same thoughts, and very nearly spoken the same words to both Ruth and Edwin. Ruth has always echoed my words; Edwin has always been in agreement with me, though, of course, what we were seeing was not new to him by any means. But he still marvelled at all things here, as indeed do we all, whether we have but just arrived, or whether we have been over here many years of earth time.

As we walked along after the concert, Edwin pointed out to us the dwelling places of many of the teachers in the various halls of learning, who preferred to live close to the seats of their work. They were, for the most part, unpretentious houses, and it would have been comparatively easy to guess the occupation of the owner, so we were told, from the various evidences within of their work. Edwin said that we should always be welcome should we ever wish to call upon any of the teachers. The exclusiveness which must necessarily surround such people when they are incarnate vanishes when they come into spirit. All values become drastically altered in such matters. The teachers themselves do not cease their own studies because they are teaching. They are ever investigating and learning, and passing on to their pupils what they have thus gained. Some have progressed to a higher realm, but they still retain their interest in their former sphere, and continuously visit it—and their many friends—to pursue their teaching.

But we have already spent some time on this subject, and Edwin is waiting to take us on to other places of importance in the city.

VIII. PLANS FOR FUTURE WORK

A SHORT walk brought us to a large rectangular building which, our friend informed us, was the hall of science, and my fair companion and I were at a loss to know how science, as we always understood the word on earth, could have any place in the spirit world. However, we were soon to learn many things, the chief of which was that the earth world has the spirit world to thank for all the major scientific discoveries that have been made throughout the centuries.

The laboratories of the world of spirit are many decades in advance of those of the earth-plane. And it will be years before many revolutionary discoveries are allowed to be sent through to the earth world, because the earth has not yet sufficiently progressed.

Neither Ruth nor I had any very great leaning towards science and engineering, and Edwin, knowing our taste in this direction, proposed that we should give but a moment or two to this particular hall.

In the hall of science every field of scientific and engineering investigation, study, and discovery was covered, and here were to be seen so many of those men whose names have become household words, and who, since passing into spirit, have continued their life's work with their fellow scientists with the full and immense resources of the spirit world at their command. Here they can solve those mysteries that baffled them when they were on earth. There is no longer any such thing as personal rivalry. Reputations have no more to be made, and the many material handicaps are abandoned forever. It follows that where such a gathering of savants can exist, together with their unlimited resources, the results must be correspondingly great. In the past ages all the epoch-making discoveries have come from the spirit world. Of himself, incarnate man can do very little. Most people are content to consider the earth-world as sufficient unto itself. Indeed it is not! The scientist is fundamentally a man of vision; it may be limited, but it is there nevertheless. And our own spirit scientists can—and do—impress their earthly colleagues with the fruits of their investigation. In many cases where two men are working upon the same problem, the one who is in spirit will be far ahead of his confrere who is still on earth. A hint from the former is very often enough to set the latter upon the right track, and the result is a discovery for the benefit of humanity. In so many cases humanity has so benefited, but, alas, in so many cases humanity has suffered sorrow and tribulation through the devilish perversion of those discoveries. Every one of them that is sent from the spirit world is for the advantage and spiritual progression of man. If perverted minds use those same things for the destruction of man, then man has only himself to blame. That is why I affirmed that the earth world has not spiritually progressed enough to have many more splendid inventions that have already been perfected here. They are ready and waiting, but if they were sent through to the earth-plane in its present state of spiritual mind, they would be misused by unscrupulous people.

The people of the earth have it in their power to see that modern inventions are employed solely for their spiritual and material good. When the time comes that real spiritual progress is made, then the earth-plane can expect a flood of new inventions and discoveries to come through from the scientists and engineers of the spirit world. But the earth-plane has a long and sorrowful way to go before that time comes. And in the meantime the work of the spirit scientist continues.

We in spirit do not require the many inventions of the earth-plane. I think I have sufficiently indicated that our laws are totally different from those of the earth-plane. We have no use for inventions that will increase our speed of travel as with you. Our own method of transit is as rapid as thought, because thought is the motive power. We have no need for methods of saving life, because we are indestructible. We have no need for the hundreds of inventions to make life easier, safer, more comfortable and enjoyable, because our life is all that, and more than that already. But in this hall of science many, many devoted men were working for the betterment of the earth-plane through the medium of their researches, and lamenting that so much could not be given to the earth because it would not be safe as yet to do so.

We were permitted to see the progress that had been made in locomotion, and we were amazed at the advance that had been made since the days when we were on the earth-plane. But that is as nothing to that which is to come. When man exercises his will in the right direction, there will be no end to the enormous rewards that he will gain in material progress, but material progress must go hand in hand with spiritual progress. And until they do the earth world will not be permitted to have the many inventions that are ready and waiting to be sent through.

The generality of people of the earth world are very stubborn. They resent any encroachment on their preserves, or upon what they have presumptuously claimed as their preserves. It was never intended that when the results of our scientists' researches are communicated to the earth they were to be seized upon by the few to the exclusion of all others. Those that have done so find that they have to pay a very heavy price for their brief span of earthly prosperity. Neither was it intended that the two worlds, ours and yours, should be as they are now—so far apart in thought and contact. The day will assuredly come when our two worlds will be closely interrelated, when communication between the two will be a commonplace of life, and then the great wealth of resources of the spirit world will be open to the earth world, to draw upon for the benefit of the whole human race.

The sight of so much activity on the part of my fellow inhabitants of this realm had set my mind to thinking about my own future work and what form it could take. I had no very definite idea upon the matter, and so I mentioned my difficulty to Edwin. Ruth, it seems, was troubled similarly, so there were the two of us, having, for the first time since our arrival, some small feelings of restlessness. Our old friend was not the least surprised; he would have been more surprised, he said, if we had felt otherwise. It was a sensation common to all, sooner or later—the urge to be doing something useful for the good of others. It was not that we were tired of seeing our own land, but that we had rather a self-conscious feeling. Edwin assured us that we could continue to go upon our explorations indefinitely if we so wished, and that none would criticize or comment upon our actions. It would thus be treated as a matter of our own concern. However, we both felt that we should like to settle the question of our future work, and we appealed accordingly for the guidance of our good friend. Edwin suggested at once that we repair to the borders of the higher realms, where, it will be recalled, he said earlier we should be able to go into this matter. And so we left the hall of science, and once more we found ourselves on the outskirts of our realm.

We were taken to a very beautiful house, which from its appearance and situation was clearly of a higher degree than those farther inland. The atmosphere was more rarefied, and as far as I could observe we were approximately upon the same spot as on our first visit to the boundary. Edwin led us into the house with all the freedom in the world, and bade us welcome. As soon at we entered I knew instinctively that he was giving us welcome to his own home. Strange to say, we had never inquired about his home or where it was situated. He said he had purposely kept our minds off the subject, but that was only his natural diffidence. Ruth was enchanted with everything she saw, and scolded him for not telling us all about it much sooner. The house was built of stone throughout, and although to the eye it might have appeared somewhat bare, yet friendliness emanated from every corner. The rooms were not large, but of medium size, and suitable for all Edwin's purposes. There were plenty of comfortable chairs, and many well-lined bookshelves. But it was the general feeling of calm and peace that pervaded the whole dwelling that struck us most forcibly.

Edwin bade us be seated and make ourselves at home. There was no need for us to hurry, and we could discuss our problem in extenso. At the outset I frankly admitted that I had no particular ideas upon what I could do. While on earth I had been fortunate enough to be able to follow my own inclinations, and I had had, consequently, a busy life. But my work was finished—at least in one respect—when my earthly life ended. Edwin then proposed that perhaps I would like to join him in his work, which was principally concerned with taking in hand newly-arrived souls whose religious beliefs were the same as we had held upon earth, but who, unlike ourselves, were unable as yet to realize the truth of the change they had made, and of the unreality of so much of their religion.

Much as I liked my friend's proposal, I did not feel competent enough to undertake such work, but Edwin waved aside my objection. I should, he said, work with him—at first at any rate. When I had become used to the task I could continue independently if I so wished. Speaking from experience, Edwin said that two or more people—and here he glanced at Ruth— could very often give far greater help to an individual soul than could one working entirely alone. The weight of numbers seemed to have a greater power of conviction upon one who was particularly stubborn in holding on to his old earthly religious ideas. Since Edwin felt that I would be of real service to him, I was very pleased to accept his offer to join forces with him. And here Ruth brought herself forward as another candidate for service under him, subject, of course, to his approval. Not only was the latter instantly forthcoming, but her offer was gratefully accepted. There was much, said he, that a young woman could do, and the three of us, working in such complete harmony and amity, should be able to do some useful work together. I was more than glad that Ruth was to join us, since it meant that our happy party would not be broken up.

There was, however, another matter that was in my mind, and it concerned that one particular book that I wished I had not written when I was on earth. I was not rendered unhappy by the thought of this still persisting, but I wanted to be free of it, and although, no doubt, my new work would eventually bring me that complete peace of mind, I felt that I would like to deal with the matter in a more direct way. Edwin knew what I was hinting at, and he recalled to me what he had already said about the difficulties of communication with the earth world. But he had also mentioned that we might seek guidance from higher up. If I still wished to try my hand at communication then we might appeal for that guidance and advice now, and thus we could settle the whole question of my future work.

Edwin then left us and retired into another room. I had hardly been chatting with Ruth for a moment about our new occupation when our old friend returned bringing with him a very striking looking man who, I knew at once, had come from a higher sphere in answer to Edwin's call. He did not appear to be one of our own countrymen, and my observation was correct, since he was an Egyptian, as Edwin told us later on. He spoke our own tongue perfectly. Edwin introduced us, and explained my wishes and the possible difficulties of their fulfillment.

Our visitor was possessed of a very strong personality, and he gave one the strong impression of calmness and placidity. This would, one imagined, always remain perfectly unruffled.

We all seated ourselves comfortably, and Edwin acquainted him with the extent of my knowledge concerning communication with the earth world.

The Egyptian placed some considerations before me. If, said our visitor, I was fully determined that by returning to the earth-plane to speak I should retrieve the situation that was giving me cause to regret, then he would do everything to assist me to achieve my purpose. It would not be possible to do what I wanted, though, for some years to come. But in the meantime I was to accept his definite assurance that I should eventually be able to communicate, and he made me a promise to that effect. If I would have patience all should be as I wished. I was to leave the whole matter in the hands of those who had the ordering of these things, and all would be well. The time—to use an earthly term—would soon pass, and the occurrence of certain events, meanwhile, would make the path clear and would provide the requisite opportunity.

It must be remembered that what I was asking was not merely to return to the earth-plane to endeavor to record the fact that I still lived! What I wanted was to try to undo something that I wished I had never done. And it was a task, I could see, that could not be accomplished in a moment. What I had written I could never unwrite, but I could ease my mind by telling the truth, as I now know it, to those who were still on the earth-plane.

The kindly Egyptian then rose and we shook hands. He congratulated us on the way we had accustomed ourselves to our new conditions of life, wished us joy of our new work whenever we should start, and finally gave me a repeated promise that my own particular wishes should have their certain fulfillment. I tried to express my gratitude for all his help, but he would not hear of it, and with a wave of the hand he was gone. We remained for a while discussing our plans—I was looking forward keenly to starting our work.

It must not be thought that we were part of a campaign to convert people, in the religious sense in which that word is used on earth. Far from it. We do not interfere with people's beliefs nor their viewpoints; we only give our services when they are asked for in such matters, or when we see that by giving them we can effect some useful purpose. Neither do we spend our time walking about evangelizing people, but when the call comes for help then we answer it instantly. But there comes a time when spiritual unrest will make itself felt, and that is the turning point in the life of many a soul who has been confined and restricted by wrong views, whether religious or otherwise. Religion is not responsible for all mistaken ideas!

There is a surprising number of people who do not realize that they have passed from the earth in the death of the physical body. Resolutely they will not believe that they are what the earth world calls 'dead'. They are dimly aware that some sort of change has taken place, but what that change is they are not prepared to say. Some, after a little explanation and even demonstration—can grasp what has actually happened; others are stubborn, and will be convinced only after prolonged reasoning. In the latter case we are oft-times obliged to leave such a soul for a while to allow a little quiet contemplation to work its way. We know we shall be sought out the instant that soul feels the power of our reasoning. In many respects it is tiring work, though I use the word 'tiring' in its strictly limited sense of the spirit world.

Ruth and I were both more than grateful to Edwin for his generous help in our affairs, and I was particularly so, both to him and the Egyptian, for the excellent prospect of communicating with the earth world. In view of our decisions to co-operate with Edwin in his work he made the suggestion that as we had seen a little—but only a very little of our own realm, we might now profitably make a visit to the dark realms. Ruth and I both concurred, adding that we had by now sufficient self-confidence to withstand anything of an unpleasant nature that might be before us. We should, of course, be under the immediate protection and guidance of our old friend. Needless to say that without this we should not have attempted to go, even had we been permitted.

We left Edwin's beautiful house, quickly traversed our own realm, and again we were on the borders of the lower realms. Edwin warned us that we should feel that sense of chilling which we experienced before, but that by an effort of will we could throw it off. He placed himself in the middle of us, Ruth and I each taking one of his arms. He turned and looked at us, and was apparently satisfied with what he saw. I glanced at Ruth and I noticed that her robe as had Edwin's had taken on a dull color, approaching almost grey. Looking at myself I discovered that my own dress had undergone a similar change. This was certainly perplexing, but our friend explained that this toning down of our natural colors was but the operation of a natural law, and did not mean that we had lost what we had already gained. The practical application of such a law meant that we should not be conspicuous in uncongenial surroundings, nor should we carry the light of our realm into those dark places to blind the vision of those who dwelt there.

We were walking along a great tract of barren country. The ground was hard under foot; the green of trees and grass was gone. The sky was dull and leaden, and the temperature had dropped very considerably, but we could feel an internal warmth that counteracted it. Before us we could see nothing but a great bank of mist that gathered in density as we advanced, until finally we were within it. It swirled round in heavy, damp clouds, and it seemed almost like a dead weight as it pressed upon us.

Suddenly a figure loomed out of the mist and came towards us. He was the first person we had met as yet, and recognizing Edwin, he gave him a friendly greeting. Edwin introduced us and told him of our intentions. He said he would like to join us, as perhaps he could be of some help to us, and we readily accepted his kind offer. We resumed our journey, and after a further passage through the mist, we found that it began to clear a little until it vanished altogether. We could now see our surroundings clearly. The landscape was bleak in the extreme with, here and there, a dwellinghouse of the meanest order. We came closer to one of the latter and we were able to examine it better.

It was a small, squat house, squarely built, devoid of ornament, and looking altogether thoroughly uninviting. It even had a sinister look in spite of its plainness, and it seemed to repel us from it the nearer we approached it. There was no sign of life to be seen at any of the windows or round about it. There was no garden attached to it; it just stood out by itself, solitary and forlorn. Edwin and our new friend evidently knew both the house and its inmate quite well, for upon going up to the front door, Edwin gave a knock upon it and without waiting for an answer opened it and walked in, beckoning us to follow. We did so and found ourselves in the poorest sort of apology for a house. There was little furniture, and that of the meanest, and at first sight to earthly eyes one would have said that poverty reigned here, and one would have felt the natural sympathy and urge to offer what help one could. But to our spirit eyes the poverty was of the soul, the meanness was of the spirit, and although it roused our sympathy it was sympathy of another kind, of which material help is of no avail. The coldness seemed almost greater within than without, and we were told that it came from the owner of the house himself.

We passed into a back room and met the sole occupant seated in a chair. He made no attempt to rise or give any sign of welcome. Ruth and I remained in the background while the other two went forward to speak to our unwilling 'host'. He was a man just past middle years. He had something of an air of faded prosperity and the clothes he wore had been obviously neglected, whether through indifference or other causes in the light of my earthly recollections I was unable to say. He rather scowled at the two of us as Edwin brought us forward as new visitors. It was a moment or two before he spoke, and then he railed at us rather incoherently, but we were able to gather that he deemed himself to be suffering under an injustice. Edwin told him in plain terms that he was talking nonsense, because injustice does not exist in the spirit world. A heated argument followed, heated, that is to say, on the part of our host, for Edwin was calm and collected, and in truth, wonderfully kind. Many times did the former glance at Ruth, whose gentle face seemed to brighten the whole dingy place. I, too, looked at Ruth, who held my arm, to see how this strange man was affecting her, but she was unperturbed.

At length he quieted down and seemed much more tractable, and then he and Edwin had some private conversation together. At the end of it he told Edwin that he would think about it, and that he could call again if he wished and bring his friends with him. Upon this he arose from his chair, escorted us to the door, and showed us out. And I observed that he was almost becoming affable—though not quite. It was as if he was reluctant to submit to being pleasant. He stood at his front door watching us as we walked away, until we must have been nearly out of sight.

Edwin seemed very pleased with our visit, and then he gave us some particulars of the strange man.

He had, he said, been in spirit some years now, but in his earth life he had been a successful business man—successful, that is as far as the earth-plane judges such things. He had not thought of much else than his business, and he always considered that any means were justified in gaining his own ends, provided they were legal. He was ruthless in his dealings with all others, and he elevated efficiency to the level of a god. In his home all things—and people—were subservient to him. He gave generously to charity where there was likely to accrue the greatest advantage and credit. He supported his own religion and church with vigor, regularity, and fervor. He felt that he was an ornament to the church, and he was much esteemed by all those connected with it. He added some new portions to the edifice at his own expense, and a chapel was named after him as the donor. But from what Edwin had been able to glean from his story, he had scarcely committed one decent, unselfish action in the whole of his life. His motive was always self-aggrandizement, and he had achieved his purpose on earth at the absolute expense of his life in the spirit world.

And now his grievance was that after having lived such an

exemplary life—in his own estimation—he should be condemned to live in such comparative squalor. He refused to see that he had condemned himself to it, and that there was none other to blame but himself. He complained that the church had misled him all along, since his munificence had been received in such fashion that he believed his gifts to the church would weigh heavily in his favor in the 'hereafter'. Again he could not see that it is motive that counts, and that a happy state in the spirit world cannot be bought for hard cash. A small service willingly and generously performed for a fellow mortal builds a greater edifice in spirit to the glory of God than do large sums of money expended upon ecclesiastical bricks and mortar erected to the glory of man—with full emphasis upon the donor.

This man's present mood was anger, which was all the greater because he had never been denied anything whilst upon the earth. He had never been accustomed to such degrading circumstances as those at present. His difficulties were increased by the fact that he did not know quite whom to blame. Expecting a high reward, he had been cast into the depths. He had made no real friends. There seemed to be no one—of his own social position, he said—who could advise him in the matter. Edwin had tried to reason with him, but he was in an unreasoning frame of mind, and had been so for some long time. He had had few visitors because he repelled them, and although Edwin had made many visits to him, the result was always the same—a stolid adherence to his sense of injustice.

Upon Edwin's latest call, in company with Ruth and myself, and with the friend whom we had met on the way, there were distinct symptoms of a coming change. They were not manifest at first, but as our visit drew to a close he had shown signs of relenting from his stubborn attitude. And Edwin was sure that it was due as much to Ruth's softening presence as to his own powers of reasoning with him. He felt sure, too, that were we to return to him on our way back, we should find him in a different frame of mind altogether. He would be unwilling to admit too soon that the fault was his entirely, but perseverance will work wonders.

Ruth was naturally pleased that she had been able to be of service so quickly, though she disavowed any claim to have done anything but merely stand there as an observer! Edwin, however, at once pointed out to her that while she disclaimed any action of an external order, she had shown a real sympathy and sorrow for this unhappy man. That explained his frequent glances at her. He had felt that commiseration, and it had done him good, although he was unaware of the cause of it. And here Ruth begs me to add that her very small share would have been of little use in this man's recovery had it not been for Edwin's long and unceasing work on his behalf.

This was our first encounter with unfortunates of the lower spheres, and I have been somewhat protracted in giving details of it. It was, in many respects, straightforward by comparison with what we met later, and in recounting it I have done so because it was an introduction to our future work. For the present, however, it was not intended that we should do anything but make our observations of the dark realms.

The four of us resumed our journey. There were no paths to follow, and the ground was becoming decidedly rocky in formation. The light was rapidly diminishing from a sky that was heavy and black. There was not a soul, not a house, nor any sign of life to be seen. The whole district seemed colorless and empty, and we might have been wandering in another world. We could see dimly ahead of us, after the passage of some time, something which had the appearance of dwellings, and we moved in their direction.

The terrain was now rocks and nothing else, and here and there we could see people seated with their heads down, seemingly almost lifeless, but in reality in the depths of gloom and despair. They took no notice of us whatever as we passed them, and very soon we drew level with the dwellings we had viewed distantly.

I. THE DARK REALMS

AT CLOSE view it became clear that these dwellings were nothing more than mere hovels. They were distressing to gaze upon, but it was infinitely more distressing to contemplate that these were the fruits of men's lives upon earth. We did not enter any of the shacks—it was repulsive enough outside, and we could have served no useful purpose at present by going in. Edwin therefore gave us a few details instead.

Some of the inhabitants, he said, had lived here, or hereabouts, year after year—as time is reckoned upon earth. They themselves had no sense of time, and their existence had been one interminable continuity of darkness through no one's fault but their own. Many had been the good souls who had penetrated into these Stygian realms to try to effect a rescue out of the darkness. Some had been successful; others had not. Success depends not so much upon the rescuer as upon the rescued. If the latter shows no glimmer of light in his mind, no desire to take a step forward on the spiritual road, then nothing, literally nothing, can be done. The urge must come from within the fallen soul himself. And how low some of them had fallen! Never must it be supposed that those who, in the earth's judgment, had failed spiritually, are fallen low. Many such have not failed at all, but are, in point of fact, worthy souls whose fine reward awaits them here. But on the other hand, there are those whose earthly lives have been spiritually hideous though outwardly sublime; whose religious profession designated by a Roman collar, has been taken for granted as being synonymous with spirituality of soul. Such people have been mocking God throughout their sanctimonious lives on earth where they lived with an empty show of holiness and goodness. Here they stand revealed for what they are. But the God they have mocked for so long does not punish. They punish themselves!

The people living within these hovels that we were passing were not necessarily those who upon earth had committed some crime in the eyes of the earth people. There were many people who, without doing any harm, had never, never done any good to a single mortal upon earth. People who had lived entirely unto themselves, without a thought for others. Such souls constantly harped upon the theme that they had done no harm to anyone. But they had harmed themselves.

As the higher spheres had created all the beauties of those realms, so had the denizens of these lower spheres built up the appalling conditions of their spirit life. There was no light in the lowest realms; no warmth, no vegetation, no beauty. But there is hope—hope that every soul there will progress. It is in the power of each soul to do so, and nothing stands in his way but himself. It may take him countless thousands of years to raise himself one inch spiritually, but it is an inch in the right direction.

The thought inevitably came into my mind of the doctrine of eternal damnation, so beloved by orthodox religion, and of the everlasting fires of so-called hell. If this place we were now in could be called hell and no doubt it would be by theologians—then there was certainly no evidence of fire or heat of any kind.

On the contrary, there was nothing but a cold, dark atmosphere. Spirituality means warmth in the spirit world; lack of spirituality means coldness. The whole fantastic doctrine of hell-fire—a fire which burns but never consumes—is one of the most outrageously stupid and ignorant doctrines that has ever been invented by equally stupid and ignorant churchmen. Who actually invented it no one knows, but it is still rigorously upheld as a doctrine by the church. Even the smallest acquaintance with spirit life instantly reveals the utter impossibility of it, because it is against the very laws of spirit existence. This concerns its literal side. What of the shocking blasphemy that it involves?

When Edwin, Ruth, and I were on earth we were asked to believe that God, the Father of the Universe, punishes, actually punishes people by condemning them to burn in the flames of hell for all eternity. Could there ever-be any grosser travesty of the God that orthodoxy professes to worship? The churches—of whatever denomination—have built up a monstrous conception of the Eternal Father of Heaven. They have made of Him, on the one hand, a mountain of corruption by shallow lip service, by spending large sums of money to erect churches and chapels to His 'glory', by pretending a grovelling contrition for having 'offended Him', by professing to fear Him—fear Him Who is all love! And on the other hand, we have the picture of a God Who, without the slightest compunction, casts poor human souls into an eternity of the worst of all sufferings—burning by fires that are unquenchable.

We are taught glibly to beg for God's mercy. The church's God is a Being of extraordinary moods. He must be continually placated. It is by no means certain that, having begged for mercy, we shall get it. He must be feared—because He can bring down His vengeance upon us at any moment; we do not know when He will strike. He is vengeful and unforgiving. He has commanded such trivialities as are embodied in church doctrines and dogmas that at once expose not a great mind, but a small one. He has made the doorway to 'salvation' so narrow that few, very few souls will ever be able to pass through it. He has built up on the earth-plane a vast organization known as 'the Church', which shall be the sole depository of spiritual truth—an organization that knows practically nothing of the state of life in the world of spirit, yet dares to lay down the law to incarnate souls, and dares to say what is in the mind of the Great Father of the Universe, and dares to discredit His Name by assigning to Him attributes that He could not possibly possess. What do such silly, petty minds know of the Great and Almighty Father of love? Mark that!—of love. Then think again of all the horrors I have enumerated. And think once more. Contemplate this: a heaven of all that is beautiful, a heaven of more beauty than the mind of man incarnate can comprehend; a heaven, of which one tiny fragment I have tried to describe to you, where all is peace and goodwill and love among fellow mortals. All these things are built up by the inhabitants of these realms, and are upheld by the Father of Heaven in His love for all mankind.

What of the lower realms—the dark places we are now visiting? It is the very fact that we are visiting them that has led me to speak in this fashion, because standing in this darkness I am fully conscious of one great reality of eternal life, and that is that the high spheres of heaven are within the reach of every mortal soul that is, or is yet to be, born upon earth. The potentialities of progression are unlimited, and they are the right of every soul. God condemns no one. Man condemns himself, but he does not condemn himself eternally; it rests with himself as to when he shall move forward spiritually. Every spirit hates the lower realms for the unhappiness that is there, and for no other reason. And for that reason great organizations exist to help every single soul who is living in them to rise out of them into the light. And that work will continue through countless ages until every soul is brought out from these hideous places, and at last all is as the Father of the Universe intended it to be.

This, I am afraid, has been a long digression, so let us return to our travels. You will recall my mention of the many heavenly perfumes and scents that come from the flowers and that float upon the air. Here in these dark places the very opposite was the case. Our nostrils were first assailed by the most foul odors, odors that reminded us of the corruption of flesh in the earth world. They were nauseating, and I feared that it would prove more than Ruth—and indeed I, myself—could stand, but Edwin told us to treat them in the same way as we had mastered the coldness of the temperature—by simply closing our minds to them—and that we should be quite unaware of their existence. We hastened to do so, and we were perfectly successful. It is not only 'sanctity' that has its odor!

In our travels through our own realm we can enjoy all the countless delights and beauties of it, together with the happy converse of its inhabitants. Here in these dark lands all is bleak and desolate. The very low degree of light itself casts a blight upon the whole region. Occasionally we were able to catch a glimpse of the faces of some unfortunates as we passed along. Some were unmistakably evil, showing the life of vice they had led upon the earth; some revealed the miser, the avaricious, the 'brute beast'. There were people here from almost every walk of earthly life, from the present earthly time to far back in the centuries. And here was a connecting link with names that could be read in those truthful histories of nations in the library we visited in our own realm. Both Edwin and his friend told us that we should be appalled at the catalogue of names, well known in history, of people who were living deep down in these noxious regions—men who had perpetrated vile and wicked deeds in the name of holy religion, or for the furtherance of their own despicable, material ends. Many of these wretches were unapproachable, and they would remain so—perhaps for numberless more centuries—until, of their own wish and endeavor, they moved however feebly in the direction of the light of spiritual progression.

We could see, as we walked along, whole bands of seemingly demented souls passing on their way upon some prospective evil intent—if they could find their way to it. Their bodies presented the outward appearance of the most hideous and repulsive malformations and distortions, the absolute reflection of their evil minds. Many of them seemed old in years, but I was told that although such souls had been there perhaps for many centuries, it was not the passage of time that had so dealt with their faces, but their wicked minds.

In the higher spheres the beauty of mind rejuvenates the features, sweeps away the signs of earthly cares and troubles and sorrows, and presents to the eye that state of physical development which is at that period of our earthly lives which we used to call 'the prime of life'.

The multitudinous sounds that we heard were in keeping with the awful surroundings, from mad raucous laughter to the shriek of some soul in torment—torment inflicted by others as bad as himself. Once or twice we were spoken to by some courageous souls who were down there upon their tasks of helping these afflicted mortals. They were glad to see us and to talk to us. In the darkness we could see them and they could see us, but we were all of us invisible to the rest, since we were provided with the same protection for the dark lands. In our case Edwin was taking care of us collectively as new-comers, but those whose work lies in rescue had each his own means of protection.

If any priest—or theologian—could have but one glimpse of the things that Edwin, Ruth, and I saw here, he would never say again, as long as he lived, that God, the Father of Love, could ever condemn any mortal to such horrors. The same priest, seeing these places, would not himself condemn anyone to them. Is he more kind and merciful than the Father of Love Himself? No! It is man alone who qualifies himself for the state of his existence after he passes into spirit.

The more we saw of the dark lands the more I realized how fantastic is the teaching of the orthodox church to which I belonged when on earth, that the place which is referred to as eternal hell is ruled over by a Prince of Darkness, whose sole aim is to get every soul into his clutches, and from whom there is no escape once a soul has entered his kingdom. We can afford to laugh at the absurdities of such teachings. It is no novelty for some wondrous and illustrious spirit to be called a devil! We still retain our sense of humor, and it causes us very great amusement, sometimes, to hear some stupid priest, spiritually blind, professing to know about things of the spirit of which, in reality, he is totally and completely ignorant. The spirit people have broad backs, and they can support the weight of such fallacious rubbish without experiencing anything but pity for such poor blind souls.

It is not my intention to go into further details of these dark spheres. At least, not at present. The Church's method of frightening people is not the method of the spirit world. Rather would we dwell upon the beauties of the spirit world, and try to show something of the glories that await every soul when his earthly life is ended. It remains with every single soul individually whether this beautiful land shall be his lot sooner, or whether it shall be later.

We held a short consultation together, and decided that we should now like to return to our own realm. And so we made our way back to the land of mist, passed quickly through, and once again we were in our own heavenly country with the warm, balmy air enveloping us. Our new friend of the dark realms then left us after we had expressed our thanks for his kindly services. I then bethought me that it was high time I went to have a peep at my house, and so I asked Ruth and Edwin to join me, as I had no wish to be alone or separated from their pleasant company. Ruth had not yet seen my home, but she had often wondered—so she said—what it would be like. And I thought that a little of the fruit from the garden would be most acceptable after our visit—short though it was—to the lower realms.

Everything in the house was in perfect order—as I left it to go upon our travels—as though there were someone permanently looking after it. Ruth expressed her complete approval of all she saw, and congratulated me upon my choice of a home.

In reply to my query as to the invisible agency that was responsible for the good order of the house during my absence, Edwin answered me by himself asking the question: what is there to disturb the order of the house? There can be no dust, because there is no decay of any sort whatsoever. There can be no dirt, because here in spirit there is nothing to cause it. The household duties that are so very familiar and so very irksome on the earth-plane, are here non-existent. The necessity for providing the body with food was abandoned when we abandoned our physical body. The adornments of the home, such as the hangings and upholstery, do not ever need renewal, because they do not perish. They endure until we wish to dispense with them for something else. And so what remains that might require attention! We have, then, but to walk out of our houses, leaving all doors and windows open—our houses have no locks upon them and we can return when we wish—to find that everything is as we left it. We might find some difference, some improvement. We might discover, for instance, that some friend had called while we were away, and had left some gift for us, some beautiful flowers, perhaps, or some other token of kindness. Otherwise we shall find that our house bids us welcome itself, and renews our feeling of 'being at home'.

Ruth had wandered all over the house by herself—we have no stupid formalities here, and I had asked her to make the whole house her own whenever she wished, and to do whatever she liked. The antique style of the architecture appealed to her artistic nature, and she revelled in the old wooden panelling and carvings—the latter being my own embellishments—of the past ages. She eventually came to my small library, and was interested to see my own works among the others upon the shelves. One book, in particular, she was attracted to, and was actually perusing it when I entered. The title alone revealed much to her, she said, and then I could feel her sweet sympathy pouring out upon me, as she knew what was my great ambition, and she offered me all the help which she could give me in the future towards the realization of this ambition.

As soon as she had completed her inspection of the house, we forgathered in the sitting-room, and Ruth asked Edwin a question which I had been meaning to ask him myself for some time: Was there a sea somewhere? If there were lakes and streams, then, perhaps there was an ocean? Edwin's answer filled her with joy: Of course, there was a seaside—and a very beautiful one, too! Ruth insisted upon being conducted there at once, and, under Edwin's guidance, we set forth.

We were soon walking along a beautiful stretch of open country with the grass like a green velvet carpet beneath our feet. There were no trees, but there were many fine clumps of healthy looking shrubs, and, of course, plenty of flowers growing everywhere. At length we arrived at some rising ground, and we felt that the sea must be beyond it. A short walk brought us to the edge of the grassland, and then the most glorious panorama of ocean spread out before us.

The view was simply magnificent. Never had I expected to behold such sea. Its coloring was the most perfect reflection of the blue of the sky above, but in addition it reflected a myriad rainbow tints in every little wavelet. The surface of the water was calm, but this calmness by no means implies that the water was lifeless. There is no such thing as lifeless or stagnant water here. From where we were, I could see islands of some considerable size in the distance—islands that looked most attractive and must certainly be visited! Beneath us was a fine stretch of beach upon which we could see people seated at the water's edge, but there was no suggestion of over-crowding. And floating upon this superb sea, some close at hand—others standing a little way out, were the most beautiful boats—though I think I am not doing them full justice by calling them mere boats. Ships would be more apposite. I wondered who could own these fine vessels, and Edwin told us that we could own one ourselves if we so wished. Many of the owners lived upon them, having no other home but their boat. It made no difference. There they could live always, for here it is perpetual summer.

A short walk down a pleasant winding path brought us to a sandy seashore. Edwin informed us that it was a tideless ocean, and that at no place was it very deep by comparison with terrestrial seas. Storms of wind being impossible here, the water was always smooth, and in common with all water in these realms, it was of a pleasantly warm temperature that could occasion no feelings of cold—or even chilliness—to bathers. It was, of course, perfectly buoyant, possessed no single harmful element or characteristic, but it was, on the contrary, life-sustaining. To bathe in its waters was to experience a perfect manifestation of spiritual force. The sand upon which we were walking had none of the unpleasant features associated with the seashore of the earth-plane. It was never tiring to walk on. Although it had every appearance of sand as we had always known it, yet to the tread it was firm in consistency although soft to the touch of the hand. In fact, this peculiar quality rendered it more like well-kept lawns to walk on, so closely did the grains hold together. We took some handfuls of the sand, and allowed it to run through our fingers, and great was our surprise to find that it lacked every trace of grittiness, but seemed to the touch more akin to some smooth, soft powder. Yet examined closely it was undeniably solid. It was one of the strangest phenomena we had met so far. Edwin said that that was because we had, in this particular instance, carried out a more minute examination of what we were beholding than we had done hitherto in other things. He added that if we chose to make a close scrutiny of all that we saw, whether it be the ground we walked on, the substance of which our house were made, or the thousand and one other objects that go to make up the world of spirit, we should be living in a state of continual surprise, and there would be revealed to us some small idea—but only a very small idea— of the magnitude of the Great Mind—the Greatest Mind in the Universe—that upholds this and every other world. Indeed, the great scientists of the earth-plane find, when they come to live in the spirit world, that they have a completely new world upon which to commence a fresh course of investigations. They begin de novo as it were, but with all their great earthly experience behind them. And what joy it brings them, in company with their scientific colleagues, to probe the mysteries of the spirit world, to collect their data, to compare their new knowledge with the old, to record for the benefit of others the results of their investigations and discoveries. And all through they have the unlimited resources of the spirit world upon which to draw. And joy is in their hearts.

Our little experiment with the sand led us to place our hands in the sea. Ruth fully expected it to taste of salt, but it did not, much to her surprise. As far as I could observe, it had no taste at all! It was sea more by virtue of its great area and the characteristics of the adjacent land than anything else. In all other respects it resembled the water of the brooks and lakes. In general appearance the whole effect was totally unlike the earthly ocean, due, among other things, to the fact that there was no sun to give its light from one quarter only and to cause that change of aspect when the direction of the sunlight changes. The overspreading of light from the great central source of light in the spirit world, constant and unmoving, gives us perpetual day, but it must never be assumed that this constancy and immobility of light means a monotonous and unchanging land—or seascape. There are changes going on the whole time; changes of color such as man never dreamt of—until he comes to the spirit world. The eyes of the spirit person can see so many beautiful things in the world of spirit that the eyes of incarnate man cannot see—unless he be gifted with the psychic eye.

We wanted very much to visit one of the islands that we could see in the distance, but Ruth felt that it would be a nice experience to travel over the sea in one of the fine vessels that were close to the shore. But the difficulty arose—that is, it seemed as though it might arise!—as to the boat. If, as I understood, these were 'privately' owned, we should first have to become acquainted with one of the owners. Edwin, however, could see how Ruth was so longing to go upon the water that he soon explained the exact position—to her unbounded joy.

It seemed that one of these elegant boats belonged to a friend of his, but had it been otherwise we should have found that we would be welcome to go aboard any one of them, introducing ourselves—if we wished to observe that formality, though it was unnecessary—to whomsoever we found on board. Had we not already received, wherever we went, that friendly reception and assurance that we were welcome? Then why should there be any departure, in the case of the boats of the sea, from the fundamental rule of hospitality that operates in the spirit world. Edwin drew our attention to a very beautiful yacht that was riding 'at anchor' close to the shore. From where we were she had all the appearance of having had much attention devoted to her—our opinion was afterwards confirmed. She was built on the most graceful lines, and the grand upward sweep of her bows held the promise of power and speed. She looked much the same as an earthly yacht, that is, externally.

Edwin sent a message across to the owner, and in reply received an instantaneous invitation to us all. We therefore wasted no time, and we found ourselves upon the deck of this most handsome vessel, being greeted with great good cheer by our host, who immediately took us off to present us to his wife. She was very charming, and it was obvious to see that the two made a perfect couple. Our host could see that Ruth and I were both very keen to see over the boat, and knowing from Edwin that we had not been long in spirit, he was so much the more pleased to do so.

Our first observations at close hand showed us that many devices and fittings that are essential to earthly ships were here absent. That indispensable adjunct, an anchor, for instance. There being no winds, tides, or currents in spirit waters, an anchor becomes superfluous, though we were told that some boat-owners have them merely as an ornament and because they did not feel their vessels would be complete without them. There was unlimited space on deck, with a copious provision of very comfortable looking chairs. Below deck were well-appointed saloons and lounges. Ruth, I could see, was disappointed because she could see no evidence whatever of any motor power to drive the vessel, and she naturally concluded that the yacht was incapable of independent movement. I shared her disappointment, but Edwin had a merry twinkle in his eye which ought to have told me that things are not always what they seem to be in the spirit world. Our host had received our thoughts, and he immediately took us up into the wheelhouse. What was our astonishment when we saw that we were slowly and gently moving away from the shore! The others laughed merrily at our bewilderment, and we ran to the side to watch our progress through the water. There was no mistake about it, we were really on the move, and gathering speed as we went. We returned at once to the wheelhouse, and demanded an instant explanation of this apparent wizardry.

X. A VISITATION

Our host told us that the power of thought is almost unlimited in the spirit world, and that the greater the power of any particular effort or concentration of thought the greater the results. Our means of personal locomotion here is by thought, and we can apply that same means to what the earth world would call 'inanimate objects'. Of course, in the spirit world nothing is inanimate, and because of this, then our thoughts can have a direct influence upon all the countless things of which the world of spirit is composed. Ships are meant to float and move upon the waters; they are animated by the living force that animates all things here, and if we wish to move them over the water we have but to focus our thoughts in that direction and with that intention, and our thoughts produce the desired result of movement. We could, if we wished, call upon our scientific friends to provide us with splendid machinery to supply the motive power, and they would be only too pleased to oblige us. But we should have to focus our thoughts upon the machinery to make it generate the necessary driving force. Why, then, go this long way round to produce the same result, when we can do so directly and just as efficiently?

But it must not be concluded that anyone can move a boat through the water merely by thinking that it shall do so. It requires, like so many other things, the requisite knowledge, its application upon well-ordered lines, and practice in the art. A natural aptitude greatly helps in these matters, and our host told us that he mastered the subject in a very short time. Once the ability has been gained, it gives one, so he said, a most satisfying feeling of power rightly applied, and not only of power, but the power of thought, in a way that is not perhaps possible in some other ways. Perfect as the movement of ourselves can be through the realms, yet the movement of such a large object as a boat, simply and easily, magnifies the wonder of the whole of spirit life. Our host explained that this was only his own point of view, and was not to be taken as an axiom. His enthusiasm was increased by his enthusiasm for the water and a love of ships.

We noticed that he guided the boat in the usual manner, with a rudder operated by the wheel in the deck-house. That, he said was because he found it sufficient work to provide the movement of the boat. In time, if he wished, he could combine the two actions in one. But he much preferred to use the old method of steering by hand as it gave him physical work to do, which was, in itself, such a pleasure. Once having given motion to the ship, he could forget about it until he wished to stop. And the mere wishing to stop, however suddenly or gradually, brought the vessel to a standstill. There was no fear of accidents! They do not—cannot—exist in these realms.

All. the while our host was explaining these matters to Ruth and me—Edwin was busily engaged in conversation with our host's wife—our speed had increased to a steady rate, and we were moving in the direction of one of the islands. The yacht was travelling through the sea with the most perfect, steady motion. There was no vibration, naturally, from any machinery, but the very movement through the water could be perceptibly felt, while the sounds from the gentle waves as the boat cut along made the loveliest musical notes and harmonies as the many colors of the disturbed water changed their tints and blends. We observed that in our wake the water quickly settled into its former state, leaving no appearance of our having passed through it. Our host handled his craft skillfully, and by increasing or diminishing its speed he could create by the different degree of movement of the water, the most striking alternations of color and musical sound, the brilliant scintillations of the sea showing how alive it was. It responded to the boat's every movement as though they were in complete unison—as indeed they were.

Ruth was simply ecstatic in her enjoyment, and ran to our host's wife in the full ardor of her new experience. The latter, who fully appreciated her young friend's feelings, was just as enthusiastic. Although it was no novelty, in the sense of a first experience, she said she could never cease to marvel, however familiar she should become with her ship-home, at the glorious dispensation that provided such beauties and pleasures for the dwellers in spirit lands.

We had by now approached sufficiently near to the island to be able to view it quite well, and the boat turned in her course and followed the coast-line. After continuing along in this fashion for a little while, we sailed into a small bay which formed a picturesque natural harbor.

The island certainly came up to our expectations in its scenic beauty. There were not many dwellings upon it; those that were to be seen were more summer-houses than anything else. But the great feature of the place was the number of trees, none of them very tall, but all were of particularly vigorous growth. And in the branches we could see scores of the most wonderful birds, whose plumage presented a riot of color. Some of the birds were flying about, others—the larger variety—were walking majestically along the ground. But all of them were unafraid of us. They walked with us as we strolled along, and when we held up our hands, some small bird would be sure to perch upon our fingers. They seemed to know us, to know that any harm coming to them was an utter impossibility. They did not require to make a constant search for food nor exercise a perpetual vigilance against what on earth would be their natural enemies. They were, like ourselves, part of the eternal world of spirit, enjoying in their way, as we do in ours, their eternal life. Their very existence there was just another of those thousands of things that are given to us for our delight.

The birds which had the most gorgeous plumage were evidently of the kind that live in the tropical parts of the earth-plane, and which are never seen by the eye of man until he comes to the spirit world. By the perfect adjustment of temperature they were able to live in comfort with those of less spectacular appearance. And all the while they were singing and twittering in a symphony of sound. It was never wearying, in spite of the quantity of sound that was going on, because in some extraordinary fashion the musical sounds blended with each other. Neither were they piercing in quality despite the fact that many of the small birds' songs were themselves high-pitched. But it was their trusting friendliness that was so delightful by comparison with the earthly birds, whose life there takes them into another world almost. Here we were part of the same free world, and the understanding between the birds and ourselves was reciprocal. When we spoke to them we felt that they knew just what we were saying, and in some subtle way we seemed to know just what their thoughts were. To call to any particular bird meant that that bird understood, and it came to us.

Our friends, of course, had encountered all this before, but to Ruth and me it was a new and very wonderful experience. And the thought came to me that had I really considered the matter, and perhaps used my mind a little more, I might have known that we should eventually see something of this sort. For why, I asked myself, should the Great Father of Heaven create all the beautiful birds solely for the earth-plane?—and make them to live in places that are frequently quite inaccessible to man, where he can never see them and enjoy them? And even those that he can see and enjoy—are they to perish forever? Would the far greater world of spirit be denied the beautiful things that are given to the earth world? Here was the answer before and around us. It is in the conceit and self-importance of man that he should think that beauty is expressly created for his pleasure while on earth. Incarnate man thinks he has the monopoly of beauty. When he becomes discarnate he eventually wakes up to the fact that he has never really seen how great beauty can be, and he becomes silent and humble, perhaps for the first time in his life! It is a salutary lesson, the awakening in spirit, believe me, my dear friend—with many a shock to accompany it.

The perfect blaze of color from all the birds we could see about us was almost too much for us to take in at one visit. They were beyond description, and I shall not even attempt it. We strolled on through delightful groves, past the musical murmuring of the many brooks, through glades of velvet grass, as in an absolute fairyland of nature. We met people on the way, who called a greeting to us, or waved their hands. They were all happy among the birds. We were told that this part of the island was exclusive to the birds, and that no other form of animal life intruded upon them. Not that there was any fear or danger that they would come to harm, because that would be impossible, but because the birds were happier with their own kind.

We eventually returned to the boat, and put to sea again. We were interested to discover whence our host had acquired his floating home. Such an intricate piece of building would require experts, most surely, to plan it, and others to build it. He told us that a boat was evolved under precisely the same conditions as our spirit houses, or any other buildings. A prerequisite is that we must earn the right to possess it. That we understood. What, then, of the many people in spirit who on earth designed and built boats of every description either as a means of livelihood or as a form of recreation? Would the latter, particularly, abandon such pleasure when they could continue in their handicraft? Here they have the means and the motive to carry on with their task, whether it be for work or for pleasure. And it can be said that though many build their boats for the pleasure of doing so, yet they give great pleasure to many others who have a fondness for the sea and ships. Their pleasure becomes their work, and their work is pleasure.

The task of actually constructing a craft is highly technical, and the methods of the spirit world, so entirely different from those of the earth-plane, have to be mastered. Although we must earn the right to possess in the spirit world, we have the aid of our friends in the actual building. We can form in our minds, when on earth, the shape of something we long to have—a garden, a home, or whatever it may be. It will then be a thought-form, and will be converted from that into actual spirit substance by the help of experts.

Our return was as delightful as our outward journey. When we drew into the land again, our host extended a permanent invitation to us to visit them on board whenever we wished, and enjoy with them all the recreation of sailing on the sea.

As we walked along the sandy beach Edwin recalled to our minds the great building in the center of the city, by telling us that very shortly there would be a visitation from a being of the higher realms, and for which many would be forgathering in the domed temple. Would we care to join him? It was not in any sense to be considered a specific act of worship for which this personage was visiting the realm. Such things as worship do not require conscious effort (they come spontaneously from the heart), but our visitant would bring with him not only his own radiance, but the radiance of the heavenly sphere which he graced. We at once expressed our eagerness to go with him, as we both felt that we would not have ventured there alone, since we had all along been under Edwin's guidance.

As we walked down the broad avenue of trees and gardens, we formed part of a great concourse of people who were all proceeding in the same direction, and obviously for the same purpose. Strange to say, that although we were among so many people, yet we never experienced the feeling, so common on earth, of being amongst a large crowd. It was an extraordinary feeling, which Ruth shared with me. We supposed that we had expected our old earthly sensations would have overcome us; the fear that in such an immense assembly of people there would be something of the confusion that one is accustomed to on the earth-plane; the jostling and the noise, and above all the sense of time passing, when our enjoyment would be over and passed. To have such ideas as these was quite ridiculous, and Ruth and I laughed at ourselves—as did Edwin—for expressing such notions, or entertaining them for an instant. We felt— because we knew—that everything was in perfect order; that everyone knew what to do or where to go; that there was no question of another's superiority over ourselves for reasons of privilege. We felt that we were expected for the support we should give, and that a personal welcome was waiting for us.

Was not this sufficient to banish all feelings of discomfort or uneasiness.

There was, moreover, a unity of mind among us that is not possible on the earth-plane even with those of the same religious beliefs. What earthly religion is there where all its adherents are entirely of one mind? There is none. It has been thought essential on earth that to offer up thanks and worship to the Supreme Being there must be a complexity of ritual and formularies and ceremonies, with creeds and dogmas and strange beliefs, over which there is as much diversity of views as there are numbers of different religions.

It may be said that I have already told of the establishment of communities of those same religions here in the spirit world, so that the spirit world is in no better case than the earth world. When the earth world becomes really enlightened these communities here will disappear. It is the blindness and stupidity of the earth world that causes them to be here at all. They are given tolerance, and they must exercise tolerance themselves, otherwise they would be swept away. They must never attempt to influence or coerce any soul into believing any of their erroneous doctrines. They must confine themselves strictly to themselves, but they are perfectly and absolutely free to practice their own false religion among themselves. The truth awaits them on the threshold of their churches as they leave their places of worship, not when they have entered. When a soul at length perceives the futility of his particular and peculiar religious beliefs he quickly dissociates himself from them, and in full freedom and complete truth—which has no creeds or ecclesiastical commandments—he offers up his thoughts to his Heavenly Father just as they flow from his mind, free and unaffected, stripped of all jargon, simple and heartfelt

But we have our temples where we can receive the great messengers from the highest realms, fitting places to receive the Father's representatives, and where such messengers can send our united thanks and our petitions to the Great Source of all. We do not worship blindly as on earth.

As we drew close to the temple we could already feel ourselves being, as it were, charged with spiritual force. Edwin told us that this was always the case because of the immense power, brought by the higher visitants, which remained undiminished within a wide circle of the temple. It was for this reason that the temple stood completely isolated, with no other buildings near it. Gardens alone surrounded it—a great sea of flowers, extending, it almost seemed, as far as the eye could see, and presenting such a galaxy of brilliant color, in great banks and masses, as the earth could never contemplate. And arising from all this were the most heavenly sounds of music and the most delicate perfumes, the effect upon us being that of pure exaltation of the spirit. We felt that we were lifted up above ourselves right out into another realm.

The building itself was magnificent. It was stately; it was grand; it was an inspiration in itself. It appeared to be made of the finest crystal, but it was not transparent. Massive pillars were polished until they shone like the sun, while every carving flashed its brilliant colors until the whole edifice was a temple of light. Never did I think such scintillations possible, for not only did the surfaces reflect the light in the ordinary way, they gave out a light of their own that could be felt spiritually.

Edwin took us to some seats which we knew to be our own—we had that feeling of familiarity with them as one does with a favorite chair at home.

Above us was the great dome of exquisitely wrought gold, which reflected the hundreds of colors that shone from the rest of the building. But the focus of all attention was upon the marble sanctuary—which word I must use for want of a better—at the end of the temple. It had a shallow balustrade with a central opening at the head of a flight of steps leading down on to the floor. We could hear the sounds of music, but whence it came I knew not, because there was no sign of any musicians. The music was evidently provided by a large orchestra—of strings only, for there were no sounds of the other instruments of the orchestra.

The sanctuary, which was of spacious dimensions, was filled with many beings from higher realms, with the exception of a space in the center, which I guessed was reserved for our visitant. We were all of us seated, and we conversed quietly amongst ourselves. Presently we were aware of the presence of a stately figure of a man with jet-black hair, who was closely followed—very much to my surprise—by the kindly Egyptian whom we had met in Edwin's house on the boundary of our realm. To those who had already witnessed such visitations, their arrival was at once the indication of the coming of the high personage, and we all accordingly rose to our feet. Then, before our eyes, there appeared first a light, which might almost be described as dazzling, but as we concentrated our gaze upon it we immediately became attuned to it, and we felt no sensation of spiritual discomfort. In point of fact—as I discovered later—the light really became attuned to us; that is to say, it was toned down to accord with ourselves and our realm. It grew in shade to a golden hue upon the extremities, gradually brightening towards the center. And in the center there slowly took shape the form of our visitant. As it gained in density we could see that he was a man whose appearance was that of youth—spiritual youth—but we knew that he carried with him to an unimaginable degree the three comprehensive and all-sufficing attributes of Wisdom, Knowledge, and Purity. His countenance shone with transcendental beauty; his hair was of gold, while round his head was a lustrous diadem. His raiment was of the most gossamer-like quality, and it consisted of a pure white robe bordered with a deep band of gold, while from his shoulders there depended a mantle of the richest cerulean blue, which was fastened upon his breast with a great pink pearl. His movements were majestic as he raised his arms and sent forth a blessing upon us all. We remained standing and silent while our thoughts ascended to Him Who sent us such a glorious being. We sent our thanks and we sent our petitions. For myself, I had one boon to ask, and I asked for it.

It is not possible for me to convey to you one fraction of the exaltation of the spirit that I felt while in the presence, though distant, of this heavenly guest. But I do know that not for long could I have remained in that temple while he was there without undergoing the almost crushing consciousness that I was low, very, very low upon the scale of spiritual evolution and progression. And yet I knew that he was sending out to me, as to us all, thoughts of encouragement, of good hope, of kindness in the very highest degree, that made me feel that I must never, never despair of attaining to the highest spiritual realm, and that there was good and useful work ready for me to do in the service of man, and that in the doing thereof I would have the whole of the spiritual realms behind me—as they are behind every single soul who works in the service of man.

With a final benediction upon us, this resplendent and truly regal being was gone from our sight.

We remained seated for a while, and gradually the temple began to empty. I had no inclination to move, and Edwin told us we could stay there as long as we wished. The building was, therefore, practically empty when I saw the figure of the Egyptian approaching us. He greeted us warmly, and asked me if I would be good enough to go with him, as he wished to introduce me to his 'master'. I thanked him for his continued interest in me, and what was my astonishment when he led me into the presence of the man with whom he had entered the sanctuary. I had only been able to see him from my seat, but close to I could see that a pair of dark sparkling eyes matched his raven hair, which was made the more pronounced by the slight paleness of his complexion. The colors of his attire were blue, white, and gold, and although these were of a very high order, they were not of such intensity as were those of the principal visitor. I had the impression that I was in the presence of a wise man—which indeed he was—and of a man with a great sense of fun and humor. (It must be ever remembered that fun and humor are not, and never will be, the sole prerogative of inhabitants of the earth-plane, however much they may like to claim a monopoly of them, and however much they may like to deny us our lighthearted merriment. We shall continue to laugh in spite of their possible disapproval)

The kind Egyptian presented me to his master, and the latter took me by the hand and smiled upon me in such a manner as to take away, completely, any feelings of diffidence that I had. In fact, he simply diffused assurance in one's self, and he placed one perfectly at ease. One would, without disrespect, call him the perfect host. When he spoke to me his voice was beautifully modulated, soft in tone, and so very kindly. His words to me filled me with joy even as they left me filled with wonder: 'My beloved master,' he said, 'whom you have just seen, bids me tell you that your prayer is answered, and that you shall have your desire. Fear not, for promises that are made here are always fulfilled.' Then he told me that I should be asked to wait for a period before the fulfillment, because it was necessary that a chain of events should take place before the right circumstances were brought about in which my desires should find fruition. The time would soon pass he said, and I could, meanwhile, carry on with my intended work with my friends. If at any time I wished for advice my good Edwin would always be able to call upon our Egyptian friend whose guidance was ever at my service. Then he gave me his blessing, and I found myself alone. Alone with my thoughts, and with the abiding memory and the celestial fragrance of our transplendent visitants.

I rejoined Edwin and Ruth, and told them of my happiness. They were both overjoyed at my great good news which had come from so exalted a source. I felt now that I would like to return to my house, and I asked Edwin and Ruth if they would accompany me. Thither we repaired, and we walked straight into my library. Upon one of the shelves was a particular book written by myself when upon the earth-plane, and which I wished that I had never written. I removed the book that was immediately next to it, leaving the space unoccupied. According to my answered prayer I should fill that space with another book, written after I had come to spirit, the product of my mind when I had seen the truth.

And linking arms together, we all three walked out into the garden—and into the heavenly sunshine of eternity.

PART II

The World Unseen

I. THE FLOWERS

After I had passed into the spirit world, one of my earliest experiences was the consciousness of a feeling of sadness, not of my own sadness, for I was supremely happy, but of the sadness of others, and I was greatly puzzled to know whence it came.

Edwin told me that this sadness was rising from the earth world, and was caused by the sorrow felt at my passing. It soon ceased, however, and Edwin informed me that forgetfulness of me by the earth people had already set in. That experience alone, my good friend, is one that can be relied upon to induce feelings of humility, if no humility before existed!

I had, I assure you, set small store by popularity. The discovery, therefore, that my memory was fast fading from the minds of earth people occasioned me no distress whatever. I had written and preached for the good they might do, and that, as I now learned, was microscopically small. I was told that many people, whose public favor was considerable when they were incarnate, discovered, when they had shed their earthly bodies, that their fame and high favor had not preceded them into the world of spirit. Gone was the admiration which had been their common everyday experience. It naturally saddened such souls to leave behind them their earthly prominence, and it gave them something of a sense of loneliness, the more so when, in addition, the earth world quickly forgot all about them.

My own earthly reputation had been of no very great magnitude, but I had managed to carve a niche for myself among my co-religionists.

My transition had been calm and peaceful, and unattended by any unpleasant circumstances. It was no wrench for me to leave the earth world. I had no ties but my work. I was, therefore greatly blessed. Edwin told me of others whose passing was extremely unhappy, and whose spiritual state upon their arrival here was still more unhappy. Many, who were great upon earth, found themselves very small in spirit. And many, who were unknown upon earth, found themselves here so spiritually well known as to be almost overcome by it. It is not all, by any means, who are destined for the beautiful realms of eternal sunshine and summer.

I have already given you a glimpse of those realms of darkness and semi-darkness, where all is cold and bleak and barren, and wherein souls have their abode, souls who can rise up out of the darkness if they so wish it and will work for that end. There are many who spend their heaven visiting these dim regions to try to draw out of their misery some of these unfortunates, and to set them upon the path of light and spiritual progression. It has been my privilege to go with Edwin and Ruth to visit the dark places beyond the belt of mist that separates them from the light. It is not my purpose to take you into those realms of misery and unhappiness just yet. Later on I shall hope to give you some account of our experiences. For the moment there are other—and pleasanter—matters upon which I should like to speak.

There are many souls upon the earth-plane who seek to

probe the manifold mysteries of life. They propound theories of divers kinds purporting to explain this or that, theories which, in the course of time, come to be looked upon as great truths. Some of these hypotheses are as remote from the truth as it is possible to imagine; others are merely nonsensical. But there are also people who refuse even to think for themselves, and who stolidly uphold the belief that while they are incarnate they are not meant to know anything of the life of spirit that lies before them all. They affirm that it is not God's purpose that they should be told of such matters, and that when they come to spirit they will know all things.

There are two extremes of thought—the theorists and the partisans of the 'closed door'. Both schools receive some severe shocks when they enter spirit lands to live for all time. Individuals with strange theories find those theories demolished by the simple fact of finding themselves faced with the absolute truth. They discover that life in the spirit world is not nearly so complex as they would have it to be. In so many instances it is vastly simpler than life upon earth, because we do not have the problems that constantly harass and worry earth people, problems, for example, of religion and politics, which throughout the ages have caused social upheavals that are still having their repercussions in the earth world at the present time. The student of occult matters is apt to fall into the same error as the student of religious matters. He makes assertions every bit as dogmatic as those that emanate from orthodox religion, assertions that are mostly, far from the truth.

The period of time in which I have lived in the spirit world is as nothing—nothing—by comparison with some of the great souls with whom it has been my privilege to speak. But they have shown me something of their vast store of knowledge, things, that is, that my mind was capable of understanding. For the rest, I—in company with millions of others—am perfectly contented to wait for the day when my intelligence is sufficiently advanced to grasp the greater truths.

A matter that gives rise to some perplexity concerns the flowers that we have in the spirit world. Some would ask: why flowers What is their purpose or significance? Have they any symbolical meaning?

Let us put the same questions to earth people concerning the flowers that grow upon the earth-plane. Have the earthly flowers any special significance? Have they some symbolical meaning?

the answer to both questions is No! Flowers are given to the earth world to help to beautify it, and for the delight and enjoyment of those who behold them. The fact that they serve other useful purposes is an added reason for their existence. Flowers are essentially beautiful, evolved from the Supreme Creative Mind, given to us as a precious gift, showing us in their colorings, in their formations, and in their perfumes an infinitesimally small expression of that Great Mind. You have this glory upon the earth-plane. Are we to be deprived of it in the spirit world because it is considered that flowers are rather earthy, or because no deep, abstruse meaning can be assigned to their existence?

We have the most glorious flowers here, some of them like the old familiar cherished blooms of the earth-plane, others known only to the spirit world, but all alike are superb, the perpetual joy of all of us who are surrounded with them. They are divine creations, each single flower breathing the pure air of spirit, and upheld by their Creator and by all of us here in the love that we shower upon them. Had we no wish for them—an impossible supposition!—they would be swept away. And what should we have in their stead? Where, otherwise, would the great wealth of color come from which the flowers provide?

And it is not only the smaller growing flowers that we have here. There is no single flowering tree or shrub that the mind can recall that we do not possess, flourishing in superabundance and perfection, as well as those trees and shrubs that are to be seen nowhere else but in the spirit world. They are always in bloom, they never fade or die, their perfumes are diffused into the air where they act like a spiritual tonic upon us all. They are at one with us, as we are with them.

When we are first introduced to the flowers and trees and all the luxuriance of spirit nature, we instantly perceive something that earthly nature never seemed to possess, and that is an inherent intelligence within all growing things. Earthly flowers, although living, make no immediate personal response when one comes into close touch with them. But here it is vastly different. Spirit flowers are imperishable, and that should at once suggest more than mere life within them, and spirit flowers, as well as all other forms of nature, are created by the Great Father of the Universe through his agents in the realms of spirit. They are part of the immense stream of life that flows directly from Him, and that flows through every species of botanic growth.

That stream never ceases, never falters, and it is, moreover, continuously fed by the admiration and love which we, in this world of spirit, gratefully shed upon such choice gifts of the Father. Is it, then, to be wondered at, when we take the tiniest blossom within our hands, that we should feel such an influx of magnetic power, such a revivifying force, such an upliftment of one's very being, when we know, in truth, that those forces for our betterment are coming directly from the Source of all good. No, there is no other meaning behind our spirit flowers than the expressed beauty of the Father of the Universe, and, surely, that is enough. He has attached no strange symbolism to His faultless creations. Why should we?

A large majority of the flowers are not meant to be picked. To pick them is not to destroy them—it is to cut off that which is in direct contact with the Father. It is possible to gather them, of course; no disastrous calamity would follow if one did. But whosoever picked them would certainly regret it very deeply. Think of some small article that you possess and treasure above all your other earthly possessions, and then consider deliberately destroying it. It would cause you extreme sadness to do so, although the loss incurred might be intrinsically trifling. Such would be your emotions when you heedlessly culled those spirit flowers that are not intended for gathering.

But there are blooms, and plenty of them, that are expressly there to be picked, and many of us do so, taking them into our houses just as we used to do on earth, and for the same reason.

These severed flowers will survive their removal for just so long as we wish to retain them. When our interest in them begins to wane they will quickly disintegrate. There will be no unsightly withered remnants, for there can be no death in a land of eternal life. We simply perceive that our flowers have gone, and we can then replace them if we so wish.

II. THE SOIL

To obtain an adequate idea of the ground upon which we walk and on which our houses and buildings are erected, you must clear your mind of all mundane conceptions. First of all, we have no roads as they are known on earth. We have broad, extensive thoroughfares in our cities and elsewhere, but they are not paved with a composite substance to give them hardness and durability for the passage of a constant stream of traffic. We have no traffic, and our roads are covered with the thickest and greenest of grass, as soft to the feet as a bed of fresh moss. It is on these that we walk. The grass never grows beyond the condition of being well-trimmed, and yet it is living grass. It is always retained at the same serviceable level, perfect to walk upon and perfect in appearance.

In such places where smaller paths are desirable, and where grass would seem unsuitable, we have such pavements as are customary in the earth world. But they are constructed of very different materials. The paving is, for the most part, a description of stone, but it is without the usual dull drabness of color. It closely resembles the alabaster-like material of which so many of the buildings are constructed. The colors vary, but they are all of delicate pastel shades.

This stone, like the grass, is very pleasant to walk upon, though, naturally, it is not as soft. But there is a certain quality about it, a certain springiness, if one may so term it, something like the resilience of certain earthly timber that is utilized in the making of floors. That is the only way in which I can convey any idea of the difference between earthly stone and spirit stone.

There is never, of course, any unsightly discoloration to be observed upon the surface of these stone walks. They always preserve their initial freshness. Often the pavements reveal a network of delightful designs formed by the use of different colored materials, and blending harmoniously with their immediate surroundings.

As one approaches the boundaries to the higher realms, the pavements become noticeably more translucent in character, and they seem to lose some of their appearance of solidity, though, indeed, they are solid enough!

When one draws near the boundaries of the lower realms, the pavements become heavy in appearance, they begin to lose their color until they look leaden and opaque, and they have the semblance of extreme solidity—almost like the granite of the earth-plane.

Round about our own individual homes we have lawns and trees and flower-beds, with trim garden paths of stone similar to that which I have just described to you. But of bare 'earth' you would see little or none. Indeed, I cannot call to mind ever having seen any such bare plots, for here there is no neglect through indifference or indolence, or from other causes that are all too familiar to specify. Where we have earned the right to possess our spirit home we have also within us the constant desire to maintain and improve upon its beauty. And that is not very difficult to accomplish, since beauty responds to, and thrives upon, the appreciation of it. The greater attention and recognition we give to it, so much the greater will be its response, and it assumes to itself still greater beauty. Spirit beauty is no abstract thing, but a real living force.

The view from my own home here is one of green fields, of houses of charm pleasantly situated amid woods and gardens, and with a distant view of the city. But nowhere are there to be seen any ugly tracts of bare or barren ground. Every inch that presents itself to the eye is cared for, so that the whole landscape is a riot of color, from the brilliant emerald green of the grass to the multi-colored flowers in the gardens, coronated by the blue of the heavenly sky above.

It may be wondered of what is the actual ground composed in which the flowers and trees are growing—is it earth of some sort?

There is soil, certainly, but it has not the same mineral constituents as that of the earth-plane, for it must be understood that life here is derived directly from the Great Source. The soil varies in color and density in different localities in just the same way as upon the earth-plane. I have not investigated it closely, any more than I took particular heed of earthly soil. I can, however, give you some small idea of its appearance and characteristics.

Firstly, then, it is perfectly dry—I could detect no trace of moisture. I found that it ran off the hand in much the same way that dry sand will do. Its colors vary in a wide range of tones, but never does it approach the dark heavy look of earthly soil. In some places it is of fine granular formation, while in others it is composed of much coarser particles—that is, relatively coarser.

One of the unexpected properties of this soil is the fact that, while it can be taken into the hand and allowed to run from it smoothly and freely, yet when it is undisturbed it remains fully cohesive, supporting as firmly as the earthly soil all that is growing within it.

The color of the 'earth' is governed by the color of whatever botanic life it supports. And here again there is no special significance, no deep symbolical reason for this particular order of things. It is simply that the color of the soil is complementary to the color of the flowers and trees, and the result, which could not be otherwise, is that of inspiring harmony—harmony to the eye, harmony to the mind, and the most soothing musical harmony to the ear. What better reason could there be? And what simpler?

Assuredly, this world of spirit is not made up of a bewildering series of profound and complex mysteries, explicable only to the few. There are mysteries, certainly, just as there are upon the earth-plane. And just as there are great brains upon the earth-plane who can solve those mysteries, so here there are greater brains still—immeasurably greater—who can provide an explanation when our intellects are ready to receive it and understand it.

But there are many people in the earth world who earnestly believe that we in spirit live in a continual state of perfervid religious emotion, that every concomitant of spirit life, every form and degree of personal activity, every atom of which the great world of spirit is composed, must have some pious, devotional signification. Such a stupid notion is wide, very wide of the mark. Search through the earth world, and do you find any such unnatural ideas attached to the multiplicity of life that lies within it? There is no religious import in a beautiful earthly sunset. Why should our spirit flowers—to take one instance among many—have any other reason for their existence than that which I have already given you, namely, a magnificent gift to us all from the Father of us all for our greater happiness and enjoyment?

There are still many, many souls on earth who solemnly uphold it as an article of 'faith' that paradise, as they call it, will be one long interminable round of singing 'psalms and hymns and spiritual canticles'. Nothing could be more fantastic. The spirit world is a world of activity, not indolence; a world of usefulness, not uselessness. Nothing in the spirit world is useless; there is a sound reason and purpose for everything. Neither the reason nor the purpose may be plain to everyone at first, but that does not alter the truth of the matter.

Boredom can find no place here as a general state of affairs. People have been known to become bored, but that very boredom begets their first step—or their next step—in spiritual progression through their engaging in some useful work. There are myriads of tasks to be performed—and myriads of souls to perform them, but there is always room for one more, and it will ever be so. Am I not living in a world that is both unlimited and illimitable?

We do not inhabit a land that bears all the outward marks of an Eternal Sunday! Indeed, Sunday has no place, no existence even, in the great scheme of the spirit world. We have no need to be forcibly reminded of the Great Father of the Universe, by setting aside one day to Him, and forgetting Him for the rest of the week. We have no week. With us it is eternal day, and our minds are fully and perpetually conscious of Him, so that we can see His hand and His mind in everything that surrounds us.

I have deviated a little from what I set out to tell you, but it is expedient to emphasize certain features of my narrative, because so many souls of the earth world are almost shocked to be told that the spirit world is a solid world, a substantial world, with real, live people in it! They think that that is far too material, far too like the earth world, hardly in fact, one step removed from it, with its spirit landscape and sunshine, its houses and buildings, its rivers and lakes, inhabited by sentient, intelligent beings!

This is no land of 'eternal rest'. There is rest in abundance for those who need it. But when the rest has restored them to full vigor and health the urge to perform some sensible, useful task rises up within them, and opportunities abound.

To return to the particular characteristics of spirit soil.

As we approach the dark regions the soil, such as I have described to you, loses its granular quality and its color. It becomes thick, heavy, and moist, until it finally gives place entirely to stones, and then rock. Whatever grass there is looks yellow and seared.

As we draw closer to the higher realms the particles of the soil become finer, the colors more delicate, with a hint of translucency. A greater degree of resilience is at once observable underfoot when walking upon the thresholds of these higher realms, but the resilience comes as well from the nature of the realm as from the distinct change in the ground.

On close examination the fine soil reveals almost jewel-like qualities both of color and form. The particles are never misshapen, but conform to a definite geometric plan.

Ruth and I plunged our hands into some of the soil and allowed it to trickle through our fingers in a gentle stream. As it descended there issued from it the sweetest musical tones, as though it were falling upon some tiny musical instrument and causing the keys to produce a ripple of sound.

A keen ear will hear many musical sounds upon the earthly seashore as the water sweeps back and forth over the beach, but no keen ear is necessary to hear the rich harmonics when the ground of the spirit world is made to speak and sing.

The sounds emitted in this way vary as much as the colors and elements themselves vary. They are there for all to hear, and they can be produced at will by the very simple action I have described.

How is this brought about, you will ask?

Color and sound—that is, musical sound—are interchangeable terms in the spirit world. To perform some act that will produce color is also to produce a musical sound. To play upon a musical instrument, or to sing, is to create color, and each creation is governed and limited by the skill and proficiency of the instrumentalist or singer. A master musician, as he plays upon his instrument, will build above himself a most beautiful musical thought-form, varying in its colors and blends of shades in strict accordance with the music he plays. A singer can create a similar effect in relation to the purity of the voice and the quality of the music. The thought-form thus erected will not be very large. It is a form in miniature. But a large orchestra or body of singers will construct an immense form, governed, of course, by the same law.

The musical thought-form produces no sound itself. It is the result of sound, and is, as it were, a self-contained unit. Although music will bring forth color, and color will yield music, each is restricted to the one resultant form. They will not go on reproducing each other in a constant, unending, or gradually diminishing, alternation of color and sound.

It must not be thought that with all the vast galaxy of colors from the hundreds of sources in the spirit world, our ears are being constantly assailed with the sounds of music; that we are living, in fact, in an eternity of music that is sounding and resounding without remission. There are few minds—if any—that could possibly endure such a continuous plethora of sound, however beautiful it may be. We should sigh for peace and quietness; our heaven would cease to be heaven. No, the music is there, but we please ourselves entirely whether we wish to hear it or listen to it. We can completely isolate ourselves from the sound, or we can throw ourselves open to all sound, or just hear that which pleases us most.

There are times upon the earth-plane when you can hear the

strains of distant music without being in any way disturbed by it; on the contrary, you may find it very pleasant and soothing. So it is with us in spirit. But there is this great difference between our two worlds—our potentialities for music of the highest order are immeasurably greater than are yours upon the earth-plane. The mind of a spirit person who has a deep love of music will naturally hear more, because he so wishes, than one who cares little for it.

To revert to the experiment that Ruth and I carried out when we let the soil run through our fingers. We both of us derive great enjoyment from listening to music, Ruth much more so than myself, since she has been trained in the musical art and therefore has a higher appreciation and grasp of musical technicalities. I have told you how, the instant the soil left our hands, we could hear the delightful sounds issuing from it. Another person performing the same action, but who possessed no particular musical susceptibilities, would scarcely be conscious of any sound at all.

The flowers and all growing things respond immediately to those who love them and appreciate them. The music that they send out operates under precisely the same law. An attunement upon the part of the percipient, with that with which he comes into contact or relationship, is a prerequisite condition. Without that attunement it would be impossible to be conscious of the musical strains that issue forth from the whole of spirit nature. By spirit nature I mean, of course, all the growing things, the sea and lakes—indeed, all water—the soil, and the rest.

The greater the power of the individual of appreciating and understanding beauty in all its multivarious forms, the greater will be the outflowing of magnetic force. In the spirit world nothing is wasted nor expended uselessly. We never have forced upon us something that we do not want, whether it be music or art, entertainment or learning. We are free agents, in every sense of the term, within the confines of our own realm.

It would be a most terrifying thought to imagine that the spirit world is one immense pandemonium of music, continuing ceaselessly, totally unavoidable, presenting itself on every conceivable occasion and in every possible place and situation! No!—the spirit world is conducted on much better lines than that! The music sounds are most certainly there, but it rests solely with ourselves whether we shall hear them or not. And the secret is personal attunement.

There are people upon the earth-plane who possess the ability of mentally isolating themselves from their surroundings to such a degree that they can become oblivious to all sounds, however intense, that might be going on around them. This state of complete mental detachment will serve as an analogy—though a rather elementary one—of the effect that we can produce upon ourselves in spirit, to the exclusion of such sounds as we have no wish to hear. Unlike the earth world, we do not need to bring to bear any great force of concentration. It is but another process of thought, just as we use our minds to effect personal locomotion, and after a brief sojourn in spirit we are soon able to perform these various mental functions without any conscious effort. They are part of our very nature, and we are merely applying, in an extended form, without earthly limitations and restrictions, mental methods that are perfectly simple to apply. On the earth-plane our physical bodies, in a heavy physical world, prevented similar mental processes from producing any physical result. In the spirit world we are free and unfettered, and those actions of the mind show an instant and direct result, whether it be to move us with the quickness of our thought, or whether it be to shut out any sight or sound that we do not wish to experience.

On the other hand, we can—and do—open our minds and attune ourselves to absorb the many glorious sounds that come rising up all round us. We can open our minds—or close them—to the many delectable perfumes that spirit nature casts abroad for our happiness, and contentment. They act like a tonic upon the mind, but they are not forced upon us—we merely help ourselves to them as we wish. It must ever be borne in mind that the spirit lands are founded upon law and order. But the law is never oppressive nor the order irksome, because the same law and order have helped to provide all the countless beauties and wonders of this heavenly realm.

III. BUILDING METHODS

Not the least important, among the many 'physical' features of the realm in which I live, are the numerous buildings devoted to the pursuit of learning and the fostering of the arts familiar to the earth-plane. These magnificent edifices present to the eye all the signs one would expect of the permanence of eternity. The materials of which they are constructed are imperishable. The surfaces of the stone are as clean and fresh as on the day when they were raised up. There is nothing to soil them, no heavy smoke-laden atmosphere to eat into them, no winds and rains to wear down the works of exterior decoration. The materials of which they are built are of the spirit world, and therefore they have a beauty that is not earthly.

Although these fine halls of learning have every suggestion of permanency, they could be demolished if it were considered expedient or desirable to do so. In some cases it has been so considered. Such buildings have been removed, and others have taken their place.

The spirit world is not static. It is ever vibrant with life and movement. Contemplate, for a moment, the normal conditions of the earth world, with the many changes that are taking place continuously—the gradual reconstruction of towns and cities, the alterations in the countryside. Some of these changes have not always been deemed improvements. However that may be, changes are made, and the procedure is looked upon as one of progression. What, then, of the spirit world? Are no changes to take place in the world in which I live? Most certainly they are!

We do not exactly 'move with the times'—to use a familiar earthly phrase, because we are always very much ahead of the times. And we have every need to be—to meet the heavy demands placed upon us by the earth world.

Let us take one specific instance—just one.

As the earth world progresses in civilization—in its own estimation—the means and methods of waging war become more devastating and wholesale. In place of hundreds killed in battles in ancient times, the slain are now counted in hundreds of thousands. Every one of those souls has finished with his earthly life—though not with the consequences of it—and, in so many cases, the earth world has finished with him too. The individual may survive as a memory to those whom he has left behind him; his physical presence is gone. But his spirit presence is unalterably with us. The earth world has passed him on to us, oftentimes not really caring what has befallen him. He will leave behind him those whom he loved, and who loved him, but the earth world—so it thinks—can do nothing for him, nor for those who mourn his passing. It is we, in the spirit world, who will care for that soul. With us there is no shifting the responsibility on to other shoulders, and passing upon our way.

We are faced with strict realities here.

The earth world, in its blind ignorance, hurls hundreds of thousands of souls into this our land, but those who dwell in the high realms are fully aware long before it happens, of what is to take place upon the earth-plane, and a fiat goes forth to the realms nearer the earth to prepare for what is to come.

These dire calamities of the earth-plane necessitate the building of more and ever more halls of rest in the spirit world. That is one occasion—and perhaps the greatest—for the changes that are always taking place here. But there are others and more pleasant.

Sometimes the wish is expressed by a great number of souls for an extension to be made to one of the halls of learning. There is seldom any difficulty about such a desire, since it is in no sense a selfish one, because it will be there for all to use and enjoy.

It was in reply to a question which I put to Edwin that he told me that a new wing was to be added to the great library, where I have spent so many profitable and enjoyable moments since I came to spirit. It was suggested that perhaps Ruth and I would like to witness a spirit building in actual course of being erected. Accordingly, we made our way to the city and to the library.

There was a large number of people already gathered there with the same intent as ourselves, and while we were waiting for operations to begin, Edwin told us something of the preliminary details that are necessary before work actually begins.

As soon as some new building is desired, the ruler of the realm is consulted. Of this great soul and of others similar to him in spiritual character and capacity I will tell you later. Knowing, as he does, so intimately, the needs and wishes of all in his realm there never arises a case where some building is required for the use and service of all but that the wish is granted. The ruler then transmits the request to those in authority above him, who in turn refer it to those still higher. We then foregather in the central temple in the city where we are received by one whose word is law, the great soul who, many years ago of earthly time, made it possible for me to communicate thus with the earth world.

Now, this seemingly involved procedure of passing on our request from one to another, may suggest to the mind the tortuous methods of officialdom with its delays and protractedness. The method may be somewhat similar, but the time taken in performance is a very different matter. It is no exaggeration to say that within the space of a few earthly minutes our request has been stated, and the permission—with a gracious blessing accompanying it—has been granted. On such occasions as these we have cause for rejoicing, and we seize the opportunity to the full.

The next step is to consult the architect, and it may be readily imagined that we have a host of masters upon whom we can draw without limitation. They work for the sheer joy it brings them in the creation of some grand edifice to be used in the service of their fellows. These good men collaborate in a way that would be almost impossible upon the earth-plane. Here they are not circumscribed by professional etiquette, or limited by the narrowness of petty jealousies. Each is more than happy and proud to serve with the other, and never is there discord or disagreement through endeavoring to introduce, or force, the individual ideas of the one at the expense of another's. Perhaps you will say that such complete unanimity is far and away beyond the bounds of human nature and that such people would not be human if they did not disagree, or otherwise show their individuality.

Before you dismiss my statement as highly improbable, or all the painting of a picture of perfection impossible to attain except within the very highest realms of all, let me state the simple fact that discord and disagreement, upon such a matter as we are now considering, could not possibly exist in this realm wherein is my home. And if you still insist that this is impossible, I say No—it is perfectly natural. Whatever gifts we may possess in spirit, it is part of the essence of this realm that we have no inflated ideas of the power or excellence of those gifts. We acknowledge them in humility alone, without self-importance, unobtrusively, selflessly, and we are grateful for the opportunity of working, con amore, with our colleagues in the service of the Great Inspirer.

This, in substance, is what one of these great architects himself told me with reference to his own work.

After the plans for the new buildings have been drawn up in consultation with the ruler of the realm, there is a meeting of the master-masons. The latter were mostly masons when they were upon the earth-plane, and they continue to exercise their skill in spirit lands. They do so, of course, because the work appeals to them, even as it did when they were incarnate, and here they have faultless conditions under which they can carry on their work. They do so with a grand freedom and liberty of action that was denied them upon earth, but which is their heritage here in the spirit world. Others, who were not masons by trade, have since learned the spirit methods of building—for the sheer joy of doing so, and they give valuable aid to their more skilled confreres.

The masons, and one other, are the only people concerned in the actual construction, since spirit buildings do not require much that has to be included within the disposition of earthly buildings. Such, for example, as the necessary provision for lighting by artificial means, and for heating. Our light comes from the great central source of all light, and the warmth is one of the spiritual features of the realm.

The addition which was being made to the library consisted of an annex, and it was not of any very great dimensions. Our spirit library has at least one feature in common with earthly libraries. A time comes when the quantity of books exceeds the space in which to house them, and in our case the excess is inclined to be greater, because not only do we have copies of earthly books upon the shelves, but there are also volumes that have their source solely in spirit. By this, I mean that such books have no counterpart on earth. Included among them are works concerning spirit life alone, the facts of life here, and spiritual teachings, written by authorities who have an infallible knowledge of their subject, and who reside in the higher spheres. There are also the histories of nations and events, with the facts set down in strict accordance with the absolute truth written by men who now find that equivocation is impossible.

The building of this annex was not, therefore, what one would denominate a major effort, and it required the help of but a comparative few. It was simple in design, consisting of two or three medium-sized rooms.

We were standing fairly close to the group of architects and masons, headed by the ruler of the realm. I noticed particularly that they had all the appearance of being extremely happy and jovial, and many were the jokes that circulated round this cheerful band.

It was strange to Ruth and me—Edwin had witnessed this sort of thing before—to think that a building was shortly to go up, because since my arrival in the spirit world I had seen no signs of any building operations going on anywhere. Every hall and house was already erected, and it never occurred to me that anything further would be required in this direction. A little thought, of course, would have revealed that spirit houses are always in course of being built, while others are being demolished if they are no longer wanted. The halls of learning all looked so very permanent to my unaccustomed eyes, so very complete, that I could not think it would ever be necessary to make any additions to them.

At length there were signs that a beginning was to be made. It must be remembered that the act of building in the spirit world is essentially an operation of thought. It will not be surprising, therefore, when I tell you that nowhere were there to be seen the usual materials and paraphernalia associated with earthly builders, the scaffolding and bricks and cement, and the various other familiar objects. We were to witness, in fact, an act of creation—of creation by thought—and as such no 'physical' equipment is necessary.

The ruler of the realm stepped forward a few paces, and, with his back towards us, but facing the site upon which the new wing was to arise, he spoke a brief but appropriate prayer. In simple language he asked the Great Creator for His help in the work they were about to undertake.

His prayer brought an instantaneous response, which was in the form of a bright beam of light that descended upon him and upon those gathered immediately behind him. As soon as this happened the architects and masons moved up close beside him.

All eyes were now turned upon that vacant spot beside the main building, to which we noticed that a second beam of light was passing directly from the ruler and the masons. As the second beam reached the site of the annex it formed itself into a carpet of coruscation upon the ground. This gradually grew in depth, width, and height, but it seemed, as yet, to lack any suggestion of substance. It matched the main building in color, but that was all so far.

Slowly the form gained in size until it reached the required height. We could now see plainly that it matched the original structure in general outline, while the carved devices similarly corresponded.

While it was in this state the architects approached and examined it closely. We could observe them moving within it, until at length they passed from view. They were gone but a moment when they returned to the ruler with the report that all was in order.

Edwin explained to us that this rather ghostly edifice was in reality an adumbration of the finished structure, shaped in exact facsimile before an intensification of thought was applied to produce a solid and completed building. Any mistake or fault would be detected when the building was in this tenuous state, and corrected at once.

No rectification, however, being necessary in this particular instance, the work was proceeded with immediately.

The downstream of light now became very much more intense, while the horizontal stream from the ruler and his collaborators assumed, after the lapse of a minute or two, a similar degree of intensity. We could now perceive the nebulous form acquiring an unmistakable appearance of solidity as the concentration of united thought laid layer upon layer of increased density upon the simulacrum.

From what I observed it seemed to devolve upon the ruler to supply to each of the masons just that quantity and description of force that each required upon his separate task. He acted, in fact, as a distributive agent for the magnetic power that was descending directly upon him. This split up into a number of individual shafts of light of different color and strength, which corresponded with his direct appeals to the Great Architect. There was no faltering or diminution of the application of thought substance to be perceived anywhere. The masons themselves seemed to work with a complete unanimity of concentration, since the building attained full solidity with a remarkable degree of evenness.

After what appeared to Ruth and me a very short period, the building ceased to acquire any further density, the vertical and horizontal rays were cut off, and there stood before us the finished wing, perfect in every detail, an exact match and extension to the main edifice, beautifully alike in color and form, and worthy of the high purpose to which it was to be devoted.

We moved forward to examine more closely the results of the feat that had just been accomplished. We ran our hands over the smooth surface, as though to convince ourselves that it was really solid! Ruth and I were not the only people to do this, as there were others who were witnessing for the first time—and with equal wonderment—the immense power of directed thought.

The procedure which governs the building of our personal

houses and cottages differs a little from that which I have just described to you. An indispensable prerequisite to the ownership of a spirit home is the right to own it, a right which is gained solely by the kind of life we live when incarnate, or by our spiritual progression after our transition to the spirit world. Once we have earned that right there is nothing to prevent our having such a residence if we should wish for one.

It has often been said that we build our spirit homes during our earthly lives—or after. That is so only in a broad sense. What we have built is the right to build, for it requires an expert to erect a house that would justify the name. My own home was built for me during my earthly life by builders just as proficient as those who helped to erect the annex to the library. My friends, headed by Edwin, had looked after all the details entailed in such work. They had sought out the men to undertake the task, and the latter had carried into effect a fine piece of craftsmanship.

When that day shall dawn upon which my spiritual progression will carry me onwards, I shall leave my house. But it will rest entirely with myself whether I leave my old home as it stands for others to occupy and enjoy, or whether I demolish it.

It is customary, I am told, to make a gift of it to the ruler of the realm for his disposal to others at his discretion.

IV. TIME AND SPACE

It is commonly thought by people of the earth-plane that in the spirit world time and space do not exist. That is wrong. We have both, but our conception of them differs from that of the earth world.

We sometimes use the phrase, 'before the dawn of time', to convey an idea of the passage of eons of time, but we have no notion of what is really embodied in that phrase.

On the earth-plane the measurement of time had its source in the revolution of the earth upon its axis, giving a division of time known to us as night and day. The recurrence of the four seasons gave that larger measure, during which the earth revolved round the sun. The invention of clocks and calendars brought a convenient means of measuring time within the reach of all of us.

In the spirit world we have no clocks or other mechanical

contrivances to indicate the passage of time. It would be the simplest thing in the world for our scientists to provide us with such if we felt the need for them. But we have no such need. We have no recurrent seasons, no alternations of light and darkness as external indications of time, and, in addition, we have no personal reminders, common to all the incarnate, of hunger and thirst and fatigue, together with the ageing of the physical body. How, then, can we have any possible heed of the flight of time? How, in fact, does time exist at all?

We have two conceptions of time, one of which, as upon the earth-plane, is purely relative. Five minutes, let us say, of acute pain suffered by the physical body will so affect the mind that the passing moments will seem an age. But five minutes of intense joy and happiness will seem to have flown with the rapidity of the same number of seconds.

Those of us in the spirit world who live in the realm of happiness and perpetual summer will have no cause to find 'time hang heavily'. In this sense we are simply not conscious of the flight of time.

In the dark realms the reverse is the case. The period of darkness will seem interminable to those who live there. However much such souls may yearn for a coming of the light, yet it never comes to them. They themselves must perforce take the first step towards the light that awaits them without their low realm. A period of existence within these dark regions, amounting to nothing more than a year or two of earthly time, will seem like an eternity to the sufferers.

If, normally, we have none of the customary means of measuring time because we have no need to do so, we can— and we do—return to make contact with the earth-plane, where we can ascertain the exact time of day, the day of the year, and the year itself.

Some people, who would not otherwise have done so, have returned to the earth world for the very purpose of satisfying their curiosity as to the number of years they have been in the spirit world. I have spoken to some who have made this journey, and they were all amazed to discover the unsuspected scores of years that had passed by since their transition.

Speaking for myself, I have found the time pass rapidly since I came into spirit, but I have always known, throughout the whole of that period, what was the year of the Christian Era. The reason in my own case was simply that I had been promised that I should one day be able to communicate with the earth world. I had, therefore, been keenly interested in watching, in company with the great souls who were closely concerned, the concatenation of events that were to lead, among other things, to the achievement of my wish.

Edwin, who met me upon the threshold of the spirit world and conducted me to my new home, was similarly acquainted with the passage of time, for he, in turn, had been watching me

It may be thought that time, in the sense of being a measured succession of existence, has little or no influence beyond the earth-plane. But it most certainly does have an influence upon the spirit-plane.

All earthly events, whether concerning nations or individuals, are subject to, or governed by, time. And in so far as those events have their application to, or extension into, the spirit world, so do we in the spirit world come under the influence of time, or its operation. We might take the festival of Christmas as the simplest and readiest example. We celebrate this festival in the spirit world at the same time as do you. Whether December 25th is the correct date, historically, for the event which it commemorates, is a question we are not concerned with for our present purposes. What matters is that the two celebrations, yours and ours, are synchronized and recurrent year by year. We are not subservient to the earth world in this; our purpose is solely one of co-operation.

In normal times upon the earth-plane at that period of the year, there rises throughout the earth world a great force of good-will and kindliness. Many people, who at other seasons are inclined to be forgetful, will frequently remember those of their family and friends who have passed into spirit lands, and they will send them thoughts of affection which we in spirit are always so happy to receive and to reciprocate. The celebration of Christmas is always preceded by thoughts of pleasant anticipation. If there were nothing else to guide us, these alone would be sufficient to tell us that the time of the feast was drawing near. In the spirit world, at that time, it is common enough to hear one person say to another: 'Christmas on the earth-plane is drawing near'. But the person so addressed might have been completely unaware of the fact.

In the particular example of Christmas we are not dependent entirely upon the earth-plane for our knowledge of the approaching anniversary. On this special occasion we are always visited by great souls from the higher realms, and were all other means to fail us, this would be an infallible indication of the passing of another year in earthly time.

Those of us who are in close and constant connection with the earth will know, of course, as well as do you, the year, the month, and the day. We shall know, too, the exact hour of earth time There is no difficulty about this, nor is there any mystery. When we come into your conditions we can make use of the very means that you yourselves employ—and what could be simpler? As a rule it is not necessary for us to be continually aware of the precise day and hour, or otherwise to keep account of them. When we actively co-operate with you your thoughts to us are sufficient indication that a certain moment has recurred when we meet to work or converse together. Such thoughts are all that we need. It is in the ordinary nature of things in spirit that, generally speaking, we should lose all sense of the continuity of time in measured succession as you know it. We allow things to remain so, unless we have cause to do otherwise. When we look forward to the arrival of relative or friend into the spirit world it is towards the event that we cast our minds, not the year in which the event is to take place.

Thus far I have given you a few facts of my own knowledge derived from my own experience, and therefore what I have told you applies to the specific realm wherein I live.

Of the higher realms I have no knowledge at first hand, and the amount of information that I have gleaned from conversations with inhabitants of those realms has been governed and restricted by my ability to understand. All that I can say, therefore, concerning time in the upper spheres is that in such elevated states we come into realms where knowledge, among many other spiritual attributes, is of a very high order. Personages from those realms have more than astonished me with the accuracy of their foreknowledge of events that were to take place upon the earth-plane. Their means of acquiring this information is far beyond the comprehension of us in this realm. It is sufficient for the moment to record that it is so, and that time, therefore, is not confined to realms of a less exalted state of spiritual progression.

When we come to the subject of space we find that, broadly speaking, we are governed, to a point, by the same law as upon the earth-plane. We have eternity of time, but we have also infinity of space.

Space must exist in the spirit world. Take my own realm alone, as an example. Standing at the window of one of the upper rooms of my house I can see across huge distances whereon are many houses and grand buildings. In the distance I can see the city with many more great buildings. Dispersed throughout the whole wide prospect are woods and meadows, rivers and streams, gardens and orchards, and they are all occupying space, just as all these occupy space in the earth world. They do not interpenetrate any more than they interpenetrate upon the earth-plane. Each fills its own reserved portion of space. And I know, as I gaze out of my window, that far beyond the range of my vision, and far beyond and beyond that again, there are more realms and still more realms that constitute the designation infinity of space. I know that I can travel uninterruptedly through enormous areas of space, areas far greater than the whole of the earth world trebled in size, or greater. I have not yet traversed anything like one fraction of the full extent of my own realm, but I am free to do so whenever I wish. I have been told by good friends from the higher realms that I could penetrate even those rarefied states if occasion demanded. I should be given the facilities and the protective cloak that are necessary in such cases to make the journey, so that, potentially, my field of movement is gigantic.

Viewed with earthly eyes only, this immense region would obviously go beyond the reach of most people, since movement through such spaces on earth would be restricted by the means of transportation at their command, as well as by other considerations. One thousand miles of earthly space is a great distance, and to cover it takes some considerable time if the slower means of transport are employed. Even with the fastest method a certain time must elapse before the end of the thousand miles journey is reached. But in the spirit world thought alters the whole situation. We have space, and we have a certain cognizance of time in its relation to space. Thought can annihilate time in its relation to space, but it cannot annihilate space.

I can stand before my house and I can bethink myself that I would like to visit the library in the city which I can see some 'miles' away in the distance. No sooner has the thought passed with precision through my mind than I find myself—if I so desire it—standing before the very shelves that I wish to consult. I have made my spirit body—and that is the only body I have—travel

125

through space with the rapidity of thought, and that is so rapid that it is equivalent to being instantaneous. And what have I done, I have covered the intervening space instantaneously, but the space still remains there with everything it contains, although I had no cognizance of time or the passage of time.

When I have completed my visit to the library I meet some friends upon the steps, and they suggest that we adjourn to the home of one of them. With this pleasant prospect in view we decide to walk through the gardens and woods. The house is some 'distance' away, but that does not matter, because we never suffer from 'physical' fatigue, and we are not otherwise engaged. We walk along together, talking happily, and after a certain lapse of 'time' we arrive at the house of our friend, and we have covered the intervening space on foot. On the journey from my house to the library I overcame the distance in between, and I dispensed with time for the occasion. On the way back I experienced an intuitive apprehension of time by walking slowly, and I restored a perception of distance to my mind by moving upon the solid ground and the grassy fields of this realm.

Time—in its spirit sense—and space are relative in the spirit world, just as they are upon the earth-plane. But our conceptions of them differ widely—yours being restricted by the earthly considerations of sunrise and sunset, and the various modes of transit. We have everlasting day, and we can move ourselves slowly by walking, or we can transport ourselves instantaneously whithersoever we wish to be. In the spirit world time can thus be made to stand still, and we can restore our sense of it by quietly resting or by walking. It is only our general sense of time that we restore, not the passage of time. But when we receive your thoughts from the earth world, telling us that you are ready for us to come to you, then, once again, we are fully aware of the passage of earthly time.

And you must admit that we are invariably punctual in keeping our appointments with you!

V. GEOGRAPHICAL POSITION

WHAT is the geographical position of the spirit world in relation to the earth world? Many people have wondered this at different times—and I include myself among the many!

And that leads to a further question concerning the

disposition of other realms than those of which I have given you some details.

I have told you how, when I had reached a critical moment as I lay upon my final bed of earthly sickness, I at length felt an irresistible urge to rise up, and that I yielded to that urge easily and successfully. In this particular case the line of demarcation was very fine between the end of my earthly life and the beginning of my spirit life, because I was in full possession of my senses, fully conscious. The actual transition from one world to the other was in this respect imperceptible.

But I can narrow things down still further by recalling that there came a moment when the physical sensations attendant upon my last illness left me abruptly, and in place of them a delightful feeling of bodily ease and peace of mind completely enveloped me. I felt that I wanted to breathe deeply, and I did so. The impulse to rise from my bed, and the passing of all physical sensations, mark the instant of my physical 'death' and my birth into the world of spirit.

But when this took place I was still in my own earthly bedroom, and therefore a part, at least, of the spirit world must interpenetrate the earth world. This particular experience will give us something of a point of departure for our geographical explorations.

The next event in my transition was the arrival of my good friend Edwin, and our meeting after the lapse of years. The meeting took place seemingly in the bedroom. Then, after we had greeted each other and chatted for a brief space, Edwin proposed that we should depart from our present surroundings, which, in the circumstances, were rather doleful. He took me by the arm, told me to close my eyes, and I felt myself gently moving through space. I had no clear perception of direction. I only knew that I was travelling, but whether up or down or horizontally, it was impossible for me to say. Our rate of progress increased until at last I was told to open my eyes, and then I found myself standing before my spirit home.

Since that day I have learned many things, and one of my first lessons was in the art of personal locomotion by other means than walking. There are immense distances here to cover, and sometimes we need to cover them instantly. We do so by the power of thought as I have already outlined to you. But the strangest thing to me, at first, was the fact that when I moved myself through space at any greater speed than ordinary walking, I found that I had no sense of absolute direction, but one of movement only. If I chose to shut my eyes whilst travelling with moderate speed I merely shut out the scenery, or whatever else were my surroundings. It must not be thought that it is possible to lose one's way. That would be out of the question.

This absence of a sense of direction in no way interferes with our initial thought function in personal locomotion. Once we have determined to journey to a certain place, we set our thoughts in motion and they, in turn—instantaneously—set our spirit bodies in motion. One might almost say 'it requires no thinking about.' I have spoken to other people on these matters, and compared notes generally—it is a thing we all do when we are newly-arrived in the spirit world; and we never lack willing friends to help us in our early difficulties. I have found that it is common to all here in spirit, this absence of any directional perception when moving rapidly. Of course, when we travel instantaneously there is no 'time' to observe any object whatsoever. There is no observable interval of time between the moment we leave for, and the moment we arrive at, our destination.

It will be appreciated from this factor of directional unawareness, if I may so term it, that to assign a precise location to the spirit world, relative to the earth world, is a difficult matter. Indeed, I doubt if anyone fairly new to spirit life could possibly hazard a guess as to his relative geographical position Of course, there are scores upon scores of people who never bother their heads about such things. They have severed all connection with the earth world, and they have done with it for all time. They know positively that they are alive and in the spirit world, but as to the exact position of that world in the universe, they have no intention of troubling themselves. But our own case is different. I am in very active communion with the earth world, and I think it would be of interest if I were to try to give some idea just where the spirit lands are situated.

The spirit world is divided into spheres or realms. These two words of designation have passed into current acceptation among most of those on the earth-plane who have a knowledge of, and practice, communication, with our world. In speaking to you thus, I have used the words interchangeably. They suffice for our purpose—one can think of none better.

These spheres have been given numbers by some students,

ranging from the first, which is the lowest, up to the seventh, the highest. It is customary among most of us here to follow this system of numbering. The idea originated, I am told, from our side, and it is a very useful and convenient method of conveying the information of one's position upon the ladder of spiritual evolution.

The spheres of the spirit world are ranged in a series of bands forming a number of concentric circles around the earth. These circles reach out into the infinity of space, and they are invisibly linked with the earth world in its lesser revolution upon its axis, and, of course, in its greater revolution round the sun. The sun has no influence whatever upon the spirit world. We have no consciousness of it at all since it is purely material.

An exemplification of the concentric circles is afforded us when we are told that a visitant from a higher sphere is coming down to us. He is relatively above us, both spiritually and spatially.

The low realms of darkness are situated close to the earth-plane, and interpenetrate it at their lowest. It was through these that I passed with Edwin when he came to take me to my spirit home and it was for that reason that he recommended that I keep my eyes firmly closed until he should tell me to open them again. I was sufficiently alert—too much so, because I was fully conscious—otherwise to see some of the hideousness that the earth world has cast into these dark places.

With the spirit world made up of a series of concentric circles, having the earth world approximately at the center, we find that the spheres are subdivided laterally to correspond broadly with the various nations of the earth, each subdivision being situated immediately over its kindred nation. When you consider the enormous variety of national temperament and characteristics distributed throughout the earth-plane, it is not surprising that the people of each nation should wish to gravitate to those of their own kind in the spirit world, just as much as they wish to do when upon the earth-plane. Individual choice, of course, is free and open to every soul; he may live in whatsoever part of his own realgm that he pleases. There are no fixed territorial frontiers here to separate the nations. They make their own invisible frontiers of temperament and customs, but the members of all the nations of the earth are at liberty to intermingle in the spirit world, and to enjoy unrestricted and happy social intercourse. The language question presents no difficulty, because we are not obliged to speak aloud. We can transmit our thoughts to each other with the full assurance that they will be received by the person whom we are mentally addressing. Thus language constitutes no barrier.

Each of the national subdivisions of the spirit world bears the characteristics of its earthly counterpart. That is but natural. My own home is situated in surroundings that are familiar to me and that are a counterpart of my earthly home in general appearance. These surroundings are not an exact replica of the earthly surroundings. By which, I mean that my spirit home is located in the type of countryside with which I and my friends are very familiar.

This dividing of the nations extends only to a certain number of realms. Beyond that, nationality, as such, ceases to be. There we retain only our outward and visible distinctions, such as the color of our skin, whether it be yellow, white, or black. We shall cease to be nationally conscious such as we are when upon the earth-plane and during our sojourn in the realms of less degree. Our homes will no longer have a definite national appearance, and will partake more of pure spirit.

You will recall how, in building the annex to the library, I introduced you to the ruler of the realm. Each realm has such a personage, though the term ruler is not a really good one, because it is apt to convey something of a wrong impression. It would be much happier and far more exact to say that he presides over the realm.

Although each realm has its own resident ruler, all the rulers belong to a higher sphere than that over which they preside.

The position is such that it calls for high attributes on the part of its holder, and the office is held only by those who have had long residence in the spirit world. Many of them have been here thousands of years. Great spirituality is not alone sufficient; if it were, there are many wonderful souls who could hold such office with distinction. But a ruler must possess a great deal of knowledge and experience of humanity, and in addition he must always be able to exercise wise discretion in dealing with the various matters that come before him. And all the ruler's experience and knowledge, all his sympathy and understanding, are ever at the disposal of the inhabitants of his realm, while his kindness and infinite patience are always in evidence. This great soul is ever accessible to any who wish to consult him, or who bring him their problems for solution.

We have our problems, just as do you upon the earth-plane although our problems are very different from yours. Ours are never of the nature of those harassing worries and cares of the earth world. Speaking for myself, my first problem, soon after my transition, was how to set right what I considered to be a wrong I had done when I was incarnate. I had written a book in which I had treated the truth of communication with the earth world with great unfairness. When I spoke to Edwin upon the subject he—all unknown to me—had sought the advice of the ruler of the realm, and the result was that another great soul had come to discuss the matter with me, and to offer help and advice in my difficulty. It was the ruler's knowledge of my affairs in the first instance that eventually brought about a happy ending to my trouble.

It will be seen from this that a ruler's knowledge of the people over whom he presides is vast. Lest it should be thought that it is humanly impossible for one mind to carry so much knowledge of the affairs of so many people as there must be in one realm, it must be understood that the mind of the incarnate is limited in its range of action by the physical brain. In the spirit world we have no physical brain to hamper us, and our minds are fully and completely retentive of all knowledge that comes to us. We do not forget those things we have learned in the spirit world, whether they be spiritual lessons or plain facts. But it takes time, as you would say, to learn, and that is why the rulers of realms have spent many thousands of earthly years in the spirit world before they are placed in charge of so many people. For the rulers have to guide and direct them, help them in their work, and unite with them in their recreation, to be an inspiration to them, and to act towards them, in every sense of the word, as a devoted father. There is no such thing as unhappiness in this realm—if for no other reason than that it would be impossible with such a grand soul to smooth away the troubles.

Each sphere is completely invisible to the inhabitants of the spheres below it, and in this respect, at least, it provides its own boundary.

In journeying to a lower realm one sees the terrain gradually degenerating.

As we draw towards a higher realm, just the opposite takes place: we see the land around us becoming more ethereal, more refined, and this forms a natural barrier to those of us who have not yet progressed sufficiently to become inhabitants of that realm.

Now, I have already told you how the realms are one above the other. How, then, does one proceed from one to the next, either above or below. There must be some point or points in each realm where there is a distinct upward inclination to the one and a distinct declivity to the other. Simple though it sounds, that is precisely the case.

It is not difficult to imagine, perhaps a gradual descent to regions that are less salubrious. We can call to our aid our earthly experiences, and recollect some rocky places that we could visit and descend, treacherous to the feet, leading us down into dark caverns, cold and damp and uninviting, where we could imagine all manner of noisome things lurking in readiness for us. We can then remember that above us, though out of sight, there shines the sun, spreading warmth and light upon the earth, while yet we seem to be in another world altogether. We might wander about through underground caves until we become lost and are shut out completely from the land above us. But we know that there is one way up at least, if we can but find it, and if we persevere in our attempts to scale the dangerous rocky pathway.

If we commence our world of spirit in the lowest recess of this earthly picture of the subterranean caves, we can see how each of the realms is connected with the realm immediately above it. The earthly analogy is, of course, an elementary one, but the process and the principle are the same. The transition in the spirit world from one realm to another is literal—as literal as passing from the dark cavern to the sunlight above, as literal as walking from one room in your house to another, whether upstairs or down.

To pass from this realm where I live to the next higher, I shall find myself walking along gently rising ground. As I proceed I shall see all the unmistakable signs—and feel them—of a realm of greater spiritual refinement. There will eventually come a point in my walking when I can go no further because I shall feel most uncomfortable spiritually. If I should be foolish enough to try to defy these feelings, I should, at length, find that I was completely unable to venture a foot forward without undergoing sensations which I could not possibly bear. I should not be able to see anything before me, only that which lay behind me. But whether we are standing at one of the boundaries, or whether we are well within the confines of our own realm, there comes a certain line in the bridge between the realms where the higher realm becomes invisible to less spiritual eyes. Just as certain light rays are invisible to earthly eyes, and certain sounds and musical notes are inaudible to earthly ears, so are the higher realms invisible to the inhabitants of the lower realms. And the reason is that each realm possesses a higher vibrational rate than that below it, and is therefore invisible and inaudible to those who live below it. Thus we can see that another natural law operates for our own good.

VI. THE LOWEST REALMS

THERE is a very bright and beautiful sphere of the spirit world which has been given the picturesque and most apposite title of the 'Summerland'.

The dark regions might almost be called the 'Winterland', but for the fact that the earthly winter possesses a grandeur all its own, while there is nothing but abomination about the lower realms of the spirit world.

So far I have only touched briefly upon the dark realms, taking you just within the threshold, but in company with Edwin and Ruth, I have actually penetrated deeply into those regions. It is not a pleasant subject, but I have been advised that the facts should be given, not with the intention of frightening people— that is not the spirit world's methods or aims—but to show that such places exist solely by virtue of an inexorable law, the law of cause and effect, the spiritual reaping that succeeds the earthly sowing; to show that to escape moral justice upon the earth-plane is to find strict and unrelenting justice in the spirit world.

As we proceed slowly from our own realm towards these dark lands, we shall find a gradual deterioration taking place in the countryside. The flowers become scanty and ill-nourished, giving the appearance of a struggle for existence. The grass is parched and yellow, until, with the last remnants of sickly flowers, it finally disappears altogether, to be superseded by barren rocks. The light steadily diminishes until we are in a grey land, and then comes the darkness—deep, black, impenetrable darkness; impenetrable, that is, to those who are spiritually blind. Visitors from a higher realm can see in this darkness without themselves being seen by the inhabitants, unless it becomes vitally necessary so to indicate their presence.

Our visits have carried us to what we verily believe to be the lowest plane of human existence.

We began the descent by passing through a belt of mist which we encountered as the ground became hard and barren. The light rapidly dwindled, dwellings were fewer and fewer, and there was not a soul to be seen anywhere. Great tracts of granite-like rocks stretched out before us, cold and forbidding, and the 'road' we followed was rough and precipitous. By now, darkness had enshrouded us, but we could still see all our surroundings perfectly clearly. It is rather a strange experience this, of being able to see in the dark, and when one first undergoes it there seems to be an air of unreality about it. But, indeed, it is real enough.

As we climbed down through one of the numerous fissures in the rocks, I could see and feel the loathsome slime that covered the whole surface of them, a dirty green in color and evil smelling. There was, of course, no danger of our falling. That would be impossible for any dwellers in these realms.

After we had journeyed downwards for what seemed to be a great distance—I should imagine it to have been of one mile of earthly measurement, at least—we found ourselves in a gigantic crater, many miles in circumference, whose sides, treacherous and menacing, towered above us.

The whole of this area was interspersed with huge masses of rock, as though some enormous landslide or cataclysm had disrupted them from the upper rim of the crater and sent them hurtling down into the depths below, there to scatter themselves in every direction, forming natural caverns and tunnels.

In our present position we were well above this sea of rocks, and we observed a dull cloud of poisonous vapor rising from it, as though a volcano were below and upon the point of erupting. Had we not been amply protected we should have found these fumes suffocating and deadly. As it was, they left us completely unharmed, although we could perceive with our intuitive faculties the degree of malignity of the whole place. Dimly, we could see through this miasma what might have been human beings, crawling like some foul beasts over the surface of the upper rocks. We could not think, Ruth and I, that they were human, but Edwin assured us that once they had walked upon the earth-plane as men, that they had eaten and slept, and breathed the earthly air, had mixed with other men on earth. But they lived a life of spiritual foulness. And in their death of the physical body they had gone to their true abode and their true estate in the spirit world.

The rising vapor seemed to shroud them somewhat from our vision, and we descended until we were level with the tops of the rocks.

As I had expressed my willingness to be taken by Edwin whithersoever he thought would best befit my purpose, and as I knew I should be able to withstand whatever sights I saw, we moved nearer to some of these creatures of hideousness. Ruth was accompanying us, and, needless to say, she would never have been permitted to enter these noxious realms had it not been known, without any shadow of doubt, that she was fully capable of the highest degree of self-possession and fortitude. Indeed, I not only marvelled at her composure, but I was profoundly thankful to have her by my side.

We walked closer to one of the sub-human forms that lay sprawled upon the rocks. What remnant of clothing it wore might easily have been dispensed with, since it consisted of nothing but the filthiest rags, which hung together in some inconceivable way, leaving visible great gaps of lifeless-looking flesh. The limbs were so thinly covered with skin that one fully expected to see bare bones showing forth. The hands were shaped like the talons of some bird of prey, with the finger nails so grown as to have become veritable claws. The face upon this monster was barely human, so distorted was it, and malformed. The eyes were small and penetrating, but the mouth was huge and repulsive, with thick protruding lips set upon a prognathic jaw, and scarcely concealing the veriest fangs of teeth.

We gazed earnestly and long at this sorry wreck of what was once a human form, and I wondered what earthly misdeeds had reduced it to this awful state of degeneration.

Edwin, who was experienced in these sights, told us that in time we should gain certain knowledge in our work, which would enable us to read from the faces and forms of these creatures what it was that had reduced them to their present state. There would be no need to accost them to find out at least some of their life's story, for there it was written for the experienced to read. Their very appearance, too, would be a safe guide as to whether they needed help, or whether they were still content to abide in their sunken state.

The object that was now before us, said Edwin, would warrant little sympathy as he was, because he was still steeped in his iniquity, and was obviously showing not the least sign of regret for his loathsome earthly life. He was dazed at his loss of physical energy, and puzzled in his mind to know what had befallen him. His face showed that, given the opportunity, he would continue his base practices with every ounce of power that remained to him.

That he had been several hundred years in the spirit world could be seen by the few tattered remnants of his garb, which bespoke a former age, and he had spent the greater part of his earth life inflicting mental and physical tortures upon those who had the misfortune to come into his evil clutches. Every crime that he had committed against other people had, at last, reverted to, and descended upon, himself. He now had before him—he had done so for hundreds of years—the memory, the indelible memory of every act of evil he had perpetrated against his fellows.

When he was upon earth, he had acted under a false pretence of administering justice. In very truth, his justice had been nothing but a travesty, and now he was seeing exactly what true justice really meant. Not only was his own life of wickedness continually before him, but the features of his many victims were ever passing before his mind, created out of that same memory which is registered unfailingly and ineradicably upon the subconscious mind. He cannot ever forget; he must always remember. And his condition was aggravated by the anger of feeling like a trapped animal.

We stood together, a little group of three, but we could not feel one tiny vestige of sympathy for this inhuman monster. He aroused none within us. He was receiving his just merits—no more, no less. He had judged himself and condemned himself, and now he was suffering the punishment he had, solely and entirely, inflicted upon himself. Here was no case of an avenging God inflicting condign punishment upon a sinner. The sinner was there, truly, but he was the visible manifestation of the unalterable law of cause and effect. The cause was in his earthly life; the effect was in his spirit life.

Had we been able to detect one tiny glimmer of that light—it is a real light that we see—which is an unmistakable sign of spiritual stirrings within, we might have done something for this soul. As it was, we could do nothing but hope that one day this dreadful being would call for help in true earnestness and sincerity. His call would be answered—unfailingly.

We turned away, and Edwin led us down through an opening in the rocks on to more or less level ground. We could see at once that this part of the crater was more thickly peopled—if one can use the term 'people' of such as we saw there.

The inhabitants were variously occupied: some were seated upon small boulders, and gave every appearance of conspiring together, but upon what devilish schemes it was impossible to say. Others were in small groups perpetrating unspeakable tortures upon the weaker of their kind who must, in some fashion, have fallen foul of their tormentors. Their shrieks were unbearable to listen to, and so we closed our ears to them, firmly and effectively. Their limbs were indescribably distorted and malformed, and in some cases their faces and heads had retrograded to the merest mockery of a human countenance. Others again we observed to be lying prone upon the ground as though exhausted from undergoing torture, or because of expending their last remaining energy upon inflicting it, before they could gather renewed strength to recommence their barbarities.

Interspersed throughout the great area of this dreadful region were pools of some sort of liquid. It looked thick and viscid, and inexpressibly filthy, as, indeed, it was. Edwin told us that the stench that came from these pools was in keeping with all else that we had seen here, and he advised us earnestly not to dream of testing the matter for ourselves. We followed his advice implicitly.

We were horrified to see signs of movement in some of the pools, and we guessed, without Edwin having to tell us, that frequently the inhabitants slip and fall into them. They cannot drown because they are as indestructible as we are ourselves.

We witnessed all manner of bestialities and grossness, and such barbarities and cruelties as the mind can scarcely contemplate. It is not my purpose nor my wish to give you a detailed account of what we beheld. We had, by no means, reached the very bottom of this foul pit, but I have given you quite sufficient details of what is to be found in the realms of darkness

And now you will ask: how does this all come about? How or why are such places allowed to exist?

Perhaps the matter will become clearer when I tell you that every soul who lives in those awful places once lived upon the earth-plane. The thought is dreadful, but the truth cannot be altered. Do not think for one moment that I have exaggerated in my brief description of these regions. I assure you that I have not done so. I have in fact given you an understatement. The whole of these revolting regions exist by virtue of the same laws that govern the states of beauty and happiness.

The beauty of the spirit world is the outward and visible expression of the spiritual progression of its inhabitants. When we have earned the right to possess things of beauty, they are given to us through the power of creation. In this sense we can be said to have created them ourselves. Beauty of mind and deed can produce nothing but beauty, and hence we have flowers of heavenly beauty, trees and meadows, rivers and streams and seas of pure, glistening, crystal-clear water, magnificent buildings for the joy and benefit of us all, and our own individual homes where we can surround ourselves with still more beauty, and enjoy the delights of happy converse with our fellows.

But ugliness of mind and deed can produce nothing but ugliness. The seeds of hideousness sown upon the earth-plane will inevitably lead to the reaping of a harvest of hideousness in the spirit world. These dark realms have been built up by the people of the earth-plane, even as they have built up the realms of beauty.

No single soul is forced into either the realms of light or those of darkness. No soul could possibly take exception to anything he found in his realm of light, since discontent or disapproval, discomfort or unhappiness cannot exist in these realms. We are a supremely happy, united body of people, and we live together in complete harmony. No soul could, therefore, feel 'out of place'.

The denizens of the realms of darkness have, by their lives on earth, condemned themselves, each and every one, to the state in which they now find themselves. It is the inevitable law of cause and effect; as sure as night follows day upon the earth-plane. Of what avail to cry for mercy? The spirit world is a world of strict justice, a justice that cannot be tampered with, a justice which we all mete out to ourselves. Strict justice and mercy cannot go together. However wholeheartedly and sincerely we may forgive the wrong that has been done to us, mercy is not given to us to dispense in the spirit world. Every bad action must be accounted for by the one who commits it. It is a personal matter which must be done alone, even as the actual event of death of the physical body must be gone through alone. No one can do it for us, but by the great dispensation upon which this and all worlds are founded, we can, and do, have ready and able assistance in our tribulation. Every soul who dwells in these dreadful dark realms has the power within himself to rise up out of the foulness into the light. He must make the individual effort himself, he must work out his own redemption. None can do it for him. Every inch of the way he must toil himself. There is no mercy awaiting him, but stern justice.

But the golden opportunity of spiritual reclamation is ready and waiting. He has but to show an earnest desire to move himself one fraction of an inch towards the realms of light that are above him, and he will find a host of unknown friends who will help him towards that heritage which is his due, but which in his folly he cast aside.

VII. SOME FIRST IMPRESSIONS

To FIND oneself suddenly transformed into a permanent inhabitant of the spirit world is, at first, an overwhelming experience. However much one may have read about the conditions of life in the world of spirit, there still remains an almost illimitable number of surprises in store for every soul.

Those of us who have returned to earth to tell about our new life are faced with the difficulty of trying to describe in terms of the earth what is essentially of a spirit nature. Our descriptions must fall short of the reality. It is difficult to conjure up in the mind a state of beauty greater than we have ever experienced upon earth. Magnify by one hundred times the beauties that I have told you about, and you would still be far short of a true appraisement.

A question, therefore, that might come into the minds of not a few people would perhaps be this: What was it that struck you most forcibly and most pleasurably when you first arrived in the spirit world, and what were your first impressions?

Let me place myself in the position of one seeking information, and interview our old friends, Edwin and Ruth.

Edwin and I, as you will recall, were brother priests when we were on earth. Edwin had no knowledge whatever upon the subject of spirit return, beyond what I had tried to give him of my own experiences. He was one of the few who really sympathized with me in my psychic difficulties, one of the few, that is, who did not brandish orthodox church teachings in my face. He has since told me that he is very glad he did not do so. When he was on earth the 'life to come' was a complete mystery to him—as it unnecessarily is to many others. He naturally conformed to the church's teachings, obeyed its 'commandments', performed his duties, and, as he has since quite frankly admitted, hoped for the best—whatever that best might be.

But his earthly life had not consisted solely of religious exercises; he had helped others upon every occasion where help was needed and where he could possibly give it. Those services, unobtrusively performed, had helped him immeasurably when the time came for him to quit the earth world. Those kind actions brought him into the land of beauty and eternal sunshine.

His first impressions upon his awakening in the spirit world were—to use his own words—absolutely breathtaking. He had visualized, subconsciously perhaps, some sort of misty state as the condition of a future life, where there would be a great deal of 'prayer and praise'. To find himself in a realm of inexpressible beauty, with all the glories of earthly nature purged of its earthliness, refined and etherealised, with the enormous wealth of color all around and about him; to behold the crystal purity of the rivers and brooks, with the charm of the country dwellings and the grandeur of the city's temples and halls of learning; to find himself in the center of all such glories without an inkling of what had thus been in store for him, was to cast doubts upon the veracity of his own eyes. He could not believe that he was not in the midst of some beautiful, but fantastic, dream, from which he would shortly awaken to find himself once again in his old familiar surroundings. He thought how he would relate this dream when he returned to consciousness. Then he considered how it would be received—as very beautiful, no doubt, but just a dream.

And so he stood gazing upon all this wealth of beauty. That, Edwin said, was his first and greatest impression.

He had regarded as part of the same dream all that had gone before, all that had led up to his standing and gazing in wonder upon the scene that stretched out almost unendingly before him. How he had awakened upon a comfortable couch, in a very charming house, to see sitting beside him an old friend, who performed the same office for Edwin as did Edwin for me when he came to meet me.

His friend led him out-of-doors to see the new world. Then came his friend's most difficult task—to convince Edwin that he had 'died' and yet still lived. You see, at first he took his friend and his friend's explanation to be part of the same dream, and he was nervously awaiting for something to happen that would break up the dream into returning earthly consciousness. Edwin admitted that he took some convincing, but his friend was infinitely patient with him.

The instant that he was assured that he was really and truly and permanently in the world of spirit, his heart knew no greater joy, and he proceeded to do what I afterwards did in company with Ruth—travel through the lands of the new life with the luxurious freedom of body and mind that is of the very essence of spirit life in these realms.

What most impressed Ruth upon her first awakening in the spirit world was, she said, the enormous profusion of color.

Her transition had been a placid one, and she had consequently awakened, after a very brief sleep, calmly and gently. As with Edwin, she had then found herself in a delightful house, small, neat and compact, and all her own. An old friend was beside her, ready to help in the inevitable perplexities that accompany so many awakenings in the spirit world.

Ruth is by nature rather reserved, especially, as she said, when it came to talking about herself. In Edwin's case I knew so much of his earth life that it was easy for me to draw upon my own knowledge of him. Ruth, however, I had never seen until vexations met here upon that occasion beside the lake. After much persuasion I managed to extract from her one or two details concerning her earthly life.

She had never, she said, been an active church-goer, not because she despised the church, but because her own views upon the 'hereafter' did not agree with what her own church taught. She saw too much of faith required, and too little of fact being given, and altogether she had encountered so much of the troubles and afflictions of others in her daily life that the vague, but rather terrifying, picture of the world to come, the dreadful 'Judgment Day' that was so constantly held before her in the church's teaching, she instinctively felt to be wrong. The emphasis laid so strongly upon the word 'sinner' with the almost wholesale condemnation of everyone as such, she also felt to be wrong. She was not foolish enough, she declared, to believe that we are all saints, but, at the same time, we are not all sinners. Of the many people she knew, she could recall none who could ever be so branded and condemned in the religious sense. Where, then, were all these people going after they had 'died?'

She could never imagine herself sitting in judgment upon these souls and passing sentence upon them as 'sinners'. It would be preposterous to contemplate, Ruth added, that she could be more 'merciful' than God. It was unthinkable. So she had built up for herself a simple 'faith'—a practice that the theologian would at once say was highly dangerous and never for one moment to be encouraged. He would have spoken of the 'peril' in which her 'immortal soul' stood by entertaining such ideas. But Ruth never for an instant considered her 'immortal soul' to be in 'peril'. Indeed, she went happily along, living her life according to the dictates of her gentle nature, helping others in her daily life, and bringing a little sunshine into the drab lives of others. And she was firmly convinced that when her time came to leave the earth-plane she would take with her into the new life the affection of her many friends.

She had no fear of death of the physical body, nor could she imagine it to be the terrifying experience that so many people anticipate and dread. She had no absolute grounds for this belief, and she has since concluded that she must have been drawn to it intuitively.

Apart from the glorious colors of the realm in which she found herself, what struck Ruth very forcibly was the astonishing clearness of the atmosphere. There was nothing like it to be seen on earth. The atmosphere was so free from the slightest trace of mistiness, and her own vision seemed to be so intensified in power and extent, that the enormous range of colors became doubly vivid. She had a naturally keen eye for color, and she had undergone considerable musical training when she was upon earth. When she came into the spirit world these two faculties had combined, and the color and music of the new land had burst upon her with all the luxuriance of their superb beauty.

At first, she could scarcely believe her senses, but her friends had soon explained to her just what had happened, and as she had so few fixed ideas about the future life, so had she so little to unlearn. But, she said, it took her many days of earth time before she could fully grasp or absorb all the wonders that lay around her. When once she had fully realized the significance of her new life, and that all eternity lay before her in which to sample the marvels of this land, she was able to restrain her excitement, and, as she said, 'take things a little more quietly'.

It was while she was in process of the latter that we first met. Once, when the three of us were seated in the garden pleasantly discussing all manner of things, we espied, walking up the garden path, a figure that was well known to Edwin and myself. He had been our ecclesiastical superior when we were upon the earth-plane, and he was what is known as a 'Prince of the Church'. He was still attired in his customary habiliments, and we were all agreed—when we came to compare notes afterwards—that they eminently suited both the place and the conditions. The full-length style and the rich coloring of the robes seemed to blend most harmoniously with all about us. There was nothing incongruous about it, and as he was at full liberty to wear his robes in the spirit world he had done so; not because of his former position, but through long custom, and because he felt that he thus, in some small measure, helped to add to the colorful beauty of his new habitation.

Now, although the high office, which he held with distinction upon earth, has no counterpart or significance in the spirit world, yet he was well known to many here by name and by sight and by repute. This provided a further good reason for his retaining his earthly style of clothing, at least for the present. But the deference that his position upon earth had always evoked, he utterly cast aside when he came into the world of spirit. He would have none of it, and he was very insistent that all who knew him—and those who did not—should be strictly attentive to his wishes in this respect. He was very much loved when he was incarnate, and it is but natural that, with his advent into spirit lands, those who knew him should show the same respect as before. Respect is one thing, for we all respect each other in these realms; but deference that should be given to others of greater spirituality is another thing altogether. He early recognized this, so he told us, and from my own personal knowledge of his innate humility I could guess that such would be the case with him.

Our first meeting led to others, and many have been the occasions—and we shall enjoy many more—when he has joined

Edwin, Ruth and myself, where we have sat in the garden, or gone forth together. It was during one of our peregrinations together that I asked our former superior if he would give me some brief sketch of his first impressions of the spirit world.

What struck him so forcibly when he found himself here was not only the immensity and beauty of the spirit world, but the very description of this world itself in relation to the earth world, and most particularly in relation to the life he had left behind him. First of all, there came the feeling, an almost crushing one, of having wasted his earthly life upon seemingly nonessentials, irrelevancies and a great deal of useless formularies and formalism. But friends had come to his rescue intellectually, and they had assured him that the time in its personal application had not been wasted, although his life had been encompassed by the pomp and pageantry of his office. However much the latter had engrossed those about him, he had personally never let them become an absorbing factor in his life. He derived much comfort from this reflection.

But what he found to be most mentally disturbing was the invalidity of the doctrines which he had perforce upheld. So many of them were tumbling in ruins about him. But again he found friends to guide him. And they did so in a simple and direct manner, such as would appeal to his alert mind, namely: to forget the religious teachings of the earthly life and become acquainted with spirit life and its laws. Discard the old, and accept the new. He had therefore made every endeavor to do so, and he had been completely successful. He swept his mind clear of all that had no foundation in truth, and he made the very pleasant discovery that, at last, he was in full enjoyment of absolute spiritual freedom. He found it was so much easier to obey the natural laws of the spirit world than to obey the church's 'commandments', and it was very pleasant to be rid of the formalities of his earthly position. He could at last speak with his own voice freely, and not with the voice of the church.

Altogether, said our former superior, he thought that his greatest impression upon his arrival in the spirit world was this splendid sense of freedom, first of mind and then of body, and made so much the greater in the spirit world by the measure of its absence in the earth world.

VIII. RECREATIONS

I HAVE used the word 'recreation', once or twice, but I have not given you any specific details upon this relatively important subject.

The merest suggestion that we should have recreations in the spirit world will, most assuredly, come to some minds as an unpleasant shock. Those same minds will instantly think of the many and varied sports and pastimes that are usefully and profitably indulged in upon the earth-plane. To transplant, as it were, such fundamentally earthy things into a world of pure spirit is inconceivable. Inconceivable, perhaps, because the whole idea is far-fetched, or because the spirit world should be regarded as a higher state. A state, that is, in which we shall leave behind us all our earthly habits, and live perpetually in a condition of high ecstasy, caring only for those vague, unsubstantial things that our respective religion hinted to us as being the reward of the good.

To entertain such suppositions about this life is to suggest that, by the very fact of our coming into the spirit world to live, we are at once in the presence of God, or that at least we are within the realm wherein God dwells, and therefore anything even remotely suggestive of earthly customs or manners would be rigidly excluded as too unholy for admission.

Such ideas as these are, of course, pure nonsense, since God is no nearer to us in the spirit world than He is to us in the earth world. It is we who are nearer to Him, because, among other things, we can see more clearly the Divine Hand in this world, and the expression of His Mind. That, however, is a deeper subject which it is not within our province to go into just now.

Many of us find our recreation in another form of work. In the spirit world we do not suffer fatigue either of body or mind, but to continue unremittingly in the pursuit of any one occupation, without any intermittent change, would soon produce feelings of mental dissatisfaction or unrest. Our powers of application to any given task are immense, but at the same time we draw a very clear line of limitation for any period of our work, in respect to the whole, and beyond that line we do not go. We will exchange our present task for another form of work, we can cease work altogether and spend our time reclining in our homes or elsewhere; we can occupy ourselves in study; or we can engage ourselves in the amusing recreations that abound in these realms.

When we have ceased our work for the time being, we are much in the same case as are you who are still upon the earth-plane. What shall you do to amuse yourself? You may feel that physical rest is necessary, and so you will incline towards intellectual recreation. And so it is precisely with us here. Intellectual recreation, which may take diverse forms, is amply provided for in the halls of learning, because learning can itself be a recreation.

Ruth and I have spent many happy hours in the library and the hall of art, but there have been numberless occasions when we felt the need for something more sturdy, and we have walked down to the sea and gone aboard one of the fine vessels there, and thence paid a visit to one of the islands. And here at the seaside we have one of the most entertaining of our sports.

I have already told you how vessels in the spirit world are propelled purely by the process of thought, and I have further indicated how it takes a little time to become proficient in the art of personally applying such propulsion. Such proficiency is ultimately achieved, but we can test our progress and receive valuable aid in our endeavors by taking part in contests upon the water.

A clear distinction must be drawn between such contests upon the earth-plane and those in the spirit world. Here we are assured, because we know, that all rivalry is purely friendly. There is no gain attached whatever, beyond the experience and the acquisition of greater skill, and there are no prizes to be fought for and won. At the end of every race we shall be sure of the greatest help to make us more expert in the increasing and handling of our vessel's speed.

One particular diversion that finds a very considerable measure of favor with us here is that of dramatic representation of different kinds.

We have beautiful theaters situated in environments just as beautiful, worthy buildings devoted to a worthy purpose. The architects who design the buildings do so with the same meticulous care as is shown in all their endeavors, and the results, as usual, reveal the degree of active co-operation that exists between the masters of the craft. The garniture within is the product of skilled artists from the Hall of Fabrics; the gardens without have the same devoted care lavished upon them. The result is as far removed from an earthly theater as it is possible to imagine.

Before I speak further upon this subject I would like to observe that I am fully aware that there are people upon the earth-plane who totally disapprove of theaters and everything connected with them. In most instances such aversion is the outcome of religious upbringing. I cannot alter the truth, as I find it in the spirit world, to accord with certain religious views held by people still incarnate. I speak of those things which I have witnessed in company with thousands of others, and the fact of strong disapproval, by earth people, of what I have described as existing in the spirit world, in no way proves such things to be non-existent, and therefore my statement to be false. My position for observation is incomparably superior to theirs, because I have left the earth world and become an inhabitant of the spirit world. If our descriptions of the world we now inhabit were to be altered to suit every individual taste and every preconception of what the spirit world ought to be, we might just as well cease, forthwith, to give any further descriptions, since, after being so tampered with, they would be worthless. Lest I should have conveyed any false impression in saying this, let me add that anyone who expressed disapproval of all, or any, form of recreation he found here, such a person would never be asked to indulge in them. With others of similar views, he would find himself in a little community apart, there to remain, safely out of range of all supposed earthly things, and able to live in such a place as he thought 'heaven' ought to be. I have met such people, and it was not long, as a rule, before they abandoned their home-made heaven, and walked abroad into the finer, greater heaven, which is the work of the Greatest Mind.

Each theater of this realm is familiar to us by the type of play that is presented in it. The plays themselves are frequently vastly different from those that are customary upon the earth-plane. We have nothing that is sordid, nor do the authors of plays insist upon harrowing their audiences. We can see many problem plays where social questions of the earth-plane are dealt with, but unlike the earth-plane our plays will provide a solution to the particular problem—a solution which the earth is too blind to adopt.

We can go to see comedies where, I do assure you, the laughter is invariably much more hearty and voluminous than is ever to be heard in a theater of the earth-plane. In the spirit world we can afford to laugh at much that we once, when incarnate, treated with deadly seriousness and earnestness!

We have witnessed grand historical pageants showing the greater moments of a nation, and we have seen, too, history as it really was, and not as it is often so fancifully written about in history books! But surely the most impressive, and, at the same time, interesting experience is to be present at one of these pageants where the original participants themselves re-enact the events in which they were concerned, first as the events were popularly thought to have occurred, and then as they actually took place. These representations are among the most widely attended here, and never are there more attentive and rapt members of the audience than those players who, during their earthly lives, played the parts, in stage plays, of the famous characters whom they are now seeing 'in the flesh'.

In such pageants the coarser, depraved and debased incidents are omitted entirely, because they would be distasteful to the audience, and, indeed, to all in this realm. Nor are we shown scenes which are, in the main incidents, nothing but battle and bloodshed and violence.

At first, one experiences a strange feeling in beholding, in person, the bearers of names famous throughout the earth world, but after a time one becomes perfectly accustomed to it, and it becomes part of our normal existence.

The most noticeable difference between our two worlds, in this matter of recreations, is created by our respective requirements. We have no need here to take bodily exercise, vigorous or otherwise, nor do we need to go out into the 'fresh air'. Our spirit bodies are always in perfect condition, we suffer no disorders of any kind, and the air, which cannot be other than fresh penetrates into every corner of our homes and buildings, where it fully retains its purity. It would be impossible for it to become vitiated or contaminated in any way. It is to be expected, then, that our recreations should be more upon the mental plane than upon the 'physical'.

As most of the outdoor games of the earth world involve the use of a ball, it will be appreciated that here, where the law of gravity operates under different conditions from yours anything in the nature of propelling a ball by striking it, would lead to quite hopeless results. I am speaking now of games of a competitive nature.

On the earth-plane skill in games is acquired by the mastery of the mind over the muscles of the body, when once the latter has been brought to a healthy condition. But here we are always in a healthy condition, and our muscles are always under the complete and absolute control of our minds. Efficiency is quickly gained, whether it is in playing upon a musical instrument, painting a picture, or in any other pursuit that requires the use of the limbs. It will be seen, therefore, that most of the usual games would lose their point here.

And it must be remembered that indoors or outdoors are precisely one to us here. We have no changes of weather during recurrent seasons. The great central sun is forever shining; it is never anything but delightfully warm. We never feel the necessity for a brisk walk to set our blood circulating the better. Our homes and our houses are not necessities, but additions to an already enjoyable life. You will find many people here who do not possess a home; they do not want one, they will tell you, for the sun is perpetually shining and the temperature is perpetually warm. They are never ill, or hungry, or in want of any kind, and the whole beautiful realm is theirs to wander in.

It must also be remembered that viewpoints change very much when one comes to live here. What we deemed so very important when we were incarnate, we find is not nearly so important when we arrive in the spirit world. And many of our erstwhile earthly games seem rather tame and trivial beside our greatly increased powers in the spirit world. The fact that we can move ourselves through space instantaneously is enough to make the greatest earthly athletic skill recede into insignificance, and our mundane sports and games are in similar case. Our recreations are more of the mind, and we never feel that we must expend a superfluity of physical energy upon some strenuous action, for our energy is at a constant level according to our individual requirements. We find that we have so much to learn, and learning is in itself such pleasure that we do not need the number or variety of recreations that you do. We have plenty of music to listen to, there are such wonders in these lands that we want to know all about, there is so much congenial work to be done, that there is no cause to be cast down at the prospect of there being few of the earthly sports and pastimes in the spirit world. There is such a superabundant supply of vastly more entertaining things to be seen and done here, besides which a great deal of the earthly recreations appear sheer trivialities.

IX. SPIRIT PERSONALIA

WHAT does it feel like to be a spirit person?

That is a question that has arisen in the minds of many people. If, in turn, one were to ask: what does it feel like to be an earth person? You might be inclined to reply that the question is rather a foolish one, because I have been incarnate myself once, and therefore I should know. But before the question is dismissed as foolish, let us see what it can provide by way of an answer.

First of all, consider the physical body. It undergoes fatigue for which it is vitally necessary to have rest. It gets hungry and thirsty, and it must be provided with food and drink. It can suffer pains and torments through a great variety of illness and disease. It can lose its limbs through accidents, or from other causes. The senses can become impaired through increasing age; or accident can cause it to lose the faculty of sight or hearing; or the physical body can be born into the world without either or both of those senses, and, in addition, it may be powerless of speech. The physical brain may be so affected that we are incapable of any sane action, and we have, in consequence, to be taken care of by others.

What a gloomy picture, you will say! That is so, but anyone can be the victim to some, at least, of the catalogue of disabilities I have mentioned. At least three of them are common to every single soul upon the earth-plane—hunger, thirst, and fatigue. And that by no means exhausts the list. But it will suffice for our purpose.

Now, eliminate, completely and entirely, every one of these unpleasant disabilities that I have enumerated; exclude, infallibly and everlastingly, the cause of them, and you should have in your mind some idea of what it feels like as a spirit person.

When I was upon the earth-plane I suffered from some of the ailments that are common to most of us, ailments that are not necessarily serious, and that we take rather as a matter of course; the minor aches and pains that most of the incarnate, at one time or another, manage to put up with. In addition to those minor ailments, I was, of course, conscious of my physical body by the intrusion of hunger, thirst, and fatigue. The final illness—the serious one—was too much for the physical body, and my

150

transition took place. And immediately I knew what it felt like to be a spirit person.

As I stood talking to Edwin I felt, physically, a giant, in spite of the fact that I had just departed from a bed of sickness. As time went on I felt even better. I had not the slightest suspicion of a twinge of pain, and I felt light in weight. Indeed, it did not seem as though I were encased in a body at all! My mind was fully alert, and I was aware of my body only in so far as I could move my limbs and myself wherever I wished, apparently without any of the muscular actions that were but so recently familiar. It is extremely difficult to convey to you this feeling of perfect health, because such a thing is utterly impossible on earth, and therefore I have nothing with which to draw a comparison, or form an analogy for you. This state belongs to the spirit alone, and completely defies any description in earthly terms. It must be experienced, and that you will not be able to do until you become one of us here yourself.

I have said that my mind was alert. That is an understatement. I discovered that my mind was a veritable storehouse of facts concerning my earthly life. Every act I had performed, and every word that I had uttered, every impression I had received; every fact that I had read about, and every incident I had witnessed, all these, I found, were indelibly registered in my subconscious mind. And that is common to every spirit person who has had an incarnate life.

It must not be supposed that we are continually haunted, as it were, by a wild phantasmagoria of miscellaneous thoughts and impressions. That would be a veritable nightmare. No. Our minds are like a complete biography of our earthly life, wherein is set down every little detail concerning ourselves, arranged in an orderly fashion, and omitting nothing. The book is closed, normally, but it is ever there, ready to hand, for us to turn to, and we merely recall the incidents as we wish. I am now speaking personally, and as it governs the folk with whom I live in this realm.

The description that I gave you of that particular soul's memory in the lowest realms, brings into force other laws, as I attempted to show you. I am not prepared to say how it happens; I can only tell you what happens.

This encyclopedic memory, with which we are endowed, is not so difficult to understand when you pause to consider your own average earthly memory. You are not continuously bothered by the incidents of the whole of your life, but they are simply there for you to recall, when and where you wish, and they may arise out of the occasions of the moment. One incident will set a train of thought going in which the memory will have its share. Sometimes you cannot recall what is in your memory, but in the spirit world we can recall instantly, without any effort, and unfailingly. The subconscious mind never forgets, and consequently our own past deeds become a reproach to us, or otherwise, according to our earthly lives. The recordings upon the tablets of the real mind cannot be erased. They are there for all time, but they do not necessarily haunt us, because in those tablets are also set down the good actions, the kind actions, the kind thoughts, and everything of which we could justly be proud. And if they are written in larger and more ornate letters than those things we regret, we shall be so much the happier.

Of course, when we are in the spirit world our memories are persistently retentive. When we follow a course of study in any subject whatsoever, we shall find that we learn easily and quickly because we are freed from the limitations that the physical body imposes upon the mind. If we are acquiring knowledge we shall retain that knowledge without fail. If we are following some pursuit where dexterity of the hands is required, we shall find that our spirit bodies respond to the impulses of our minds immediately and exactly. To learn to paint a picture, or to play upon a musical instrument, to mention two familiar mundane activities, are tasks which can be performed in a fraction of the time that they would take when we are incarnate. In learning to lay out a spirit garden, for example, or to build a house, we shall find that the requisite knowledge is gained with equal ease and speed—in so far as our intelligence will allow; for we are not all endowed with keen intellects the moment we shake off the physical body. If that were the case, these realms would be inhabited by supermen and superwomen, and we are very far from that! But our intelligence can be increased; that is part of our progression, for progression is not only of a spiritual nature. Our minds have unlimited resources for intellectual expansion and improvement, however backward we may be when we come into the spirit world. And our intellectual progression will advance surely and steadily, according to our wish for it to do so, under the learned and able masters of all branches of knowledge and learning. And throughout our studies we shall be assisted by our unfailingly retentive memories. There will be no forgetting.

Now to come to the spirit body itself. The spirit body is, broadly speaking, the counterpart of our earthly bodies. When we come into the spirit world we are recognizably ourselves. But we leave behind us all our physical disabilities. We have our full complement of limbs, our sight and our hearing; in fact, all our senses are fully functioning. Indeed, the five senses, as we know them upon earth, become many degrees more acute when we are discarnate. Any supernormal or subnormal conditions of the physical body, such as excessive stoutness or leanness, vanish when we arrive in these realms, and we appear as we should have appeared on earth had not a variety of earthly reasons caused us to be otherwise.

There is a stage in our lives on earth which we know as the prime of life. It is towards this that we all move. Those of us who are old or elderly when we pass into spirit will return to our prime-of-life period. Others who are young will advance towards that period. And we all preserve our natural characteristics— they never leave us. But we find that many minor physical features that we can profitably dispense with, we shake off with our earthly bodies certain irregularities of the body with which, perhaps, we have been born, or that have come upon us during the course of the years. How many of us, are there, I wonder, when we are incarnate, who could not think of some small improvement that we should like to make in our physical bodies, were it at all possible? Not many!

I have told you how the trees in these realms grow in a state of perfection—upright and clean-looking and well-formed, because they have no storms of wind to bend and twist the young branches into malformations. The spirit body is subject to just the same law here in spirit. The storms of life can twist the physical body, and if that life has been spiritually ugly the spirit body will be similarly twisted. But if the earth life has been spiritually sound, the spirit body will be correspondingly sound. There is many a fine soul inhabiting a crooked earthly body. There is many a bad soul inhabiting a well-formed earthly body. The spirit world reveals the truth for all to see.

How does the spirit appear anatomically, you will ask? Anatomically, just exactly the same as does yours. We have muscles, we have bones, we have sinews, but they are not of the earth; they are purely of spirit. We suffer from no ailments— that would be impossible in the spirit world. Therefore our bodies do not require constant looking after to maintain a state of good health. Here our health is always perfect, because we have such a vibrational rate that disease, and the germs that cause it, cannot enter. Malnutrition, in the sense that you know it, cannot exist here, but spiritual malnutrition—that is, of the soul—does most certainly exist. A visit to the dark realms and their neighborhood will soon reveal that!

Does it seem strange that a spirit body should possess finger nails and hair? How would you have us to be? Not different from yourselves in this respect, surely? Would we not be something of a revolting spectacle without our usual anatomical features and characteristics? This seems an elementary statement, but it is sometimes necessary and expedient to voice the elementary.

How is the spirit body covered? A great many people—I think it would be true to say the great majority—wake up in these realms dressed in the counterpart of the clothes they wore when upon the earth-plane at the time of their transition. It is reasonable that they should, because such attire is customary, especially when the person has no foreknowledge whatever of spirit world conditions. And they may remain so attired for just as long as they please. Their friends will have told them of their true state of being, and then they can change to their spirit clothing if they so wish. Most people are only too glad to make the change, since their old earthly style of clothing looks very drab in these colorful realms. It was not long before I discarded my old clerical attire for my true raiment. Black is altogether too somber amongst such a galaxy of color

Spirit robes vary in themselves almost as much as the realms vary. There always seems to be some subtle difference between one person's spirit robe and another's, both in color and form, so that there is an endless variety in the two particulars of color and form alone.

All spirit robes are of full length; that is, they reach down to the feet. They are sufficiently full to hang in graceful folds, and it is these very folds that present the most beautiful shades and tones of color by the effect of what on earth would be called 'light and shade'. It would be impossible to give you anything like a comprehensive account of the different additional features that go to make up the whole composition of spirit vesture.

Many people will be found wearing a girdle or sash around the waist. Sometimes these will be of material, sometimes they appear to be of gold or silver lace or tissue. In all cases of the latter, they are rewards for services performed. No possible conception can be formed of the superlative brilliance of the golden or silver girdles that are worn by the great personages from the higher realms. They are usually adorned with the most beautiful of precious stones, fashioned in various shapes, and mounted in beautifully wrought settings, according to the rulings that govern such matters. The higher beings, too, will be seen to be wearing the most magnificent diadems as brilliant as their girdles. The same law applies to these. Those of us of lesser degree may perhaps be wearing some such embellishment as I have just described, but in a greatly modified form.

There is an enormous wealth of spirit lore behind the whole subject of spirit adornments, but one fact can be plainly stated: all such adornments must be earned. Rewards are given only upon merit.

We may wear what we like upon our feet, and most of us prefer to wear a covering of some sort. It usually takes the form of a light shoe or sandal. I have seen numbers of people here who have a predilection for going barefooted, and they do so. It is perfectly in order, and it excites no comment whatever. It is natural and commonplace with us.

The material of which our robes are made is not transparent, as some would perhaps be inclined to imagine! It is substantial enough. And the reason why it is not transparent is that our clothing possesses the same vibrational rate as the wearer. The higher one progresses the higher this rate becomes, and consequently dwellers in those elevated spheres will take on an unimaginable tenuousness both of spirit body and clothing. That tenuousness is the more apparent to us than to them, that is, externally apparent, for the same reason that a small light will seem so much the brighter by virtue of the surrounding darkness. When the light is magnified a thousand times—as it is in the case of the higher realms—the contrast is immeasurably greater.

We seldom wear any covering upon our heads. I do not remember seeing anything of the sort anywhere in this realm. We have no need for protection against the elements!

I think you will have concluded by now that to be a spirit person can be a very pleasant experience.

And in my travels through these realms of light I have yet to find a single solitary individual who would willingly exchange this grand, free life in the spirit world for the old life upon the earth-plane. Experto crede!

X. THE CHILDREN'S SPHERE

ONE of the innumerable questions that I put to Edwin, shortly after my arrival in the spirit world, concerned the destiny of children who, as such, passed into spirit lands.

There is a period of our earthly lives which we are accustomed to call 'the prime of life'. There is also a prime of life here in spirit, and it is towards that period that all souls either advance or return, according to the age at which their transition takes place. How long it will take rests entirely with themselves, since it is purely a matter of spiritual progression and development, though with the young this period is usually much shorter. Those who pass into spirit after the prime of life period has been reached, whether they be elderly or extremely aged, will, in due time, become younger in appearance, although they will grow older in knowledge and spirituality. It must not be assumed from this that we all eventually reach a dead level of commonplace uniformity. Outwardly, we look young; vexations lose those signs of the passage of years which cause some of us no little disturbance of mind when we are incarnate. But our minds become older as we gain knowledge and wisdom and greater spirituality, and these qualities of the mind are manifest to all with whom we come into contact.

When we visited the temple in the city, and, from a distance, beheld the radiant visitor whom we had come to honor, he presented to the eye the appearance of perfect—and eternal—youth. Yet the degree of knowledge and wisdom and spirituality which he diffused, and which we could feel with our minds, was almost overpoweringly great. It is the same, in varying degrees, with all those who visit us from the higher realms. If, therefore, there is this rejuvenation of fully grown people, what of the souls who pass over as children; indeed, what of those, even, who pass into the spirit world at birth?

The answer is that they grow as they would have grown upon the earth-plane. But the children here—of all ages—are given such treatment and care as would never be possible in the earth world.

The young child, whose mind is not yet fully formed, is

uncontaminated by earthly contacts, and on passing into the spirit world it finds itself in a realm of great beauty, presided over by souls of equal beauty. This children's realm has been called the 'nursery of heaven', and surely anyone who has been fortunate enough to have visited it will say that a more apposite term could not be found. It was, therefore, in response to my original question that Edwin proposed that Ruth and I should accompany him on a visit to the nursery of heaven.

We walked towards the boundary between the higher realm and our own, and we turned in the direction of Edwin's house. Already we could feel the atmosphere more rarified, though it was not sufficiently pronounced to cause us any inconvenience or discomfort. I noticed that this atmosphere had a great deal more color in it, much more than in the depths of the realm. It was as though a great number of shafts of light were meeting and spreading their broad beams over all the landscape. These shafts of light were forever on the move, interweaving themselves and producing the most delicate and delightful blending of color, like a succession of rainbows. They were extremely restful, but they were also filled with vitality and, as it seemed to Ruth and me, lightheartedness and merriment. Sadness and unhappiness, one felt, would be utterly impossible here.

The countryside took upon itself a much brighter green in its verdure, the trees were not so tall, but they were as shapely as every other tree in these realms, and they were growing as perfectly.

After we had proceeded a little distance the atmosphere became clear of the colored beams, and it more resembled that of our own sphere. But there was a strange and subtle difference which was puzzling to the visitor upon his first visit, and it arose, so Edwin told us, from the essential spirituality of the children who live there. Something akin to this is to be encountered when one is privileged to journey to a higher realm than that in which one normally resides. It is almost as though there were a greater degree of buoyancy in the air, apart altogether from a noticeable effect of elevation of the mind.

We saw many fine buildings before us as we walked along the soft grass. They were not of any great height, but they were broad in extent, and they were all most pleasantly situated among trees and gardens. Flowers, needless to say, were growing prolifically everywhere, in artistically-arranged beds, as well as in large masses upon the grassy slopes and beneath the trees. I noticed that in some instances flowers that have their counterpart upon the earth-plane, were growing by themselves, those that were proper to the spirit world being separated from them. We were told that there was no special significance in this segregation, but that it was done solely to show the distinction between the two classes of flowers, the spirit and the earthly. Beautiful as the earthly flowers are that grow here, there can be no comparison with those that belong alone to spirit lands. Here again one is limited by earthly experience in any attempt to describe them. Not only are the colorings richer, but the conformations of the flowers and foliage present such an abundance of unparalleled beauty of design that we have no earthly example to adduce by way of comparison. But it must not be supposed that these magnificent flowers remotely suggested the rare hot-house bloom. Far from it. The superabundance of them, together with the great strength and variety of their perfumes, would instantly dispel any thought of rarity. It was no case of cultivating the beauty of the bloom at the expense of its perfume. They all possessed the quality common to all growing things here, that of pouring out energizing force, not only through the medium of their aromas, but through personal contact. I had already tried the experiment of holding a flower within the cupped hands—it was Ruth who had instructed me—and I had felt the stream of life-force flowing up my arms.

We could see delightful ponds and small lakes, upon the surface of which were flourishing the most beautiful water flowers in the gayest colors. In another direction we could see larger expanses of water like a series of lakes, with many small boats gliding serenely along.

The buildings were constructed of a substance that had all the appearance of alabaster, and they were all tinged with the most delicate colors, such as one is accustomed to seeing in the subtle blending of an earthly rainbow. The style of architecture resembled, for the most part, that of our own sphere; that is to say, some of the buildings bore upon their surface the most exquisite carvings of such natural objects as abound in the trees and flowers, while others drew for their relief upon the normal features particular to the spirit world.

But what gave us the most enjoyable surprise was to see, interspersed throughout the woods, the quaintest little cottages such as one was always inclined to believe only belonged to the pages of children's story-books. Here were diminutive houses with crooked timbers—beautifully crooked—with bright red roofs and lattice-windows, and each with a charming little garden, all its own, surrounding it.

It will at once be concluded that the spirit world has borrowed from the earth world in these fanciful creations for the children's delight, but such is not the case. In truth, this whole conception of miniature houses emanated, in the first instance, from the spirit world. Whoever was the artist who received our original impression, she has been lost to the earth world through the course of the years. That artist is known to us here, though, where she continues her work in the children's sphere.

These little houses were large enough to allow a grown person plenty of room in which to move without appearing to knock his head! To the children they seemed to be of just the right size, without their feeling lost within them. I learned that it was for this same reason that all the large buildings in this realm were without any appreciable height. By thus not making them too high, nor the rooms too large, they conformed with the child's mind, as yet not fully formed, where spaces seem greater than they really are, and where buildings too spacious would have the effect upon the little mind of seeming to dwarf it.

Great numbers of children live in these tiny dwellings, each being presided over by an older child, who is perfectly capable of attending to any situation that might arise with the other 'residents'.

As we walked along we could see groups of happy children, some playing games with their fellows, others seated upon the grass while a teacher was reading to them. Others, again, were to be observed listening attentively and with marked interest to a teacher who was explaining the flowers to them, and giving them something of a lesson in botany. But it was botany of a very different order from that of the earth-plane, in so far as the purely spirit flowers were concerned. The distinctions between the earthly flowers and the spirit flowers were amply demonstrated by the two orders of flowers being separated.

Edwin took us to one of the teachers, and explained the reason of our visit. We were instantly made welcome, and the teacher was kind enough to answer a few questions. Her enthusiasm for her work added to her pleasure, she said, in telling us anything we wished to know. As to herself, she had been in the spirit world a goodly number of years. She had had children of her own when upon the earth-plane, and she was still keenly interested in their welfare, and that had led her to take on her present work. So much she told us of herself. It was not very informative, and we knew as much without her having to tell us. What she did not tell us—it was Edwin who later gave us the details—was that she had made such a success with her own children upon earth, who now joined their mother in her work, that it had been obvious from the commencement just what her work would be in spirit lands. Needless to say, it was the very work upon which she had set her heart—the care of children.

It needed no one to tell us that she was admirably suited for such work. She radiated that charm and confidence, kindliness and mirthfulness of nature that so appealed to the children. She understood the child mind—she was, in fact, just a grown-up child herself! She possessed a wide knowledge of the most interesting things, especially of those things that appeal most to children; she had an inexhaustible fund of capital stories for her small charges, and, most important of all, she could be—and showed herself to be—at one with them. I do not think we had as yet seen anyone so superlatively happy as this gracious soul.

In this sphere, our new friend told us, there were to be found children of all ages, from the infant, whose separate existence upon the earth-plane had amounted to only a few minutes, or who even had had no separate existence at all, but had been born 'dead', to the youth of sixteen or seventeen years of earth time.

It frequently happens that as the children grow up they remain in this same sphere, and themselves become teachers for a period, until other work takes them elsewhere.

And what of the parents? Were they ever the teachers of their own children? Seldom, or never, our friend informed us. It was a practice that would scarcely ever be feasible, since the parent would be more inclined to be prejudiced in favor of her own child, and there might be other embarrassments. The teachers are always souls of wide experience, and there are not many parents upon the earth-plane who would be capable of undertaking the care of spirit children immediately upon the transition of the former. Whether the teachers were themselves parents upon the earth-plane or not, they all undergo an extensive course of training before they are adjudged fit to fill the post of teacher to the children, and to conform with, and uphold, the rigidly high standards of the work. And, of course, they must all be temperamentally fitted to hold the position of teacher.

The work is not arduous, as you would judge it in the earth world, but it demands a multiplicity of special attributes.

The mental and physical growth of the child in the spirit world is much more rapid than in the earth world. You will recall what I told you about the absolute retentiveness of the memory here. That retentiveness begins as soon as the mind is capable of grasping anything at all, and that is very early. This seeming precocity is perfectly natural here, because the young mind absorbs knowledge evenly. The temperament is carefully guided along purely spirit lines, so that the possession of knowledge in one so young never takes upon it the obnoxiousness of earthly precociousness. The children are trained in strictly spirit matters first, and then they are usually taught about the earth world, if they have not already lived in it, or if their earthly lives were very brief.

The ruler of the realm acts, in a general sense, in loco parentis, and all the children, indeed, look upon him as a father.

The children's studies have an extremely wide range. They are taught to read, but many other subjects of the earthly curricula are entirely omitted as being superfluous in the world of spirit. It would be more exact to say that the children are given knowledge of a particular subject rather than taught it.

As they grow they are able to choose for themselves the type of work that appeals to them, and so by specializing in their studies the children can become equipped with the necessary qualifications. Some of them, for instance, elect to return to the earth-plane temporarily to work with us in the exercise of communication, and they make highly efficient instruments, and thoroughly enjoy their visits. Such visits have the advantage of adding widely to their experience. It increases their depth of understanding of the trials and tribulations—and the pleasures—of being incarnate.

There is always one question that arises in the minds of earth people in connection8 with children who have passed on: Shall we be able to recognize our children when we ourselves arrive in the spirit world? The answer is, most emphatically, Yes, beyond all shadow of doubt. But how, if they have grown up in the spirit world and out of our sight, can that possibly be? To answer that, it is necessary to know a little more about one's self.

You must know that when the physical body sleeps, the spirit body temporarily withdraws from it, while still remaining connected to it by a magnetic cord. This cord is the veritable life-line between the spirit body and the earth body. The spirit thus situated will either remain in the vicinity of the earth body, or it will gravitate to that sphere which its earthly life, so far, has entitled it to enter. The spirit body will thus spend part of the lifetime of the earthly body in spirit lands. And it is upon these visits that one meets relatives and friends who have passed on before, and it is similarly upon these visits that parents can meet their children, and thus watch their growth. In the majority of cases the parents are not allowed within the children's own sphere, but there are plenty of places where such meetings can take place. Remembering what I have said about the retentiveness of the subconscious mind you will see that, in such cases, the problem of recognizing a child does not arise, because the parent has seen the child and observed its growth throughout the whole of the intervening years, in just the same way as the parent would have done if the child had remained in the earth world.

There must be, of course, a sufficient bond of attachment between the parent and child, or else this law will not come into operation. Where such does not exist the conclusion is obvious. That link of affection or kindly interest must also exist between all human relationships in the spirit world, whether it be with husband and wife, parent and child, or between friends. Without that interest or affection it is problematical whether there would ever be any meeting at all, except fortuitously.

The children's realm is a township in itself, containing everything that great minds, inspired by the greatest Mind, could possibly provide for the welfare, comfort, and education, and the pleasure and happiness of its youthful inhabitants. The halls of learning are as fully equipped as are those larger establishments in our own sphere. Indeed, in many respects, they are more so, since they have all the equipment for the diffusion of knowledge and learning to those who are possessed of neither in the slightest degree, and who must therefore start at the very beginning, as they would have done had they remained upon the earth-plane. This concerns those children who have passed into the spirit world in their extreme infancy. Children who leave the earth world in their early years will continue their studies from where they left off eliminating from the latter all that are of no further use, and adding those that are spiritualistically essential. As soon as they reach a suitable age the children can choose their future work, and study for it accordingly. What that work can be, I will recount to you later.

The whole question of infant survival had puzzled me considerably when I was incarnate. Ruth said she had no ideas upon the matter whatever, beyond supposing that children must survive, because she felt intuitively that grown people did so. The survival of the one would pre-suppose the survival of the other in a world of anything like law and order—which she presumed the spirit world to be.

Edwin was as perplexed as I was. You can imagine our surprise, then, when we were introduced into the children's realm, to behold the more than adequate provision made for the young folk who have passed into spirit lands in their tender years. It is a provision instituted under the greatest and wisest dispensation—that of the Father, Himself—involving no creeds or belief, no doctrines or dogmas, no ritual or formulary. It involves nothing more, in fact, but the plain act of undergoing the 'death' of the physical body, and the operation of the same laws that govern us all, whether infants or aged—just the casting off of the physical body, and entering, for all time, the world of spirit.

And the children as might be expected, have the same opportunities, the same rights to their spiritual heritage as we all have here, young and old.

And we all have the same great goal—perfect and perpetual happiness.

XI. OCCUPATIONS

THE spirit world is not only a land of equal opportunity for every soul, but the opportunities are upon so vast a scale that no person still incarnate can have the least conception of its magnitude. Opportunities for what?—it will be asked. Opportunities for good, useful, interesting work.

I hope that, by now, I have sufficiently indicated that the spirit world is not a land of idleness, not a land where its inhabitants spend the whole of their lives in a super-ecstatic atmosphere of religious exercises, formally offering up 'prayer and praise' to the Great Throne in a never-ceasing flow. There is an uninterrupted flow, most certainly, but it comes about in a very different way. It surges up from the hearts of us all, who are happy to be here, and thankful withal.

I want to try to give you some slight idea of the immensity of the range of occupations in which one can become engaged here in these realms.

Your thoughts will at once turn to the many and varied occupations of the earth world, covering every shade of earthly activity. But behind the earth world's occupations is the ever-driving necessity of earning a living, of providing the physical body with food and drink, clothing and a habitation of some sort. Now, you already know that these last four considerations have no existence whatever with us here. Food and drink we never need; the clothing and the habitation we have provided for ourselves by our lives upon earth. As our lives have been on earth, so will our clothing and our domicile be when we come to spirit lands. We have, as you see, no physical necessity to work, but we do have a mental necessity to work, and it is because of the latter that all work is a pleasure with us here.

Imagine yourself in a world where no one works for a living, but where everyone works for the sheer joy of doing something that will be of service to others. Just imagine that, and you will begin to understand something of the life in spirit lands.

A great many earthly occupations have no application whatever to the spirit world. Useful and necessary as they are, they belong essentially to the earthly period of life. What, then, becomes of people who occupied such a position as I have just mentioned? They will discover, immediately they are fully aware of their new state, that they have left their earthly avocation behind forever. They will see that the spirit world does not offer the same or similar work for them. But this does not cause regret or unhappiness, because the need for physical subsistence no longer exists with them, and in place of it such people feel gloriously free to engage themselves in some new work. They need never wonder what they are fitted for; they will soon find something which attracts their attention and draws their interest. And it will not be long before they are joining their fellows in learning some new occupation, and thoroughly enjoying themselves.

So far, I have merely referred to work in the abstract. Let us be more specific, and consider some of the business of the spirit world. First, let us take what we might call the purely 'physical' side of spirit life, and for the purpose we might pay another visit to the city.

On the way there we walk through many beautiful gardens, which at some period have all been designed and created. Here, shall we say, is the first means of employment that we come across. Scores of people upon the earth-plane love gardens and gardening. Some have engaged in the latter as their calling, and enjoyed doing it. What better than to continue with their work here in the spirit world, unrestrained by physical exigencies, free and unhampered, and with the inexhaustible resources of the spirit world at their command? Their occupation is their own. They can—and do—stop whenever they wish, and they can resume whenever they wish. And there is no one to exert his will upon them. And what is the result? Happiness for themselves, because by creating a beautiful work of horticultural art they have added more beauty to an already beautiful realm, and in doing so they have brought happiness to others. So their task goes on, altering, rearranging, planning, beautifying, building anew, and ever acquiring skill and still greater skill. Thus they continue until such time as they wish to change their work, or until their spiritual progression carries them on to fresh fields of endeavor in other realms.

Now let us go into the hall of music, and see what work we can find there. Someone, of course, had to plan, and others to build, the hall itself. I have already given you an account of the building of an annex to the library. In all major building operations the method followed is the same, but the methods of the spirit world have to be learned, and the work of the architects and builders, with their various expert assistants, is among some of the most important in the spirit world. As all descriptions of employment are open to anyone who has the taste for such work, that of the architect and builder is, likewise, free to all who express a preference for continuing their earthly occupation, or who wish to turn to something new. The wish to do so is really all that is required, although, naturally, an aptitude is a great help. But it is very surprising how quickly efficiency is gained by the stimulus of desire. The 'wish to do' becomes translated into the 'ability to do' in a very short time. Keen interest and predilection for the work are all that are asked.

Inside the hall of music we find libraries of music, where students are busy at their studies, and pupils with their musician teachers. Most of the people whom we meet thus are learning to be practical musicians; that is, they are learning to play some one or more instruments. And someone has to provide them with the necessary instruments. The hall of music does that, but somebody must create them for the hall of music. And so the instrument makers of the earth-plane find themselves at home in their craft if they wish to continue with it in the spirit world.

Now, it may be suggested that a lifetime on earth spent in one particular form of work would be quite enough for the average person, and that when he comes into the spirit world the last thing he would want to do would be to take up again his old earthly occupation with its interminable routine and drudgery. But bear in mind all that I have told you about the freedom of these realms, and the fact that no one is compelled, either by force of circumstances, or from the mere need of subsistence, to do any work at all in the spirit world. Remember that all work is undertaken willingly, freely, for the love of doing it, for the pride in creating something, for the desire of being of service to one's fellow inhabitants and to the realm in general, and you will see that the maker of musical instruments—to adduce one occupation among thousands—is just as happy as we all are in these realms. So he continues to make his instruments, brings happiness to himself and to so many other people, who will pleasurably and usefully bring joy to still more through the creation of his mind.

Incidentally, I should mention that it is not imperative that one should acquire a musical instrument solely through the hall of music. Any person who is skilled in the fashioning of such instruments would be only too willing to provide another person with anything he might require musically. In many a home here there reposes—and not as a mere ornament!—a beautiful pianoforte, built by clever hands, who have learned the spirit methods of creation. These things cannot be bought. They are spiritual rewards. It would be useless to try to possess that to which we have no right. We should simply find ourselves without it, and with no means of getting it. No one could create it for us, whatever it might be. If they were to try, they would find that their power would not function in that direction. If you were to ask me who or what governs these things, I could only tell you that I do not know, beyond knowing the fact that it is the operation of a spirit law.

Before we pass on from the hall of music, we might just look at the library. Here are musical scores by the thousand, together with the various parts from which the instrumentalists play. Most of the large orchestras here obtain their music from the hall of music. It is free for all to borrow whenever they wish, but someone has to duplicate it. And that is another important and productive occupation. The librarians who take care of all this music, and who attend to people's wants in this connections, fulfil another useful task. And so the details could be multiplied, covering the whole range of musical endeavor, from the person who does no more than love and enjoy music to those who are instrumentalists and leaders in the musical art.

In the hall of fabrics we shall find the same industry, the same happiness among all those who are working there. At any moment I am at liberty, if I wish, to join the students who are learning to weave the most exquisite fabrics. It happens, however, that my interests lie elsewhere, and my visits to the hall are for purposes of recreation only. Ruth regularly spends a certain time there studying, and she has become an expert in weaving tapestries. It is part of her spirit-life occupation, and it is part of her recreation also. She has produced some beautiful tapestries, of which Edwin and I possess two choice specimens hanging upon our walls.

We can obtain all the different materials we need from the hall of fabrics, or, as in the case of music, we can ask some craftsman to make what we require. We shall never have a refusal, nor shall we have to wait an interminable time before we receive what we want. There are plenty of craftsmen to supply the needs of all of us.

In the same hall there are students learning the art· of designing and they are instructed by masters in the art. Experimentation is continually going on in-producing new types of cloth and new designs. These various materials have nothing whatever to do with our own spirit clothes. That is a personal matter. The products of the fabric hall are used for general purposes; such as, for instance, in the garniture of our homes and in the larger halls and buildings. In the case of the historical pageants, which I mentioned to you, those who organize them exact a heavy contribution from the hall of fabrics for all their authentic costumes.

Now, I have given only two or three examples of what it is possible for a person to do here. There are thousands more, covering as great a field of activity as there is to be found upon the earth-plane. Think of the doctors who come into the spirit world, and still carry on their work here. Not that we need doctors but they can work here with their colleagues in investigating the causes of sickness and disease upon the earth-plane, and they can help in alleviating them. Many a spirit doctor has guided the hand of an earthly surgeon when he is performing an operation. The earthly doctor is, probably, perfectly unaware of the fact, and would ridicule any suggestion that he is receiving assistance from an unseen source. The doctor in spirit is contented to serve without acknowledgment from him whom he serves. It is the successful issue that he is concerned about, not who shall have the credit. The earthly doctor, in such cases, makes some very illuminating personal discoveries when he finally comes into the spirit world.

The scientist, too, continues his researches when he comes here. In whatever branch of science he may be concerned, he will find enough, and more than enough, to engage his attention for a long time to come. And so with the engineer, and scores upon scores of others. Indeed, it would be impossible, or is not impossible, a little tedious, perhaps, to run through the long list of occupations so well known upon the earth-plane, of which we have a counterpart in the spirit world. But by now you should have some idea of what the spirit world has to offer. All that we have in our halls and our houses, in our homes and in our gardens, has to be made, to be fashioned, or created, and it requires someone to do it. The need is constant, and the supply is constant, and it will ever be so.

There is another department of industry, though, which is vitally necessary, and it is peculiar to the spirit world.

The percentage is low, deplorably low, of people who come into the spirit world with any knowledge at all of their new life and of the spirit world in general. All the countless souls without this knowledge have to be taken care of, and helped in their difficulties and perplexities. That is the principal work upon which Edwin, Ruth and I are engaged. It is a type of work that appeals to many of the ministers of the church of whatever denomination. Their experience upon earth stands them in good stead, and all of them—perhaps I should say all of us!—know that we are now members of one ministry, with one purpose, serving one cause, and all of us possessed of the same knowledge of the truth of spirit life, without creed, without doctrine or dogma, a united body of workers, men and women.

In the great halls of rest there are expert nurses and spirit doctors ready to treat those whose last earthly illness has been long and painful, or whose passing into spirit has been sudden or violent. There are many such homes, especially for the latter. These homes are a standing monument of shame to the earth world, that they should be obliged to exist at all. Passings may be sudden and violent—that is inevitable at present, but it is to the eternal shame of the earth world that so many souls should arrive here in woeful ignorance of what lies before them. These halls of rest have multiplied very considerably since I first came into the spirit world, and consequently the need for more nurses and doctors has been more pressing. But that is always supplied.

As this service belongs exclusively to the spirit world, we have special colleges where those desiring to take up this particular work can become fully conversant with it. Here they learn much that scientifically concerns the spirit body itself, and the spirit mind. They are given a general knowledge of the ways of spirit life, since they will have to deal with people who, for the most part, have no knowledge whatever of their new state. They will have to know the facts of intercommunication between our world and yours, since such numbers of people ask about this important matter the instant they realize what has taken place in their lives. It is astonishing how many of them want to rush back to the earth-plane to try to tell those they have left behind of the great discovery they have made of the fact that they are alive and in another world!

In numbers of cases people require a long rest after their dissolution. They may be awake during the whole of this period of rest, and those in attendance have to be a storehouse of information. The attention of such souls is usually about equally divided between the spirit world and the earth world. It requires a high proportion of general spirit-world knowledge, as well as tactfulness and discretion, upon the part of all the nurses and doctors.

By making mention of any particular occupation I do so entirely without prejudice to any other, and not because those which we have discussed have any pre-eminence over others. One or two of them have been chosen to present to you because they have the appearance of being so very 'material', and to point what I have tried to demonstrate repeatedly before—that we are living in a practical spirit world where we are busy upon our own individual and useful tasks, and that we are not spending the whole of our spirit lives in a high state of religiosity, nor perpetually absorbed in pious meditation.

But what of the person who has never done a useful thing during his earth life? All I can say is, that such a person will not find himself in these realms until he has worked his way here. Entrance is by service alone.

To make a complete list of all spirit occupations would take a very large volume to do so, for they seem to be inexhaustible. Indeed, my mind becomes almost numbed at the thought of their countless number, and of my inability to do justice to so vast a subject. In the scientific sphere of labor alone, thousands upon thousands of people are happily employed, whether it be upon probing the secrets of the earth-plane, or in investigating those of the spirit world.

Science and engineering being closely allied in the spirit world, far-reaching discoveries are constantly being made, and inventions are ever being perfected. These inventions are not for us, but for you—when the time is ripe, and that is not yet. The earth world has given a poor exhibition of what has been sent through to it from the spirit world, by putting to base uses what has been given for its benefit. Man has exercised his own free will, but he has been exercising it in a direction that ultimately brings destruction. The mind of man is but in its infancy, and an infant becomes dangerous when he has free use of that which can destroy. Hence, much is held back; from the earth world until man has reached a higher state of development. That day will assuredly arrive, and a torrent of new inventions will come pouring through from the spirit world to your world.

In the meantime, the work goes on, research, investigation, discovery, and invention, and it is work that absorbs great hosts of interested people, and provides them with useful employment in their spirit life. Nothing ever disturbs the ordered routine of our work. While the work continues, we may be retiring from it for a space, either to rest or to follow some other line of endeavor. We have no disputes, no domestic upheavals, no rivalries that produce dissatisfaction and unpleasantness. We have no discontented folk. We may have the urge to be doing something of greater moment, but that is not discontent, but the prompting from within that denotes the steps of our spiritual progression. The humblest of us is made to feel that whatever his work, however insignificant it may appear beside other and seemingly greater tasks, he is performing something vital and significant that will bring with it its own inevitable reward that none can withhold from us, none can take away. In the spirit world, to work is to be profoundly happy—for the many reasons that I have given you.

There is none here who would not endorse my words wholeheartedly and unreservedly!

XII. FAMOUS PEOPLE

To LEAVE the earth world and to take up permanent residence in the spirit world is not such a personal upheaval as some people might be disposed to imagine. It is true that for a great many all earthly ties are severed, but when we pass into the spirit world we meet again those of our relatives and friends who have passed over before us. In this respect we start a fresh period in our lives, apart altogether from the new life that begins with our entry into the world of spirit.

The meetings with relations and friends are something that must be experienced in order to grasp the full significance and joy of reunion. Such meetings will only take place where there is mutual sympathy and affection. We will not, for the moment, consider any other. These gatherings will continue for some while after the arrival of the new resident. It is natural that in the novelty both of surroundings and condition some time should be spent in a grand exchange of news, and in hearing of all that has transpired in the spirit lives of those who have 'predeceased' us. Eventually the time will come when the newly-arrived individual will begin to consider what he is to do with his spirit life.

Now, it might be said that with most of us on the earth-plane we have a two-fold existence—our home life and the life connected with our business or occupation. In the latter we associate, perhaps, with an entirely different group of people. It is therefore in the natural order of things, here in spirit, that much the same state of things should also exist. The scientist, for example, will meet, first of all, his own family connections. When the question of work is broached he will find himself among his old colleagues who have passed into the spirit world before him, and he will again feel more than at home. And he will be more than overjoyed at the prospect of the scientific research that stretches before him. It is the same with the musician, the painter, the author, the engineer, the doctor, the gardener, the stone mason, or the man who weaved carpets in a factory, to mention but a fraction of the many occupations both of the earth and spirit worlds. It will be seen from this that the question which puzzles many folk, namely, what becomes of the famous people in the spirit world?—practically answers itself.

Fame in the spirit world is vastly different from fame in the earth world. Spiritual fame carries with it distinctions of a very different order from the earthly distinctions, and it is gained in one way only—in service to others. It sounds almost too simple to be feasible, but such is the case, and nothing will alter it. Whether the earthly famous will reside in the realms of light immediately after their dissolution remains with themselves. The law applies to all irrespective of earthly position.

A certain inquisitiveness concerning the general fate of those well known upon the earth-plane, is possessed by most people who are in their early days of psychic study. The mere fact of their being well known is sufficient. But none calls forth more curiosity than the historically famous people. Where are they— the masters in all branches of earthly endeavor, the names that are familiar in the history books? They must be somewhere. Most certainly they are. A good number of them are to be found in the dark realms where they have been living for countless centuries, and they are more than likely so to continue for more countless centuries. Others are in those exalted realms of light and beauty, where their noble lives upon earth have found their just reward. But there are many, a great many, who will find themselves within these realms whereof I have tried to give you some account.

I cannot do better than give you an example, of which, for our present purpose, I have gathered a few details.

It concerns the passing into the spirit world.

In this particular case we knew beforehand that his personage was about to come to the spirit world. His own countrymen were naturally interested in what was about to take place. His own family, in common with any other family here, were ready and awaiting his arrival. A short illness was the occasion of his passing here, and as soon as dissolution had taken place he was taken to the home of his mother, who had everything in readiness for him. The home is an inconspicuous one, similar, broadly speaking, to others here about. The news had spread that he had at last arrived. There was no universal rejoicing, such as might take place upon the earth-plane following a safe home-coming, but happiness was felt for all those who were directly concerned with the arrival in the spirit world of this well-known and much-loved figure. And there he remained for a time, enjoying a seclusion and freedom of action and a simplicity of life that had been denied him upon the earth-plane. He needed rest after his active life and the illness that terminated its earthly span. Numbers of people who had formed part of his official circle as well as his private circle, and who had passed on before him, had called to inquire after him, but they had not seen him as yet. There had been, of course, a grand family reunion, and as soon as he had rested sufficiently, he issued forth to see the wonders of his new life.

He retained to a noticeable extent his former and usual personal appearance. The signs of illness and bodily and mental fatigue had disappeared, and he looked some years younger. The rest had achieved its purpose as unfailingly as usual.

As he walked abroad he was recognized for what he had been, and respected for it, but he was still more honored and respected and loved for what he now was. Now, you may think that as soon as he met and mingled with his own countrymen, the latter would have shown some embarrassment, perhaps, and exhibited a general air of diffidence such as they would have done, perforce, upon the earth-plane. But during that period of recuperation much had been explained to him as to the conditions of life in the spirit world, its methods, it laws, and its pleasant customs. Such revelations had filled him with happiness, and he knew that as soon as he left the seclusion of his mother's house to venture abroad, he could do so with a freedom that is only to be found in spirit lands, where the inhabitants would regard him in the light in which he would wish to be regarded—that of a plain man desirous of joining with his fellow beings in their happiness and their rejoicing. He knew that he would be treated as one of themselves. When, therefore, in company with members of his family, he walked through these realms on the voyage of discovery that is such a common sight among the newly arrived, he did not experience in himself or cause in others any feelings of mental discomfort. No one referred to his earthly position, unless he himself broached the subject, and then there was no suspicion of inquisitiveness or ignorant curiosity.

You may think that one who had occupied so elevated a position upon the earth-plane would engender in the minds of others here thoughts of sympathy with such a change of relative position that had taken place. But no such feelings of sympathy are ever wished for, nor extended, in these realms in such cases, for the very good reason that the occasion for them never arises. We have left our earthly importance behind us, and we do not refer to it except to show, by our own experiences, to others still incarnate, just what to avoid. We do not revive our memories for the purpose of self-glorification, or to impress our hearers. Indeed, they would not be in the least impressed, and we should only succeed in making fools of ourselves! We recognize the truth here, and our true worth is for all to see. It is spiritual worth, and that alone, that counts, irrespective of what we were upon the earth-plane. Perspectives and view-points are completely altered when one comes into the spirit world. However mighty we were upon the earth-plane, it is spiritual worth only that takes us to our right place in the spirit world, and it is the deeds of our life, regardless of social position, that at our transition will assign to us our proper abode. Position is forgotten, but deeds and thoughts are the witnesses for or against us, and we become our own judges.

It is not difficult to see, then, that when this royal personage arrived in the spirit world, like others of his family before him, he found himself faced with no difficulties or awkward situations. It was just the reverse, for the whole situation seemed to simplify itself, and provided its own solution. Now, what applies in this extreme case, applies equally to all who were famous upon the earth-plane. But how does this affect some well-known scientist, let us say, or a musical composer, or a painter? To us—and to themselves—they will be learners, and humble learners, too, in whatever branch of science or art their earthly lives led them. To you, still incarnate, they are famous names, and when we have occasion to refer to them in speaking to you we use those names by which they are familiar. Here, in the spirit world, they dislike to be referred to as masters or geniuses. Their names, however famous, mean nothing to them personally, and they sternly repudiate anything that even remotely approaches the hero-worship that the earth world accords them. They are just one of ourselves, and as such they wish to be—and are—so treated.

In the spirit world the law of cause and effect applies equally to all people, regardless of their former earthly status. This law is no new thing. It has always been in existence, and so every famous name that is to be found within the chronicles of nations comes strictly within the jurisdiction of this law. The soul who passes his earthly life in obscurity, known only to one or two people, is subject to this same law just as much as the soul whose name is a household word among nations. In living in these realms one is inevitably bound, sooner or later, to encounter some person whose name is known to all upon the earth-plane. But these famous folk have no attachment to the earth world. They have left it behind them, and many of those who passed to here hundreds of earthly years ago are glad to have no occasion to recall their earthly lives. Such numbers of them suffered a violent transition that they are happy to consider their present only, and leave their past sealed up in their memory.

The people of the earth world may think it strange to walk through these realms and mingle with persons who lived on the earth-plane hundreds—and, in some cases, thousands—of years ago. A meeting of the past, as it were, with the eternal present. But it is not strange to us here. It may be so for the newly arrived, but then there are many other things that may seem strange—at first. Discretion is something we soon learn to exercise, and it is embodied in our never prying into the facts and circumstances of other people's earthly lives. That does not mean to say that we are debarred from discussing our earthly lives, but the initiative always comes from the person concerned. If he wishes to tell anyone of his life on earth he will ever find a sympathetic and interested ear awaiting him.

You can see, then, that our earthly lives are very strictly our own. The discretion that we exercise is universal among us—we show it and we receive it. And whatever our former position upon earth, we are united in these realms, spiritually, intellectually, temperamentally, and in such human traits as our likes and dislikes. We are one; we have achieved the same state of being upon the same plane of existence. Every fresh face that enters these realms receives the same heartfelt welcome, without reference to what he was upon earth.

One will meet many people here, who were famous upon earth, in all sorts of places and pursuing all sorts of occupations, some of the latter a continuation of their earthly calling, and some, perforce, entirely new. All alike are approachable without formalities of any kind whatever. We need no introductions to men and women whom the earth knows as famous. Their gifts are at the disposal of all, and happy, indeed, are they to assist another who comes to them for help in any difficulties, whether it is in art or science, or in any other form of activity. The great, who have gained their greatness through the various expressions of their genius, consider themselves but the lowly units of a vast whole, the immense organization of the spirit world. They are all striving—as we are too—for the same purpose, and that is spiritual progression and development. They are grateful for any help towards that end, and they are glad to give it wherever possible.

The riches and honors of the earth world seem very tawdry and trumpery by comparison with the spiritual riches and honors that are ready to be won here. And those riches and honors are within the grasp of every soul the instant he enters the spirit world. They are his spiritual birthright, of which no one can deprive him, and it rests with himself just how long it will be before he gains them. Earthly greatness may seem very tangible while we are in the midst of it. Just how tangible it is can be seen as soon as our dissolution takes place. Then we find that it is spiritual greatness that is concrete and permanent. Our earthly prominence just melts away as we step into the spirit world, and we stand revealed for what we are, not for what we were.

Several of the earth world's famous people have spoken to me of their awakening in the spirit world, and they have told me of the shock of revelation they received when they beheld themselves for the first time as they really were.

But oft-times greatness of earthly position goes hand in hand with greatness of soul, and thus spiritual progression and development continue without intermission from the moment of dissolution.

XIII. ORGANIZATION

You will have gathered that the spirit world is a vast place, and, with the earth world in mind, you may conclude that it possesses an administrative organization in all respects proportionate to its demands. You would be right, for it does. But our needs are not as yours. With you in your corruptible world it is constant war with material decay and degeneration. With us in our incorruptible world we have neither the one nor the other. Ours is a state far beyond Utopian in quality. But it is a state where thought is its basic element.

I have recounted to you how, when I first saw my own spirit garden, I marvelled at its orderliness and excellent preservation, and I wondered just how it was maintained thus, and who was responsible for it. Edwin told me that it would require practically no effort in its upkeep. By that he meant, as I have since learned, that provided my wish remained constant for the garden to continue unaltered, and provided that I had affection for the flowers and grass and trees, the garden would respond to my thoughts and flourish under them. If I desired to alter the arrangement of the flower beds, and so on, I could easily ask some expert to come to my help—and he would be only too happy to do so. So much for the upkeep of my garden.

My house is provided for under the same law. And so it is with all gardens and houses belonging to other folk in this realm. These, however, are what you would call more or less private concerns. They are so in one respect, but the fact that I can find an expert gardener who can make radical changes in my house and garden; indeed, who can build me an entirely new and different home, with surrounding gardens wholly different from what I have now, shows that organization of some sort—and a very considerable one—must exist somewhere.

The united thoughts of the inhabitants of the whole realm will sustain all that grows within it, the flowers, and the trees and the grass, and the water, too, whether of lake, river, or sea—for water is fully alive in the spirit world. It is when we come into the city and travel through the halls of learning that the organization becomes outwardly more observable.

In the hall of music, for example, we find many students busy at work upon their lessons and studies. We find others engaged upon musical research, and delving into ancient music books; others will be arranging the music for some concert, consulting the shelves for suitable works, and sometimes discussing those works with their composers. There are many teachers, many able people ready to assist us in our inquiries or our difficulties, and they are all able to provide a solution to our problems, because the staff of this hall—as of all others—are themselves experts.

Nominally, the ruler of the realm is the principal of all the halls, and all major decisions would, of course, be referred to him. But he appoints competent people to the staffs of the halls, and extends to them a free hand in all their undertakings.

Each hall will have its own direct head, but it must not be thought that this 'official' is an unapproachable, detached personage, hidden away from all sight, and only seen on relatively rare occasions. He is just the opposite. He is always to be seen about the hall, and he welcomes, personally, anyone who comes there, either as a learner, or as a 'mere lover' of music, or to carry out musical researches.

I have recounted to you how we continue with our work for just that period during which we derive pleasure or profit from it. The moment we feel the need for a change of work or other diversion, we cease our work for the time being, and turn to whatever else we wish. The staffs of all the halls of learning are no different from others in this respect. They most certainly need change and recreation, and so we find that the staffs alternate in their personnel as occasion demands. As some retire others take their places. It is the most natural thing in the world and the most practical. We need never fear that when we call to see some particular expert we shall be disappointed because he is not there. We shall be able to have all the help we need, and if it is vitally necessary to consult the absent one, either an instantaneous thought will answer our question, or with equal rapidity we can visit his home. We need have no misgivings about our intruding upon him.

Now, when I tell you that the service in all these halls is going on unremittingly simply because we have perpetual day in these realms, I think you will appreciate that our conception of organization begins to assume its right proportions.

Many of the people attached to the halls of learning have been there a great number of years as you reckon time. So devoted are they to their work that although they have progressed and virtually belong to a higher sphere, they prefer to remain where they are for some considerable period yet. They will retire, from time to time, to their own realm, and then return to take up their labours anew. The moment will eventually arrive when they will relinquish their position altogether to reside permanently in their own sphere, and then others, equally capable, will take their place. And so it goes on, and has gone on for countless centuries, and so it will go on for countless more centuries—an unbroken continuity of service for others in these realms. And this rule applies to all the various halls of learning. The work of the spirit world functions unceasingly; the workers rest and change about, but the work never stops. The pressure of work may fluctuate, as it does with you upon earth. When we have our great celebrations and festivals, during which we are honored by the presence of visitants from the higher realms, it follows that large numbers of people will be present in the temple or elsewhere, and during that time there will be an appreciable diminution of some activities. We are naturally desirous of holding our festivals in company with one another, and we do so. But the services never suffer on that account. It so happens that the inhabitants in these realms are always considerate of others, and will never ask of others that which would entail a disappointment for them, such as would be the case if one insisted upon some attention in one of the halls when we were all, as it were, on holiday. This concerns the various halls in the city where any temporary cessation of work would be of no great consequence.

In the halls of rest, however, the doctors and nurses are always in attendance whatever else may be taking place in other parts of the sphere. Their devotion to duty is always instantly rewarded, for during the general celebrations of the realm, the illustrious visitors from the upper realms make a special journey to the rest homes where they personally greet every one of the staff. The latter can afterwards arrange amicably for their own family and friendly festivities.

All this administration belongs to the spirit world proper, so to speak, and concerns the spirit world alone. There are other services that concern the two worlds together, ours and yours. Such, for example, as the arrival, or the approaching arrival, of a soul into spirit lands. The rule is that all souls passing to here shall have some measure of attention. It depends upon themselves how much attention they shall have. Some are sunken so spiritually low as to preclude any approach to them that would be effective. We will not consider those for the moment, but only those who are destined for the realms of light.

Without anticipating what I wish to say regarding the interrelationship of our two worlds, we might, for our present purposes consider a typical inquiry in the matter of transition, such as it affects a very large number of people here.

We will suppose that you are yourself in the spirit world, and that beyond knowing the truth of communication with the earth world, you have had no experience of the close ties existing between the two worlds. You have, we will further suppose, left behind you a friend for whom you had—and still have—a warm affection, and you wonder when he will be coming to reside permanently in the spirit world. Occasionally you have received his thoughts of affection arising from the earth-plane, by which you know that he has not forgotten you. You have, we will say, never tried to communicate with him because you know from your earthly knowledge that he would rather frown upon such ideas. Is it possible to find out just when he is likely to join you in the spirit world, and if so, how does one go about it? The answer to that question reveals the existence of one of the great organizations of these lands.

In the city there is an immense building which exercises the function of an office of records and inquiries. (In the earth world you have your multifarious offices of inquiry. Why should we not have ours?) Here a great host of people is available to answer all manner of questions that are likely to arise both from the newly-arrived and from those of longer residence. Occasions will occur when we need a solution to some problem that has arisen. We may consult our friends upon the matter, only to find that they are as uninformed as we are ourselves. We could, of course, make an appeal to some higher personage, and we should receive all the help we wanted. But the higher beings have their work to do, in just the same way as we have, and we forbear to interrupt them unnecessarily. And so we take our difficulty to this grand building in the city. Among its many important duties is that of keeping a register of people newly arrived in this particular realm. It is a useful service, and full advantage is taken of it by scores of people who have an interest in that direction. But a still more important service is that of knowing beforehand of those who are about to come into this realm. This information is accurate and infallibly reliable. It is collected through a varied process of thought transmission, of which the inquirer sees little or nothing. He is merely presented with the required information. The value of this service can be readily imagined.

In normal times upon the earth-plane, when transitions maintain a fairly steady level, it is valuable enough, but in times of great wars, when souls are passing into the spirit world in thousands, the advantages of such an office are almost incalculable. Friend can meet friend, and together can unite in helping others who are passing into spirit lands.

Foreknowledge of terrestrial events both national and private is possessed by a certain order of beings in the spirit world, and when expedient this knowledge is communicated to others, who in turn pass it on to those principally concerned. Among the first to receive pre-knowledge of an impending war are the different homes of rest. The office of inquiry will be similarly informed.

You are anxious, then, to know when your friend is likely to be coming to the spirit world to reside; you want to know when his 'death' is going to take place. Your first step is to go to the inquiry office. There you will be readily assisted to consult the right person for your needs. You will not find yourself passed from one 'official' to another, nor will you be submitted to other forms of procrastination. All that will be required of you is to furnish the name of your friend, and you will be asked to focus your attention upon him to establish the necessary thought link. When this has been accomplished, you will be requested to wait for a brief period—in your time it would amount to only a few minutes. The requisite forces are put into action with astonishing rapidity, and we shall be presented with the information of the time of our friend's arrival. The actual date may mean very little to some of us, as I have already tried to make clear to you, because it is towards such an event that we cast our minds, and not towards the time of its taking place. At least, whatever our condition of proximity to the earth-plane, we shall be assured that when that event is close at hand we shall be informed of it without fail. In the meantime, we shall be given a conception of the closeness of the event or otherwise, which we shall understand according to the measure of our knowledge of the passage of earthly time.

The organization that exists behind this one service should give you some idea of the vastness of the whole office of help and inquiry. There are many others. This same building houses people who can provide answers to the innumerable questions that arise in the minds of us here, especially among the newly arrived, and its extent covers the whole range of spirit activity. But what is most to our present point, this office employs thousands of people, usefully and happily. Many souls ask to be allocated to work there, but it is necessary to have some training for it first, for however suitable may be our personal attributes, it requires absolute knowledge, in whatever department we wish to work, since we should be there for the express purpose of providing information to those in need of it.

Let us now pass to another example of spirit organization, and for the purpose we might visit the hall of science.

There are numberless people upon the earth-plane who are mechanically minded, and who pursue as a means of material livelihood one or other of the engineering arts. Others are interested in engineering as a pleasant diversion from their usual work. The opportunities in the spirit world in this field alone are enormous, and such scientific work is carried on under conditions precisely similar to all other work here—without restriction, freely, and with the limitless resources and the perfect administration of the spirit world behind it. This form of work attracts thousands, young and old alike. All the great scientists and engineers are carrying on their investigations and researches in this world of spirit, assisted by scores of enthusiastic helpers from every walk of earthly life, as well as by those whose work lay upon those lines when they were incarnate.

Most of us here are not content with one type of work; we engage in another form of labor as part of our recreation. You see, we have the constant urge to be doing something useful, something that will be of benefit to others. However small that service may be, it will be valued as a service. To have only two forms of work with which to alternate is to give the lowest estimate. So many of us have a dozen channels through which we are usefully engaged. It must be obvious, then, that the supply of useful tasks is entirely adequate to the thousands upon thousands of us here. And each and every form of work has its separate organization. There are no such things as haphazard methods. Every type of pursuit has those in charge of it who are experts, and the administration admits of no muddle or fuss. There is no mismanagement, for everything runs with the smoothness of perfectly-constructed machinery under the operation of efficient hands.

It must not be concluded from this that we are infallible. That would be a totally wrong estimation, but we know that whatever our mistakes may be we are always sure that our perfect organization will come to our rescue and help us to put things right. Mistakes are never frowned upon as a piece of glaring inefficiency, but are regarded as very good lessons for us by which we can profit to the fullest extent. But because of this sympathy with our mistakes, we are not careless on that account, for we have our natural and proper pride in our work, which spurs us on to do our best always—and free from mistakes.

To attempt to give you anything like a comprehensive survey of the administrative organization of the spirit world would be a gigantic task, and quite beyond my descriptive powers, apart altogether from the impossibility of putting into material language what can only be understood as an inhabitant of these lands.

Perhaps one of the most striking features of life in the spirit world is that the organization of life is so perfect that there never seems to be any suspicion of hurry or confusion, in spite of the fact that we can perform so many actions of a 'material' kind with the rapidity of thought, which latter is the motive force. This rapidity is as second nature to us, and we scarcely notice it. It is there, none the less, and it is because of it that our great system of life, and the organization of living generally, works so perfectly and yet so unobtrusively.

It is something of a proud boast upon the earth-plane that you have reached such an age of speed. By comparison with our rapidity of motion, why, you are scarcely moving! You must wait until you come to live here with us. Then you will know what real speed is like. Then you will know, too, what real efficiency and real organization are like.

They are like nothing upon the earth-plane.

XIV. SPIRIT INFLUENCE

IT IS the habit of most men to look upon the spirit world and the earth world as two planes apart, separate and distinct. They regard the two worlds as being each independent of the other, cut off from each other, and both entirely uninformed or unaware of what the other is doing. That the spirit world could possibly have any influence upon the earth world to the latter's advantage is demonstrated to be altogether false by the state of universal disorder that exists through the entire earth world.

There is another school of thought, consisting of those who have made a superficial study of what they call occultism. These people believe that the earth world, being indisputably very earthy, and the spirit world being incontrovertibly very spiritual, the two worlds are for these reasons automatically inhibited from anything like intercommunication.

Both these lines of thought are unquestionably wrong. The two worlds, yours and ours, are in constant and direct communication, and we are fully aware of what is occurring upon the earth-plane at all times. I do not, for one minute, say that we all of us know what is taking place with you. Those of us who are in active communion with you are conversant with your personal affairs and with the affairs of your world in general. While the rest of us here, who have no further active interest in the earth-plane since we left it, may be unaware of many things in connection with it, those wise beings in the higher realms are in possession of all knowledge of what is transpiring upon earth.

I would like to indicate one or two channels through which the influence of the spirit world is exerted upon the earth world.

First, we might take that influence in a personal way.

Every soul that has been, and is to be, born upon the earth-plane has allocated to him—or her—a spirit guide. In past ages, some such idea must have filtered through into the minds of the early churchmen, since they adopted the pious notion of giving to every incarnate person an unseen protector whom they called a 'guardian angel'. These guardian angels sometimes found their way into contemporary art, where the artists drew a somewhat vapid individual habited in glistening white garments and supporting from his shoulders a pair of enormous wings. The whole conception would suggest by its very implications a remoteness, or a great gulf, between the guardian angel and the soul he was supposed to be guarding. He would, one might say, be unable to draw very near his charge because of extreme spiritual refinement upon the one hand, and repelling earthly grossness upon the other.

Let us turn from this inaccurate figment of the artist's brain to something a little more practical.

Spirit guides constitute one of the grandest orders in the whole organization and administration of the spirit world. They inhabit a realm of their own, and they have all lived for many centuries in the spirit world. They are drawn from every nationality that exists upon the earth-plane, and they function regardless of nationality. A great many of them are drawn from eastern countries, and from the North American Indians, too, because it has always been the case that dwellers in those regions of the earth world were, and are, already possessed of psychic gifts themselves, and were therefore aware of the inter-relationship of our two worlds.

The principal guide is chosen for each individual on the earth-plane in conformity with a fixed plan. Most guides are temperamentally similar to their charges in the latter's finer natures, but what is most important the guides understand and are in sympathy with their charges' failings. Many of them, indeed, had the same failings when they were incarnate, and among other useful services they try to help their charges overcome those failings and weaknesses.

A great number of those who practice communication with the spirit world have already met their spirit guides and are in close touch with them. And fortunate, indeed, they are. The guides, too, are never happier than when they have established a direct link with those whose lives they are helping to direct. It would be safe to say that by far the greater number of spirit guides carry on their work all unknown to those whom they serve, and their task is so much the heavier and more difficult. But there are still others whose lives upon earth render it practically impossible for their guides to approach within any reasonable distance of them. It naturally saddens them to see the mistakes and follies into which their charges are plunging themselves, and to be obliged to stand aloof because of the thick wall of material impenetrability which they have built up round themselves. Such souls, when they at last arrive in the spirit world, awake to a full realization of what they have thus missed during their earth lives. In such cases the guide's work will not be entirely in vain, for even in the worst souls there comes an occasion, however transient, when the conscience speaks, and it is usually the spirit guide who has implanted the better thought within the brain.

It must never for one instant be thought that the influence of the spirit guide negatives or violates the possession or expression of free will. If, upon the earth-plane, you were to observe somebody about to take a false step into a stream of traffic upon the road, the fact that you put out your hand to stop him would in no way impinge upon his exercise of free will. A spirit guide will try to give advice when his advice can be got through to his charge; he will try to lead him in the right direction solely for his own good, and it remains for his charge, in the exercise of his free will, to take that advice or reject it. If he does the latter, he can only blame himself if disaster or trouble overtakes him. At the same time, the spirit guides are not there to live a person's life for him. That he must do himself.

It has become a habit among a certain class of individuals of the earth-plane to ridicule the whole establishment of spirit guides. There will assuredly come a time when they will bitterly repent their folly, and that day will be whereon they meet in the spirit world their own guide, who probably knows more about their lives than they do themselves! We in the spirit world can afford to pass by such ridicule as this, because we know that the day will inevitably come when they will arrive in the spirit world, and great is the remorse—and, in many instances, the self-pity—of those who have, in their supposed wisdom, made fools of themselves.

Apart from spirit guides, there is another prolific source of influence that derives from the world of spirit. I have told, for example, how earthly doctors' hands will be guided, in performing an operation, by the hand of a spirit doctor. In many other walks of life spirit inspiration is being carried on in the same way as it has been carried on since the dawn of time. Incarnate man can really do very little of himself; and he is the first to realize it when he comes here to live. Man can perform certain mechanical actions with precision and exactitude. He can paint a picture, he can play upon an instrument, he can manipulate machinery, but all the major discoveries that are of service to the earth-plane have come and always will come, from the spirit world. If man, employing his free will, chooses to put those discoveries to base ends, then he can thank himself for the calamities that follow. Inspiration devoted to whatever cause or pursuit, comes from the world of spirit, and from nowhere else. If it be for the good of mankind the source is equally good; if the inspiration is obviously not for the good of mankind, then the source is unquestionably evil. Man has it within his own hands as to which source of inspiration he will lend himself—to good or to evil.

You will remember how I have told you that a person is exactly the same spiritually the moment after he has 'died' as he was the moment before. No instantaneous change takes place to turn an earthly lifetime of evil into good.

One orthodox church takes the view, which is also an infallible teaching, that those of us who return to the earth-plane and make our presence known, are all devils! It is a pity that the church is so blind, for it can be said that they are trying—

ineffectually—to stifle the forces of good, while they are ignoring the real forces of evil. If they encouraged the forces of good to come to them, the forces of evil would soon be put to flight. The churches, of whatever denomination, suffer from abysmal ignorance. Throughout the ages right down to the present time they have gone their own blind, ignorant way, disseminating fantastic teachings in place of the truth, and paving the way, through the universal ignorance begotten of such false teachings, for the forces of evil to operate.

A minister of the church performs the services and offices prescribed by his particular sect, and he stifles all inspiration by holding to creeds and dogmas that are utterly false. If he were interrogated in the matter he would reply that he believed in inspiration—in a vague, remote way. In the long run he would find it much less trouble to borrow the religious thoughts of some other incarnate person, and rely upon his own cleverness for any original thought. But to suggest that the spirit world has any influence upon the earth world other than evil, would be totally against his principles.

It is a strange habit of mind that persists in the belief that it is always the forces of evil from the spirit world that try to make their power felt upon the earth-plane. The forces of evil are attributed with powers which, it would seem, are denied to the forces of good. Why? And why are the churches mortally afraid to 'try the spirits'—as they are advised to do in the very book upon which they place so much reliance? They ignore this text, and point a warning finger to the supposed woman of Eden.

The spirit world works constantly to make its power and force and presence felt by the whole earth world, not only in personal matters, but through individuals into a wider sphere for the good of nations and national policies. But so little can be done, because the door is usually closed to the higher beings of the spirit world, whose range of vision, and whose wisdom and knowledge and understanding are vast. Think of the evils that could be swept from the face of the earth under the immensely able guidance of wise teachers from the spirit world. The world of spirit does its best through the limited channels available. But it is safe to say that there is no problem upon the earth-plane that could not be solved by the help and advice and experience of those beings I have just mentioned. But it would involve one thing—an implicit adherence to whatever they advised or advocated. Many a leader, either of the nation's affairs or of religious thought, who is here with us in the spirit world, is filled with sorrow when he looks back upon the wasted opportunities for bringing about a revolutionary change for the betterment of his fellow countrymen. He will confess that he had the idea in his mind—he did not know then that it had been impinged thereupon by the spirit world—but he had allowed himself to be overruled. These souls sigh for the state into which humanity has degraded itself. Humanity has, in effect, allowed the evil forces to dictate to it. But the evil ones, so beloved by the churches, have appeared in a different direction from that which those same churches allege that they come. The men and women who practice communication with us in all seriousness and earnestness, and who enjoy happy meetings with their spirit friends as well as with noble teachers from the higher spheres, are accused of dealings with 'devils'. That is rubbish. The real devils are far too busy elsewhere, in places where they can produce far greater results to their own evil satisfaction.

You will say that my outlook seems rather pessimistic; that really, after all, the earth world is not so bad as I paint it. That is perfectly true, because we have managed to get through to the earth world just one or two of our ideas and thoughts and precepts. But it can safely be said that in spite of universal earth-world disorder, had we withdrawn every element of our influence, the earth world would, in a very brief time, be reduced to a state of complete and absolute barbarity and chaos. And the reason is that man thinks he can get along nicely by his own powers and volition He is conceited enough to think that he requires no help from any source whatever. As for assistance from the spirit world—if such a place exists—it is unthinkable! If there is such a place as the spirit world, it is fully time enough to begin thinking about it when one arrives there. For the present, then, they are so superior that they know everything, and can manage their own affairs perfectly well without the help of a shadowy spirit world. And when many men arrive here in the same world of spirit that they scorned, they see their own littleness and the littleness of the world they have just left. But small though the earth world may be, man still needs help in conducting its affairs—and that is another discovery that he makes when he comes here.

The earth world is beautiful, and life upon it could be beautiful as well but man steps in and prevents it. The spirit world is surpassingly beautiful, more beautiful than the mind of man incarnate can possibly imagine. I have tried to show you a glimpse or two of it. But your world looks very dark to us, and we try very hard to bring a little light to it. We try to make our presence known, our influence felt. Our influence is great, but it has yet to be increased far, far beyond its present range. When we and our world gain full acceptance you will then know what it means to live upon the earth-plane.

But we have a long, long way to go yet.

XV. THE HIGHEST REALMS

I HAVE spoken to you, on a number of occasions, of the higher spheres. There are two ways, and two ways only, of penetrating into those lofty states. The first is through our own spiritual development and progression; the second is by special invitation from some dweller in those regions. Any other way is barred to us by the invisible barriers of spiritual impenetrability.

I would like to speak to you now about a special invitation that we received to visit those high realms.

We were seated in one of the lower rooms of my house, from which all the beauties without could be viewed to perfection. Across a glittering expanse of countryside could be seen the city in the distance, as clearly as though it were close by instead of some distance away. Edwin and I were chatting, while Ruth was seated at the piano playing some pleasant work that seemed to blend so harmoniously, not only with our present mood, but with all our colorful environment.

Ruth had never really recovered from her initial surprise when she first beheld the piano in her own home. She was an accomplished performer during her earth life, and she has since told us of the thrilling moment when she seated herself before her 'spirit instrument', as she called it, and struck the first chord upon it. She said that she never precisely knew what was going to happen, or what description of sound would come forth with her striking the keys! She was consequently amazed at the result of her simple action, for the tone of her 'spirit piano' was something that she could never have imagined possible, it was so perfectly balanced and of such ringing quality. Her surprises were not ended, however. She found that her dexterity had increased a hundredfold by her casting off her physical body, and that she had taken her technique with her to the spirit world.

She further discovered that her hands, when applied to the instrument, just rippled along the keys without conscious effort, and that her memory was as sound as though she had the very music before her.

On the present occasion she was filling the air with dulcet sounds, and so helping all three of us in our rest and recreation, for we had just completed a particularly onerous task during the course of our usual work. We three worked together—we are still doing so at this moment of your time—and we usually take our rest and amusement together. In fact, Edwin and Ruth spend far more time in my home than they do in their own! Speaking for myself, I would not have it otherwise.

Suddenly Ruth ceased playing, and ran to the door. Wondering what had caused her to stop so abruptly, Edwin and I joined her. We were much surprised to see, walking across the lawn, two striking figures, of whom I have before made mention. One was the Egyptian who had given me such helpful advice when I was but recently arrived in spirit lands, and who had since taken such a kindly interest in my welfare. The other was his 'master', who had accompanied the great celestial visitor upon that occasion in the temple in the city.

The Egyptian's 'master' was a man with jet-black hair, matched in its color by a pair of eyes that bespoke the greatest sense of humor and merriment. I subsequently learned that our guest was a Chaldean.

We went forward eagerly to welcome our two visitors, and they expressed their pleasure in thus coming to see us.

We conversed happily upon various matters, and Ruth was persuaded to finish the work she had been playing when they arrived. At the finish they voiced their appreciation of her talent, and then the Chaldean broached the subject upon which they had called.

He came, he said, with an invitation from the great soul whom we had assembled to honor upon that memorable day in the temple, for us to visit him at his own home in the high realm in which he lived.

The three of us were silent for a moment. Ruth and I did not know exactly what to say beyond expressing our sense of the privilege that was contained in such an invitation. Edwin, however, came to our rescue, and acted as our spokesman. The Chaldean was much amused at our embarrassment, and he hastened to assure us that there was nothing to fear in such a meeting. That would be impossible, as we should see. I think what troubled us most, or, at least, puzzled us most, was the reason why we should be invited upon such a visit, and just how we were to get there. Indeed, we had no notion where 'there' might be. As to our first question, the Chaldean said that we should ascertain that when we arrived at our destination. As to our getting to our destination, why, that was what he and his much-loved friend, the Egyptian, had come for purposely.

We tried to speak our feelings, but we failed; at least, that is how I felt about my attempt. I think Edwin and Ruth were really much more successful than I was, although the Chaldean helped us with his delightful lightheartedness and his keen sense of fun.

I truly believe that the Chaldean is the merriest soul in the whole of the spirit realms. I mention this specifically because there would seem to be an idea in some minds that the higher one's spiritual status becomes the more serious one has to be. Such a notion is entirely false. The reverse is the truth. Lighthearted merriment that comes truly from the heart, that hurts no one and is directed against no one to their detriment, but that is indulged in for the sake of making others merry, such merriment is welcomed and encouraged in the spirit world. There is no inscription: 'Abandon all laughter, ye who enter here' written over the portals of these realms! To suggest that the greater the spirituality the grimmer one must look is altogether a horrible notion, and recalls too much the sanctimoniousness of some breeds of earthly religious piety. We know when to laugh and how to laugh, and we do so. We do not like mournful countenances with no mirthfulness behind them. So that when I tell you that our distinguished guest, the Chaldean, so elevated our minds with his gaiety—and he was very ably assisted, one might say aided and abetted, by the kindly Egyptian—you must know that he lost none of the grand dignity and stateliness of his high station. And it must not be thought that it was a case of laughing at everything he said before he had hardly spoken it! We are not living in a land of make-believe; we laughed because there was genuine cause to do so. It was not the spurious laughter of dependents upon another of greater position.

Edwin inquired when we were to make the journey. The Chaldean replied that he and his good friend the Egyptian had come to take us back with them now. I was still—we all were—in the dark as to the actual procedure in making such a journey, but the Chaldean soon took matters in hand by bidding us to 'come along'. And he led us towards the boundary of our realm.

As we walked through the woods and meadows, I asked the Egyptian if he could tell me anything about the great being whom we were about to visit. What he told me was very little, although I was certain that he knew very much more than he revealed! Most likely I should not have understood had he told me all he knew, so that he, in his wisdom, withheld further information. This, then, is what he told me.

The illustrious personage, towards whose home in the high realms we were making our way, was known by sight to every soul in the realms of light. His wish was always treated as a command, and his word was law. The blue, white and gold in his robe, evident in such enormous proportions, revealed the stupendous degree of his knowledge, spirituality, and wisdom. There were thousands who named Him as their 'beloved master', the principal among whom being the Chaldean, who was His 'right hand'. As to his special function, he was the ruler of all the realms of the spirit world, and he exercised collectively that function which the particular ruler of a realm exercises individually. All other rulers, therefore, were responsible to him, and he, as it were, united the realms and welded them into one, making them one vast universe, created and upheld by the Great Father of all.

To attempt to define the immense magnitude of his powers in the spirit world would be to essay the impossible. Even were it possible, understanding would fail. Such powers have no counterpart, no comparison even, with any administrative powers upon the earth-plane. Earthly minds can only conjure up those individuals who ruled great kingdoms upon earth, who held sway over vast territories, it may be, but who did so through fear alone, and where all who lived under him lived as serfs and slaves. No earthly king throughout the whole narrative of the history of the earth world ever presided over a state so vast as that presided over by this illustrious personage of whom I am speaking. And his kingdom is ruled by the great universal law of true affection. Fear does not, could not, exist in the minutest, tiniest fraction, because there is not, and cannot be, the slightest cause for it. Nor will there ever be. He is the great living visible link between the Father, the Creator of the Universe, and His children.

But notwithstanding the supreme elevation of his spiritual

position, he descends from his celestial home to visit us here in these realms, as I have tried to describe to you on a former occasion. And it is permissible for others of incomparably lesser degree to visit him in His own home.

There is nothing unsubstantial, vague, or unreal about this regal being. We have beheld him on those great festival days that we have in the spirit world. He is not some 'spiritual experience', some grand upliftment of the soul produced within us by some invisible means from some invisible source. He is a real living person, as firm a reality as we are ourselves—and we are more real than are you upon the earth-plane, though you are not conscious of it yet! I am putting it to you in this almost blunt way so that there will be no misunderstanding of what I am attempting to recount. There are mistaken notions that the beings of the highest realms are so ethereal as to be practically invisible except to others of their kind, and that they are utterly and completely unapproachable; that no mortal of lesser degree could possibly view them and survive. It is commonly held that these beings are so immeasurably higher than the rest of us that it will be countless eons of time before we shall ever be permitted to cast our eyes upon them even from a remote distance. That is sheer nonsense. Many a soul in these realms has been spoken to by one of these great beings, and he has been totally unaware of the fact. We all of us have certain powers which are magnified as we pass from sphere to sphere in the progressive steps of our spiritual development. And one of the principal of these powers is that of matching ourselves, of adjusting ourselves, to our surroundings. There is nothing magical about this, it is highly technical—far more so than most of the scientific mysteries of the earth world. In the spirit world we call it an equalizing of our personal vibrational rate, but I am afraid you are now none the wiser—and it is not within my province to attempt to explain it!

The Egyptian supplied me with these few details, and I have supplemented them from my own knowledge, which is very small indeed.

In the meantime I have digressed a little.

By now we were close to Edwin's house, and we were rapidly passing from our own realm into a more rarified atmosphere. In a short while it would have caused us some discomfort to proceed further. We instinctively halted in our walk, and we felt that the crucial moment of our journey had come. It was, of course, exactly as the Chaldean had said: we had nothing whatever to fear. And the procedure was perfectly normal and unsensational.

First of all he came behind us and allowed his hands to rest upon our heads for a brief moment. This, he told us, was to give us extra power to move through space. We felt a tingling sensation immediately beneath his hands that was most pleasant and exhilarating, and we felt as though we were becoming lighter, although one would scarcely have thought that would be possible. We could also feel a gentle heat running through the system. This was merely the effect of the power, and was nothing in itself. The Chaldean placed Ruth between Edwin and me, and then he stood just behind her himself. He placed his left hand upon Edwin's shoulder and his right upon mine, and as he was wearing a mantle—which we saw was richly embroidered—it formed a perfect cloak about the three of us.

It must not be assumed that a dignified silence had fallen or had been imposed upon us during these preliminaries. On the contrary, the Chaldean and the Egyptian, in fact, all the five of us were chatting away merrily, the former contributing by far the largest share to our jocundity. This was no dreary pilgrimage upon which we were embarking. Far from it. It is true that we were about to be taken into realms far, far removed from our own normal habitation, but that was no reason for a heavy solemnity nor for the assumption of an intense gravity which we did not feel. The Chaldean had done his utmost to dispel any such emotions upon our part. This visit, he said in effect, was to be a gloriously happy one. Let us have smiling faces, then, and lightness of heart. Mournfulness has no place in the high realms any more than it has in our own sphere. We shall be expected, he said, to present smiling happy faces that are a true reflection of our feelings within. But it would be impossible not to be cheerful when in the presence of the Chaldean and his companion. And I am sure we did credit to them both for all their assiduity on our behalf, for I think we did most surely present to others the very embodiment of spiritual gaiety.

The Chaldean told us that by placing his hands upon our heads it would also have the effect, in addition to giving us power to travel, of adjusting our vision to the extra intensity of light that we should encounter in the high realm. Without such counterbalancing we should find ourselves in very considerable distress. In this adjustment our sight was not dimmed from within, but a kind of film was superimposed without, just in the same way as upon earth you wear protective glass to shield the eyes from the light and heat of the sun. We did not actually wear any such apparatus, of course; the Chaldean merely applied his own powers of thought. What he did precisely, I cannot say, but the process, whatever it was, he had applied many times before, and it was, needless to say, fully effective.

The Egyptian next took our hands within his, and we perceived a fresh accession of power flowing into us.

The Chaldean asked us to make ourselves completely passive, and to remember that we were upon a journey for our enjoyment and not as a test of our spiritual endurance. 'And now, my friends,' said he, 'our arrival is awaited. So let us be off.'

We immediately felt ourselves to be floating, but this sensation ceased abruptly after what seemed but a second of time, and thereafter we had no sense of movement whatever. A light flashed before our eyes. It was extremely bright, but it was by no means startling. It vanished as quickly as it came, and coincidental with its disappearance I could feel the solid ground under my feet. And then the first vision of this high realm opened before our eyes.

We were in a dominion of unparalleled beauty. There is no imagination upon the earth-plane that can visualize such inexpressible beauty, and I can only give you some meager details of what we saw in the limited terms of the earth-plane.

We were standing within the realm of a king—that was evident to us at once. We stood upon an elevation some height above the city; our good friends had expressly taken us to this particular location to present us with this superb view. It would not be possible, they said, to spend more than a limited period here, and so it was the wish of the Chaldean's master that we should see as much as possible within that period.

Stretching before us was the wide stream of a river, looking calm, peaceful, and overwhelmingly lovely as the heavenly sun touched every tiny wave with a myriad tints and tones. Occupying a central position in the view, and upon the right bank of the river, was a spacious terrace built to the water's edge. It seemed to be composed of the most delicate alabaster. A broad flight of steps led up to the most magnificent building that the mind could ever contemplate.

It was several stories high, each of them being arranged in a series of orders, so that each occupied a gradually diminishing area until the topmost was reached. Its exterior appearance was, if anything, almost plain and unadorned, and it was obvious why this should be so. The whole edifice was exclusively composed of sapphire, diamond, and topaz, or at least, their celestial equivalent. These three precious stones constituted the crystalline embodiment of the three colors blue, white and gold, and they corresponded with the colors which we had seen before in the robe of our celestial visitor as we had seen him in the temple, and which he carried in such an immense degree. The blue, white and gold-of the jewelled palace, touched by the pure rays of the great central sun, were intensified and magnified a thousandfold, and flashed forth in every direction their beams of the purest light. Indeed, the whole edifice presented to our bewildered gaze one vast volume of sparkling irradiation. We at once thought of earthly topaz and sapphire and diamond, and we pondered how small stones of purity were only tiny objects that could be held between the forefinger and thumb. And here was an immense glittering mansion entirely built of these precious stones, and of such stones that the incarnate have never beheld—nor are they ever likely to behold while they are incarnate.

Our first question concerned the reason or significance of the especial fabric of the building that was before us. There was no special significance in the actual materials of which the palace was constructed, so the Chaldean informed us. The precious stones were proper to the realm which we were now visiting. In our own realm the buildings are opaque, albeit they have a certain translucence of surface. But they are ponderous and heavy by comparison with the upper realms. We had journeyed through many other spheres to reach this present one, but had we paused to observe the lands through which we had passed, we should have seen a gradual transformation taking place until the relatively heavy-looking materials of our own realm became transmuted into the crystalline substance upon which our gaze was now fastened.

But the colors most certainly had a special significance to which I have already alluded.

We could see, surrounding the palace, many acres of the most enchanting gardens laid out in such fashion that, from the distant and elevated viewpoint which we occupied, they presented a huge and intricate pattern as in some superbly-wrought eastern carpet. We were told that upon close view, or in walking through the gardens, the pattern would be lost, but that we should find ourselves in the midst of delicately arranged flower beds and soft velvety lawns.

Though we could scarcely remove our eyes from the superlative glory of the palace and its grounds, yet the Chaldean gently drew our attention to the remainder of the prospect.

It extended for miles upon countless miles—or so it seemed to us. The range of our vision was increased in these rarified regions beyond all human conception, and so it seemed that literally an unending vista spread before us of more earthly miles than it is possible to contemplate. And all through this wide expanse we could see other magnificent buildings built of still more precious stones—of emerald and amethyst, to name but two, and, far away, what looked like pearl. Each of the different buildings was set amid the most entrancing gardens, where trees were growing of unimaginable richness of color and grandeur of form. Wherever we cast our eyes, there we could see the flashing of jewelled buildings, reflecting back the rays of the central sun, the myriad colors from the flowers, and the scintillations from the waters of the river that flowed before us far away into the distance.

As we were gazing spellbound upon the scene a sudden flash of light seemed to come from the palace directly to the Chaldean, and it was acknowledged by an answering flash which he sent back to the palace. Our presence in the realm was known, and as soon as we had feasted our eyes upon the view, we were asked to walk within the palace where our host would be waiting to receive us. Such was the message contained in the flash of light, as interpreted by the Chaldean. We, therefore, proceeded at once towards the palace.

By the same means of locomotion that had brought us into the sphere, we quickly found ourselves walking upon the terrace beside the river, and up a broad flight of steps that led to the main entrance of the palace. The stonework of the terrace and the steps was pure white, but we were much surprised by its apparent softness under foot, for it was like walking upon the velvet softness of a well-tended lawn. Our footsteps made no sound, but our garments rustled as we walked along, otherwise our progress would have been a silent one except for our conversation. There were, of course, many other sounds to be heard. We had not stepped into a realm of silence! The whole air was filled with harmony sent forth from the volumes of color that abounded upon every hand.

The temperature seemed to us much higher than that of our own realm. The Chaldean told us that it was really much higher than we could feel, but that our minds had been attuned to the difference of temperature just as they had been attuned to the intensity of light. A gentle breeze was pleasantly perceptible as it touched our faces with its heavenly scented breath.

As we proceeded through the palace entrance, I should dearly have loved to have lingered to examine more closely the remarkable materials of which the building was composed, but time pressed. Our stay could not be prolonged beyond our capacity to resist the rarity of the atmosphere and the intensity of light, notwithstanding the charge of spiritual force that the Chaldean and the Egyptian had given us. As we passed through, therefore, we had but a fleeting glimpse of the grandeur that encompassed us.

So beautifully proportioned were the various apartments and galleries that there was no overbearing loftiness to any one of them, such as one might have expected in an edifice of such dimensions. everywhere that we cast our eyes we could see jewelled walls and jewelled floors. Upon the walls were pictures of pastoral scenes where the artist had utilized every gem known to mortal man—and many others unknown to him—as the medium for his work. These pictures were, in their execution, of a mosaic order, but the effect produced upon the beholder was one of liquid light, if I may use the term. The constituents of the pictures sent forth their rays of light in all the colors that the subject demanded, and the effect upon the eye was one of pure life. The colors themselves were exquisite, and contained many more tones and shades of tones than earthly pigments could provide. It seemed inconceivable that precious stones could exist that had such a wide variety of colors—but, then we are in the spirit world and in a high realm of the spirit world, too.

As we walked down the corridors we met and were greeted by the most friendly and gracious beings, who thus added to our welcome. Welcome, indeed, was the overmastering feeling that enveloped us as we first put foot within the palace. There was no coldness, but everywhere the warmth of friendliness and affection.

At last we paused before a small chamber, and the Chaldean

told us that we had reached the highest point of our journey. I did not feel exactly nervous, but I wondered what formalities were to be observed, and as I was totally unaware of what description these might be—as we all were, except, of course, our two cicerone—I was naturally a little hesitant. The Chaldean, however, immediately reassured us by telling us to follow him, and merely to observe those rules dictated by good taste.

We entered. Our host was seated by a window. As soon as he saw us he rose and came forward to greet us. First he thanked the Chaldean and the Egyptian for bringing us to him. Then he took us each by the hand and bade us be welcome to his home. There were several vacant chairs close to that in which he had been seated, and he suggested that we might like to sit with him there and enjoy the view. It was, he explained, his favorite view.

We drew close to the window, and we could see beneath us a bed of the most magnificent white roses, as pure white as a field of snow, and which exhaled an aroma as exalting as the blooms from which it came. White roses, our host told us, were flowers he preferred above all others.

We seated ourselves, and I had an opportunity, as our host spoke to us, of observing him at close quarters where before I had but seen him from a distance. Seeing him thus, in his own home and surroundings, his facial appearance was, in general, similar to that which he had presented when he visited us in the temple in our own realm. There were differences, however, as we saw him here; differences that were largely a matter of light intensity. His hair, for example, seemed to be golden when he came to us. Here it seemed to be as of bright golden light, rather than of the color of gold. He looked to be young, to be of eternal youthfulness, but we could feel the countless eons of time, as it is known on earth, that lay behind him.

When he spoke his voice was sheer music, his laugh as a rippling of the waters, but never did I think it possible for one individual to breathe forth such affection, such kindliness, such thoughtfulness and consideration; and never did I think it possible for one individual to possess such an immensity of knowledge as is possessed by this celestial king. One felt that, under the Father of Heaven, he held the key to all knowledge and wisdom. But, strange as it may sound, though we had been transported unfathomable distances to the presence of this transcendingly wonderful being, yet here in his very presence we felt perfectly at home, perfectly at ease with him. He laughed with us, he joked with us, he asked us what we thought of his roses, and had the Chaldean managed to keep us merry upon our way thither. He spoke to each of us individually, displaying an exact acquaintance with all our concerns, collectively and personally. Then finally he came to the reason for his invitation to us to visit him.

In company with my friends, he said, I had visited the dark realms, and I had recounted what I had seen there. He thought that it would be in the nature of a pleasant contrast if we were to visit the highest realm, and see for ourselves some of its beauties; to show that the inhabitants of such high realms are not shadowy unreal people, but, on the contrary, they are like ourselves, capable of feeling and exhibiting the emotions of their fine natures, capable of human understanding, of human thought, and as easily susceptible to laughter and free-hearted merriment as were we ourselves. And he had asked us to visit him in order to tell us himself that these realms, wherein we were now visiting, were within the reach of every soul that is born upon the earth-plane, that no one can deprive us of that right: and that although it may take countless years of time to reach those realms, yet there is all eternity in which to achieve that end, and that there are unlimited means to help us upon our way. That, he said, is the simple, great fact of spirit life. There are no mysteries attached to it; all is perfectly straightforward, plain, and unrestricted by complicated beliefs, religious or otherwise. It requires no adherence to any particular form of orthodox religion, which, of itself, has no authority to assure any single soul of its powers to secure the soul's 'salvation'. No religious body that ever existed can do that.

And so this realm of incomparable beauty was free and open to all to work their way thither from the very lowest and foulest realm. It may take eons of time to accomplish, but that is the great and superb finale of the lives of the earth world's millions of souls.

Our good friend, the Chaldean, then mentioned to his 'master' that our stay had almost reached its limit. The latter said he was sorry to observe that it was so, but that such powers as had been invoked for us had their limitations, and so, for our comfort, we must work within them. However, he added, there are other occasions, and thus he extended further invitations to us.

We now rose, and I could not resist the lure of the view of the roses from the window. I gazed out once more, then we made ready to depart.

Our gracious host said he would accompany us to the hill from which we had had our first glimpse of his kingdom. We followed a different route from that by which we had reached the palace. And what was our delight when it led us directly to the rose bed. Stooping, our host culled three of the most choice blooms that mortal eyes ever beheld, and presented one to each of us. Our joy was still further heightened by the knowledge that with the affection that we should shower upon them, the blooms would never fade and die. My one anxiety was that in taking them to our own realm we should see them crushed, perhaps, by the unaccustomed density of our heavier atmosphere. But our host assured us that they would not, for they would be borne up by our thoughts of them and of the giver, and between the one and the other they would be amply supported, and would so remain.

At length we reached our point of departure. Words would not express our feelings, but our thoughts passed unfailingly to him who had brought us this supreme happiness, this foretaste of our destiny—and of the destiny of the whole earth world and the whole spirit world. And with a blessing upon us all, and with a smile of such affection, of such ineffable benignity, he bade us God-speed, and we found ourselves once more in our own realm.

I have tried to tell you something of what we saw, but words cannot be found to describe it, because I cannot translate the purely spiritual into earthly terms. My account must therefore fall far, far short.

And so, also, in those other matters of which I have treated. To give you a comprehensive account of all that we have seen in the world of spirit would fill many volumes, and therefore I have chosen what I felt would be of most interest and benefit. My earnest wish is that I have captured your interest, taken you away for a moment, from the pressing affairs of earthly life, and given you a glimpse of the world beyond the world in which you are now living.

If I have brought a measure of comfort, or of good hope, then great is my reward, and I would say to you:

Benedicat te omnipotens Deus.